ROUTLEDGE LIBRARY EDITIONS:
LABOUR ECONOMICS

Volume 9

RECENT ADVANCES IN LABOUR ECONOMICS

RECENT ADVANCES IN LABOUR ECONOMICS

Edited by
GILLIAN HUTCHINSON AND
JOHN TREBLE

LONDON AND NEW YORK

First published in 1984 by Croom Helm Ltd

This edition first published in 2019
by Routledge
2 Park Square, Milton Park, Abingdon, Oxon OX14 4RN

and by Routledge
52 Vanderbilt Avenue, New York, NY 10017

Routledge is an imprint of the Taylor & Francis Group, an informa business

British Library Cataloguing in Publication Data
A catalogue record for this book is available from the British Library

ISBN: 978-0-367-02458-1 (Set)
ISBN: 978-0-429-02526-6 (Set) (ebk)
ISBN: 978-0-367-02613-4 (Volume 9) (hbk)
ISBN: 978-0-429-39871-1 (Volume 9) (ebk)

Publisher's Note
The publisher has gone to great lengths to ensure the quality of this reprint but points out that some imperfections in the original copies may be apparent.

Disclaimer
The publisher has made every effort to trace copyright holders and would welcome correspondence from those they have been unable to trace.

Recent Advances in Labour Economics

EDITED BY
GILLIAN HUTCHINSON
& JOHN TREBLE

CROOM HELM
London & Sydney

© 1984 G. Hutchinson and J. Treble
Croom Helm Ltd, Provident House, Burrell Row,
Beckenham, Kent BR3 1AT
Croom Helm Australia Pty Ltd, First Floor,
139 King Street, Sydney, NSW 2001, Australia

British Library Cataloguing in Publication Data

Recent advances in labour economics.
   1. Labor supply—Great Britain
   I. Title II. Hutchinson, Gillian
   III. Treble, John
   331.12'0941   HD5765.A6

   ISBN 0-7099-2460-7

Printed and bound in Great Britain

CONTENTS

Contents

ACKNOWLEDGEMENTS

We would like to thank several people for their assistance in the organisation of the Conference and the production of this volume. Margaret Parkinson at Hull University and June Murphy at Queen Mary College cheerfully bore the burden of the administration before and during the three days of the conference. This book could not have been produced without the expert typing of Kathryn Greig and draughtmanship of Derek Waite.

Finally, our sincere gratitude is extended to the S.S.R.C. for its support and encouragement over many years, and, in particular, to Wendy Thompson.

To Bernard Corry, the Founding Father and Guiding
Light of the S.S.R.C. Labour Economics Study Group.

INTRODUCTION

The E.S.R.C. Labour Economics Study Group has held regular seminar meetings since 1971. The usual format for these meetings has been for the group to gather for an afternoon on four or five occasions each year to hear and discuss two papers. This format has advantages in that it enables new work to be disseminated rapidly, while it is fresh and topical. Its disadvantage, however, is that it does not facilitate the kind of in depth discussion which is more easily available in a conference setting.

The three day conference of the group which took place in July 1983 at Hull University was an attempt to provide this kind of opportunity for labour economists from all parts of the U.K. This volume is intended to be a record of the proceedings and an indication of the current concerns in labour economics.

Six of the papers deal with issues related to the role of trade unions in the economy. These issues include distributional effects (A. & D. Ulph, and Black and Bulkley), the "wage round" (Jackman), macroeconomic policy in a unionised economy (Ellis & Fender, Driffill, and Sampson). The remaining five papers deal with a variety of issues in empirical labour economics. Blundell and Walker elucidate recent research on life-cycle labour supply, Makepeace tests for macroeconomic stability, Hughes examines new evidence on unemployment flows, Forrest attempts to disentangle the effects of demographic change on unemployment rates and Chatterji and Price provide new estimates of employment functions for Great Britain.

Introduction

Consequently we invited Andrew Oswald to give a lecture surveying this recent literature on trade unions and we also ensured that a significant proportion of the papers presented focussed on trade union behaviour.

The structure of this book reflects this division of the conference proceedings into those papers which deal with trade unions (parts I and II) and papers on other aspects of labour economics (part III). The papers in parts I and II are concerned with theoretical issues but whereas part I concentrates on the micro-economic features, part II picks up some macro-economic implications of trade union activity. Part III, in contrast, deals exclusively with empirical themes.

As a result of the discussions at the conference, most of the authors felt that their papers would benefit from some revision before publication in this book. The papers are presented here without the discussants' comments since these have largely been incorporated in the final versions.

The studies of trade union behaviour in parts I and II model, in general, fully or partially unionised economies in equilibrium. Within this common framework the papers address several different issues. A. and D. Ulph study the distributional effects of unionisation using a model with two different skill groups of labour, each of which is separately unionised. Jackman, again in the context of a general equilibrium model, examines the properties of a dynamic system with non-synchronised wage setting. The study by Ellis and Fender explores certain macro-economic implications of the Mcdonald and Solow model, while Driffill, using a different form of union utility function, argues that stabilisation policy has long run consequences for wage and employment levels which may be undesirable.

These four papers all consider economies in which every worker belongs to a union. In contrast, Black and Bulkley and Sampson assume only partial unionisation. Black and Bulkley examine the kind of contracts that would be required to obtain socially optimal employment levels in such an economy and Sampson provides a comparative study of alternative tax schemes and their distributional effects.

The first paper in part III contains an exposition by Blundell and Walker of recent literature concerning the use of micro-economic data sets for modelling life-cycle labour supply behaviour. This

Introduction

literature has expanded rapidly in recent years and
Blundell and Walker provide a lucid guide to the
main issues.
     The remaining contributions are all empirical
investigations of various macro-economic aspects of
the labour market. The disequilibrium tests carried out by Makepeace cast doubt on the existence of
long run equilibrium of wages and employment in the
U.K. economy. Hughes has compiled a new data series
of flows to and from the unemployment register. He
shows that these data appear to have bimodal properties,
implying that the male unemployment stock may consist
of two distinct types of person.
     The phenomenon of demographic change and its
relationship to the unemployment rate in Canada which
is analysed by Forrest is one that is common to most
western economies, and the distinctions made in this
paper will be of general applicability. The final
paper by Chatterji and Price estimates a reduced
form employment function using quarterly data from
1957-1982. They find little support for supply
side influences.
     A feature common to all the papers in this vol-
ume is their concern with important policy issues.
In our brief survey above we have already mentioned
distributional effects and the social welfare implications of labour contracts and the wage round. In
addition, several studies have implications for tax
and subsidy policies, the wage-unemployment trade
off, the stabilisation effects of macro-policy and
industrial relations.
     Many of the authors have suggested ways in
which future research in their topics may proceed.
An overall perspective suggests several areas which
seem ripe for further development. In particular,
it should be clear that there is a need for empirical
investigation of the many theoretical propositions
which have resulted from recent analyses of trade
union behaviour. The papers contained here are
rich in testable hypotheses. Satisfactory empirical
testing will require the extension of currently
available data sources. It is unfortunate that the
statistics currently available in Great Britain are
inadequate for this task.

Part One

MICRO-ECONOMIC STUDIES OF TRADE UNION BEHAVIOUR

UNIONS AND THE DISTRIBUTION OF INCOME AND EMPLOYMENT - A DISCRETE MODEL

Alistair Ulph and David Ulph

INTRODUCTION

The question to be considered in this paper is what
is the impact of trade unions on the distribution of
wages and employment in a general equilibrium model
where all forms of labour are unionised.

There are a number of reasons why one might be
interested in such questions. One interest derives
from the analysis of optimal income taxation made
familiar by the work of Mirrlees (1971). In that
paper there is an exogenously determined distribution
of gross wages justified by the assumptions that in
doing different jobs, workers with different skills
have absolute, but not comparative, advantage; and
that in doing the same job, workers of different
skills are perfect substitutes for each other.
The work of Allen (1982), Heady, Ulph and Carruth
(1982) has gone some way to relaxing these assumptions and thus allowing the tax system to affect the
distribution of gross wages directly. However,
these analyses are still carried out in a competitive framework, and it would be of interest to see
how such results are affected when one introduces
trade unions.

A second approach which raises the same issues
would be to extend the work of Oswald (1982b), who
considers the question of optimal intervention in a
unionised economy, by introducing distributional as
well as efficiency considerations into the design of
tax policies.

Whatever one's motivation, it is clear that the
primary need is for a well articulated model of the
way in which unions might affect the distribution of
income. In a recent paper, Ulph and Ulph (1982),
we have argued that much of the traditional literature on general equilibrium effects of trade unions

3

(e.g. Johnson and Mieskowski (1970), Diewert (1974a, b), Jones (1971), Rosen (1970) are not well suited to analyse the issue of distribution, since they focus on the issue of union/non-union wage differentials.   These models all have the implication that workers of the same skill level can be paid different wages in different sectors, so that the effects of unionisation on income distribution will depend heavily on which sector is assumed to be unionised.

A more important criticism of the traditional models is made by Pettengill (1979, 1980) who argues that the differentials alluded to are only short-run features of unionisation and must be eroded in the long-run.   Pettengill develops a model in which every sector of the economy is unionised and in which workers of the same skill level earn the same wage throughout the economy.   He then claims to demonstrate quite generally that the effect of unionisation is to worsen the distribution of income, in the limited sense of making the highest skilled workers better off and the lowest skilled workers worse off.

In our paper cited above, we have argued that this claim by Pettengill is far from convincing. This is partly because the generality of Pettengill's claim is based on a detailed misspecification of the demand for labour.   More fundamentally, however, Pettengill fails to spell out an explicit model of union behaviour, so that it is difficult to test his assertion that his model represents a genuinely long-run equilibrium model.   He assumes that for each job, unions determine the minimum wage that must be paid for the job.   Firms are then free to hire whoever they want to do that job, provided they get at least that wage.   This automatically builds in an asymmetry between skills - for if low skilled workers try to drive up their wages, firms can offset this by hiring more skilled workers: but if high skilled workers do this, firms may be deterred from hiring lower-skilled workers by the need to pay the minimum wage.   Another way of looking at this is to say that high skilled workers can prevent low skilled workers taking their jobs, but not vice versa.

This asymmetry may reflect the fact that it is always possible for high skilled workers to pretend to be low skilled, whereas the reverse is not true; but then Pettengill's results are generated not so much by unionisation but by an asymmetry of information.   For a long-run analysis it may be more

appropriate to start with a model where firms and
unions are completely informed about the skills of
the workforce, and to derive a fully specified general equilibrium model in which there is a clearly
formulated concept of equilibrium. In a companion
paper, Ulph and Ulph (1983), this is done for a
general model in which there is a continuum of jobs
and a continuum of skills. However, it is rather
difficult to derive analytic solutions in this general model. In this paper we therefore present a
simplified and more tractable model in which we have
just two discrete skills and two discrete jobs.

The essential features of the model are as
follows. Start, say, from the competitive equilibrium, which will involve a particular assignment
of workers of different skills to jobs, and a particular allocation of capital to different jobs. For
each job, the workers now form a union, and, taking
as given the assignment of capital to their job and
their current membership, choose a level of employment to maximise their expected utility. In making
this choice the union members assume that those who
do not get employed in that particular job at the
union wage will receive unemployment benefit. Following this choice, capital will be reallocated between jobs to equalise its marginal product and
workers will also shift between jobs to seek
efficiency wages and unemployment probabilities that
maximise their expected utilities.

The key assumption in our model is clearly that,
in the long run, there are no restrictions on entry
to jobs (and hence unions). Not surprisingly, this
leads us to rather different conclusions from
Pettengill, and we shall show that it is now possible, and (as we indeed shall argue) likely that
unions will improve conditions for the least skilled
worker, although it is less clear what happens to
the high-skilled worker.

The structure of this paper is as follows. In
Section 2 we set out the basic framework of the
model, and then in Section 3 we derive the competitive equilibrium for our model. Section 4 sets out
the unionised equilibrium, while in Section 5 we
compare the two equilibria.

SECTION 2: THE MODEL

There are two kinds of worker - low-skilled, $i = 1$,
and high-skilled, $i = 2$, and two kinds of jobs, easy,
$j = 1$, and difficult, $j = 2$. Within each job,

skills are perfect substitutes for each other, so
let α_{ij} denote the number of efficiency units of
labour produced when one unit of labour of type i
does job j.   The assumptions on α_{ij} are as follows:

$$\left.\begin{array}{l} \alpha_{11} < \alpha_{21} \\ \alpha_{12} < \alpha_{22} \end{array}\right\} \tag{1}$$

$$\frac{\alpha_{22}}{\alpha_{12}} > \frac{\alpha_{21}}{\alpha_{11}} \tag{2}$$

Assumption (1) says that high skilled workers have
absolute advantage in doing both jobs, while (2) says
that high-skilled workers have comparative advantage
in doing the difficult job.

If n_{ij} is the number of people of skill i who
make themselves available for job j, (the sense of
this will become clear later), then the assumption
of perfect substitution allows us to define

$$\overline{L}_j = \alpha_{1j}n_{1j} + \alpha_{2j}n_{2j}, \quad j = 1,2$$

as the available labour force for doing job j,
measured in efficiency units.   In the competitive model the actual labour force will be equal to the available labour force, but in the unionised equilibrium
some of the available labour force will typically be
unemployed, so we shall let L_j denote the actual
labour force in efficiency units for job j, with
$L_j \leqslant \overline{L}_j$. n_i, i = 1, 2 will denote the number of
people of skill i in the economy.

There is a fixed amount of capital, $\overline{K}$, available in the economy, and K_j, j = 1,2 is the amount
of capital allocated to job j.   The output of jobs
1 and 2 are given by

$$\left.\begin{array}{l} Q_1 = K_1{}^{\gamma}L_1{}^{1-\gamma} \\ Q_2 = K_2{}^{\delta}L_2{}^{1-\delta} \end{array}\right\} \tag{3}$$

and, to simplify the demand side of the economy, we
shall assume that these outputs are intermediate
goods which are combined according to the production
function

$$Y = Q_1{}^\beta Q_2{}^{1-\beta}$$

to produce Y units of the single final output good, national income, which will act as numeraire.

Let P_j be the price of output of job j, W_j the efficiency wage of labour in job j (recall that skills are perfect substitutes in each job), and r the rental rate of capital, all denoted in terms of the numeraire. Firms producing both the intermediate and final outputs take all these prices as given, and act as profit maximisers, thus generating the usual conditions

$$\left.\begin{array}{l} P_1 = \beta Q_1{}^{\beta-1} Q_2{}^{1-\beta} \\[2mm] P_2 = (1-\beta)Q_1{}^\beta Q_2{}^{-\beta} \\[2mm] r = P_1 \gamma K_1{}^{\gamma-1} L_1{}^{1-\gamma} \\[2mm] r = P_2 \delta K_2{}^{\delta-1} L_2{}^{1-\delta} \\[2mm] W_1 = (1-\gamma)P_1 K_1{}^\gamma L_1{}^{-\gamma} \\[2mm] W_2 = (1-\delta)P_2 K_2{}^\delta L_2{}^{-\delta} \end{array}\right\} \tag{5}$$

The equations in (5) can now be solved to yield

$$W_1 = \mu L_2{}^\lambda L_1{}^{\mu-1} \tag{6}$$
$$W_2 = \lambda L_1{}^\mu L_2{}^{\lambda-1}$$

where $\lambda = (1-\delta)(1-\beta)$, $\mu = (1-\gamma)\beta$

These are the general equilibrium inverse labour demand functions.

The model set out so far is a special case of the framework developed in Heady, Carruth and Ulph (1982), in which further discussion can be found.

Finally, we need to consider unemployment. People either work for one unit of time or else are unemployed. There is an exogenously fixed level of unemployment benefit of S units of the output good, which we shall assume to be financed out of a lump sum tax on capital, and we assume there will always be sufficient revenue from this source to fund all the unemployment as will occur in our models.

7

Letting every worker have a utility function $\tilde{U}(C,\ell)$ over income and leisure, we can derive a corresponding reservation wage ω defined by

$$\tilde{U}(\omega,0) = \tilde{U}(S,1)$$

Henceforth we can suppress any reference to leisure, and work solely with a utility function

$$U(W) \equiv \tilde{U}(W,0)$$

where we will only be interested in wages $W \gtreqless \omega$. We shall assume that $U' > 0$, $U'' < 0$, and to derive

$$U(W) = -\frac{1}{\nu} W^{-\nu} \qquad \nu > 0$$

where ν is the coefficient of relative risk-aversion.

We denote n_{i3} as the number of people of skill i who are "unavailable for work", i.e. who do not offer themselves for work in either job. Then, by definition,

$$n_i = n_{i1} + n_{i2} + n_{i3}$$

To close our model, we need to say how wages are determined, and we analyse this first for the competitive case, which is standard, and then for the unionised case, which is the novel part of the paper.

SECTION 3: THE COMPETITIVE MODEL

In competitive labour markets, all workers who make themselves available for a job will be employed. Workers will make themselves available for a job or choose to be unemployed so as to maximise their utility. This leads to the following complete specification of the labour market, and hence, in conjunction with equations (1) - (5), the whole economy.

$$L_1 = \bar{L}_1 = \alpha_{11} n_{11} + \alpha_{21} n_{21}$$

$$L_2 = \bar{L}_2 = \alpha_{12} n_{12} + \alpha_{22} n_{22}$$

$$W_1 = \mu L_2^{\lambda} L_1^{\mu-1}$$

$$W_2 = \lambda L_2^{\lambda-1} L_1^{\mu}$$

8

$$\alpha_{11}W_1 \leqslant y_1 \quad n_{11} \geqslant 0$$

$$\alpha_{12}W_2 \leqslant y_1 \quad n_{12} \geqslant 0$$

$$\omega \leqslant y_1 \quad n_{13} \geqslant 0$$

$$\left.\begin{array}{l}\text{complementary}\\\text{slackness}\end{array}\right.$$

$$\alpha_{21}W_1 \leqslant y_2 \quad n_{21} \geqslant 0$$

$$\alpha_{22}W_2 \leqslant y_2 \quad n_{22} \geqslant 0$$

$$\omega \leqslant y_2 \quad n_{23} \geqslant 0$$

$$n_{11} + n_{12} + n_{13} = n_1$$

$$n_{21} + n_{22} + n_{23} = n_2$$

where y_i is the income level of workers of type i.

Given the parameters of the model there are a range of different kinds of equilibrium that can occur involving different degrees of specialisation by each skill type and different levels of unemployment. It would be tedious to list all the possible equilibria and the necessary conditions for each to occur. It is clear, though, that comparative advantage ensures that both skills cannot be simultaneously employed in both jobs, while absolute advantage means that high skilled people will only be unemployed if low skilled people are wholly unemployed. Moreover, if there is any unemployment among low skilled workers, the incomes of all low skilled workers get driven to the reservation wage. These obvious comments serve to highlight the fact that in the competitive equilibrium it is the low skilled workers who bear the brunt of unemployment.

SECTION 4: THE UNIONISED ECONOMY

It is assumed that each job now has its own union, so that n_{ij} will now denote the number of people with skill i who join union j (i, j = 1, 2). For a given membership, $\bar{L}_j$ is thus the maximum amount of labour (in efficiency units) that the union could supply, L_j, the amount it actually does supply, so that $\Pi_j = L_j/\bar{L}_j$ is the employment rate in job j. We shall assume that the union decides which of its

9

members to employ at random, irrespective of skill
levels, so that Π_j is now the probability that a
member of union j will be employed, given its current membership and employment policies.
    Union j is assumed to take as given its current
membership, n_{1j}, n_{2j}, the price of its output, P_j,
and the capital stock in its sector, K_j.   With
these factors all assumed given, the union believes
it faces a partial equilibrium trade-off between the
efficiency wage and employment rate given by

$$W_1 = B_1 \Pi_1^{-\gamma} \left. \right\} $$
$$W_2 = B_2 \Pi_2^{-\delta} \qquad\qquad (8)$$

where

$$B_1 = (1-\gamma)P_1 K_1^{\gamma}\bar{L}_1^{-\gamma}$$
$$B_2 = (1-\delta)P_2 K_2^{\delta}\bar{L}_2^{-\delta}$$

The union now chooses a point on this trade-off
to maximise the total utility of its membership, so
the union will seek to

$$\max_{W_j} \left\{ \Pi_j \left[\rho_j U(W_j \alpha_{1j}) + (1-\rho_j)U(W_j \alpha_{2j}) \right] \right.$$
$$\left. + (1-\Pi_j)U(\omega) \right\}$$

s.t. $0 \leqslant \Pi_j \leqslant 1$

and (8), where

$$\rho_j = \frac{n_{1j}}{n_{1j} + n_{2j}}$$

is the proportion of union j's membership of skill 1.
For the case

$$U(W) = -\frac{1}{\nu} W^{-\nu}$$

it can be readily shown that the constant elasticity
nature of the demand function leads the union to act
as if it had the labour supply curve SS in Fig. 1.

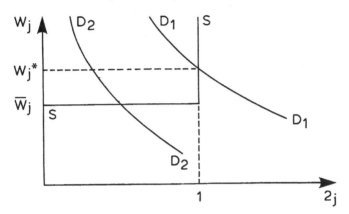

Union's Optimal Wage

Figure 1

$\bar{W}_j$ is union j's union reservation wage, where

$$\bar{W}_1 = \omega(1+\gamma\nu)^{\frac{1}{\nu}} \left[\rho_1\alpha_{11}^{-\nu} + (1-\rho_1)\alpha_{21}^{-\nu}\right]^{\frac{1}{\nu}} \Bigg\}$$

$$\bar{W}_2 = \omega(1+\delta\nu)^{\frac{1}{\nu}} \left[\rho_2\alpha_{12}^{-\nu} + (1-\rho_2)\alpha_{22}^{-\nu}\right]^{\frac{1}{\nu}} \Bigg\} \quad (9)$$

From (8) we can see that if the demand for labour is
sufficiently strong, $B_j > \bar{W}_j$, we get a demand curve
such as D_1D_1 in Fig. 1 and the union's optimal policy will lead to full employment, so that the optimal wage, W_j*, is given by $W_j* = B_j$. On the other
hand, when labour demand is low in its sector,
$B_j \leqslant \bar{W}_j$, then we have a demand curve such as D_2D_2 in
Fig. 1, then the optimal wage is $W_j* = \bar{W}_j$, and the
optimal employment rate is given by

$$\Pi_1* = (B_1/\bar{W}_1)^{\frac{1}{\gamma}}, \quad \Pi_2* = (B_2/\bar{W}_2)^{\frac{1}{\delta}}$$

Thus the union's optimal policy depends on the two

parameters B_j, the strength of demand for labour, and $\bar{W}_j$, its reservation wage.   From the definition of B_j we can see that labour demand depends positively on the price of the sector output and its capital allocation, but negatively on the size of the union in efficiency units.   To see what determines the reservation wage we can rewrite (9) as

$$\left.\begin{aligned}
\bar{\alpha}_1\bar{W}_1 &= \omega(1 + \gamma\nu)^{\frac{1}{\nu}} \\[2mm]
\bar{\alpha}_2\bar{W}_2 &= \omega(1 + \delta\nu)^{\frac{1}{\nu}}
\end{aligned}\right\} \tag{10}$$

where

$$\bar{\alpha}_j = \left[\rho_j\alpha_{1j}^{-\nu} + (1-\rho_j)\alpha_{2j}^{-\nu}\right]^{-\frac{1}{\nu}}$$

is a measure of the 'average' number of efficiency units of its current membership.

Thus (10) says that union reservation wage is such that it will yield its "average" member an income which is a markup over the level of unemployment benefit where the mark-up will increase the more inelastic is the (partial) demand for labour in that sector (see (8)), and will decrease the greater is the union's aversion to risk.   All of this is quite consistent with intuition.

Summarising, then, the optimal behaviour of unions given its current membership and the trade-off it thinks it faces will be to select optimal wage and employment rates W_j^*, Π_j^* given by

$$W_j^* = \max(B_j, \bar{W}_j)$$

$$\Pi_1^* = \min\left(1, (B_1/\bar{W}_1)^{\frac{1}{\gamma}}\right)$$

$$\Pi_2^* = \min\left(1, (B_2/\bar{W}_2)^{\frac{1}{\delta}}\right)$$

The model of union behaviour then is that of the standard textbook model.   In particular unions are supposed to act as Stackelberg leaders with respect to the employment policies of firms, rather than, say, negotiate efficient contracts as in the model of McDonald and Solow(1981), or Oswald and Ulph (1982).

To complete the model, we need to specify the

behaviour of individuals. Individuals observe the efficiency wages W_j^*, and employment rates Π_j^* negotiated by unions and decide whether to join a union or remain unemployed so as to maximise their expected utilities. Note that while the 'average' income of a union member is above the reservation wage, this may not apply to the low skilled worker in the union, so that voluntary unemployment $n_{i3} > 0$, is a real possibility.

A <u>unionised equilibrium</u> then must be such that:
1. given their current membership and partial equilibrium wage/employment trade-offs unions select an optimal wage/employment package,
2. given the wage/employment packages set by the unions individuals are making their optimal choice of union membership, and
3. the resulting wage and employment choices are consistent with general equilibrium in the output and capital markets.

Letting V_i denote the levels of expected utility obtained by persons of skill i, then a union equilibrium is given by

$$\rho_j, \bar{W}_j, W_j, \Pi_j, V_i, n_{ij}, B_j, \bar{L}_j; \quad i, j = 1, 2$$

such that

$$\bar{L}_j = \alpha_{1j} n_{1j} + \alpha_{2j} n_{2j}$$

$$\rho_j = \frac{n_{1j}}{n_{1j} + n_{2j}}$$

$$\left.\begin{aligned}
\bar{W}_1 &= \omega(1 + \gamma\nu)^{\frac{1}{\nu}} \left[\rho_1 \alpha_{11}^{-\nu} + (1-\rho_1)\alpha_{21}^{-\nu}\right]^{\frac{1}{\nu}} \\[2ex]
\bar{W}_2 &= \omega(1 + \delta\nu)^{\frac{1}{\nu}} \left[\rho_2 \alpha_{12}^{-\nu} + (1-\rho_2)\alpha_{22}^{-\nu}\right]^{\frac{1}{\nu}}
\end{aligned}\right\} \quad (11)$$

$$\left.\begin{aligned}
W_j &= \max (B_j, \bar{W}_j) \\[2ex]
\Pi_1 &= \min (1, (B_1/\bar{W}_2)^{\frac{1}{\gamma}}) \\[2ex]
\Pi_2 &= \min (1, (B_2/\bar{W}_2)^{\frac{1}{\delta}})
\end{aligned}\right\} \quad (12)$$

$$\Pi_1(W_1\alpha_{11})^{-\nu} + (1-\Pi_1)\omega^{-\nu} \geqslant V_1 \qquad n_{11} \geqslant 0$$

$$\Pi_2(W_2\alpha_{12})^{-\nu} + (1-\Pi_2)\omega^{-\nu} \geqslant V_1 \qquad n_{12} \geqslant 0$$

$$\omega^{-\nu} \geqslant V_1 \qquad n_{13} \geqslant 0$$

$$\Pi_1(W_1\alpha_{21})^{-\nu} + (1-\Pi_1)\omega^{-\nu} \geqslant V_2 \qquad n_{21} \geqslant 0 \qquad (13)$$

$$\Pi_2(W_2\alpha_{22})^{-\nu} + (1-\Pi_2)\omega^{-\nu} \geqslant V_2 \qquad n_{22} \geqslant 0$$

$$\omega^{-\nu} \geqslant V_2 \qquad n_{23} \geqslant 0$$

$$n_{i1} + n_{i2} + n_{i3} = n_i$$

$$B_1\Pi_1^{-\gamma} = \mu(\Pi_2\bar{L}_2)^\lambda (\Pi_1\bar{L}_1)^{\mu-1}$$

$$B_2\Pi_2^{-\delta} = \lambda(\Pi_1\bar{L}_1)^\mu (\Pi_2\bar{L}_2)^{\lambda-1} \qquad (14)$$

(11) is just a set of definitions; (12) are the conditions for union optimisation; (13), which holds with complementary slackness, the conditions for individual optimisation; and (14) is the condition equating the partial equilibrium labour demand functions with the general equilibrium demand function.

Again there are a large number of possible configurations for equilibrium. Note that now, unlike the competitive equilibrium, it will be possible for both skills to be simultaneously members of both unions. However, absolute advantage will ensure that if some high skilled workers do not join a union, then no unskilled workers would join either union.

SECTION 5: A COMPARISON OF EQUILIBRIA

Nothing has been said so far about the existence, uniqueness or stability of the equilibria set out in the previous sections. Given the special nature of the model, these are not issues which we wish to pursue here; a discussion, relating to the more general model, is set out in the companion paper, Ulph and Ulph (1983). We have already referred to one aspect

that could cause difficulties - the fact that unemployment benefits are assumed to be financed out of
capital taxation. Obviously if unemployment benefit
were so high that no one chose to work then the rental rate on capital would be zero and hence no equilibrium would exist.

However, for reasonable values of ω, it seems
plausible that our model will display unique equilibria for both the competitive and unionised models,
so that a comparison of the distributions of income
and employment in the two cases make sense.

To examine the implications of our model from the
distribution of income and employment, and in particular to provide counter-examples to the Pettengill
claim, it will be simplest to examine some simulation
results. It will be more illuminating if we first
consider a slight reparameterisation of the coeffi-
cients α_{ij}. We shall take α_{11} and α_{12} as fixed.
Let $a = \alpha_{21}/\alpha_{11}$ denote the degree of <u>absolute</u> advantage high skilled people enjoy over low-skilled.
With no comparative advantage one would then expect
that $\alpha_{22} = a.\alpha_{12}$, but since there is comparative advantage, $\alpha_{22} > a.\alpha_{12}$. Thus let $b = \alpha_{22}/(a.\alpha_{12})$
denote the degree of comparative advantage.

In the following simulations we shall keep fixed
throughout the parameters $\alpha_{11} = 2$, $\alpha_{12} = 2.5$, $\delta = .5$,
$n2 = 1$. What we shall be interested in is variations
in the number of unskilled workers, $n1$, the level of
the reservation wage, ω, the degree of risk aversion,
ν, the degree of absolute and comparative advantage a,
and b, and the parameters β, γ and δ which determine
the elasticity of the partial and general equilibrium
wage-employment functions.

One additional point needs to be made. We have
noted that in our model unions use the partial equilibrium wage-employment trade-off in determining their
policy. It may be argued that this is likely to
give perverse results, and unions should take account
of the general equilibrium effects of their policies.
We shall say more about this later, but for the purpose of the simulations we shall interpret this to
mean that the unions use the functions (6) and (7) as
their general equilibrium wage employment trade off,
on the assumption that the employment level in the
other section is fixed. Now it should be noted that
these partial and general equilibrium trade-offs have
the same functional forms, and differ only in the
elasticities involved. Thus the form of the equilibria are the same in both cases, so there is no need
to detail the solution of the general union equilibrium.

We consider first our 'standard' case where a = 0.05, b = 2.0, β = .9, γ = .2, δ = .5, ν = 2, ω = .55, nl = 22.   We can then compute the following equilibria.

Competitive Equilibrium

Job-Skill Allocation: $n11$ = 20.93 $n21$ = 0
$\qquad\qquad\qquad\qquad\qquad$ $n12$ =   0 $n22$ = 1
$\qquad\qquad\qquad\qquad\qquad$ $n13$ =   1.07 $n23$ = 0

Thus there is complete specialisation and unemployment of some low skilled workers of just over one unit.   Corresponding efficiency wages are $W1$ = .275, $W2$ = .152, yielding incomes $y1$ = .550 and $y2$ = .800.

Partial Union Equilibrium

Union-Skill Allocation: $n11$ = 22 $n21$ = 0
$\qquad\qquad\qquad\qquad\qquad$ $n12$ = 0 $n22$ = 1
$\qquad\qquad\qquad\qquad\qquad$ $n13$ = 0 $n23$ = 0

Thus all low-skilled workers join the 'easy' job union, all the high-skilled workers join the 'hard' job union.   This leads to unions optimal solution being to set wages equal to the union reservation wages, $W1$ = .325, $W2$ = .148, with corresponding employment probabilities $\pi1$ = .477, $\pi2$ = .610. For those in employment in job 1, their income will be .650, while for those employed in job 2 it will be .778.   Note then that low skilled workers are undoubtedly better off;   for although 62% of them are unemployed, it is only these 13.706 people who get the reservation wage of .55, while in the competitive equilibrium, all 22 got the reservation wage.   The high skilled workers are unequivocally worse off; the .61 who are employed now get a lower income, .778, then in the competitive equilibrium of .800, but now .39 only get the reservation wage of .55.   Table 1 summarises the distribution of income in the two cases.

Table 1:

Income	.55	.65	.778	.800
Competitive Equilibrium	22	-	-	1
Partial Union Equilibrium	14.096	8.294	.61	-

Finally, we consider the general union equilibrium. We get the allocation of skills to unions as in the partial case, but now the union reservation wages are W1 = .343 and W2 = .178 with corresponding employment probabilities π_1 = .367, and π_2 = .411, yielding incomes for those in employment of .687 and .937. Thus, while the unskilled workers in employment get even higher income, now the high skilled workers who are employed also get higher incomes, .937, than in both the competitive and partial cases, so it was less clear what has happened to the distribution of income for this case.

Before discussing the robustness of the example, it should be noted that the example shows why one might expect that for a wide range of plausible parameter values the least skilled worker will benefit from the move from a competitive to a unionised economy. In the competitive equilibrium, if there is any unemployment, it will be the least skilled who are made unemployed first. Even if only a few of them are unemployed, all will have their income driven down to the reservation level, so that they are indifferent between working and being unemployed. In the unionised equilibrium, however, they can certainly be made no worse off than in the competitive equilibrium, and, if they all find it advantageous to join a union, they must be better off, since those in employment will have an income above the reservation wage. In the continuum model, where there is a unique assignment of workers to jobs (unions) then either the least skilled worker will be wholly unemployed, or they must be better off than in the competitive equilibrium with unemployment (Ulph and Ulph 1983).

We now discuss the robustness of our example to variation in the parameters. Table 2 shows the effects of varying the reservation wages, the number of unskilled workers and the degree of risk aversion. Case 5 is the standard case. The effects are very much as one would expect; higher unemployment pay induces more unemployment in the competitive equilibrium, except possibly for cases where the union wage is above the reservation wage (c.f. cases 4 and 5 for the partial union model). Comparing cases 4, 5 and 6 with 10, 11 and 12, it can be seen that higher risk aversion makes unions settle for lower wages and higher employment probabilities. Case 7 is of interest for two reasons. The low skilled workers are made better off, the high skilled workers worse off in the partial union equilibrium than the competitive equilibrium and this is accentuated in

17

Table 2:

Constant Parameters	$a = 1.05$, $b = 2$, $\beta = .9$, $\gamma = .2$, $\delta = .5$, $n_2 = 1$, $a_{11} = 2$, $a_{12} = 2.5$											
Case No:	1	2	3	4	5	6	7	8	9	10	11	12
Varying Parameters												
ω	.45	.55	.65	.45	.55	.65	.45	.55	.65	.45	.55	.65
n_1	9	9	9	22	22	22	30	30	30	2	2	2
ν	2	2	2	2	2	2	2	2	2	4	4	4
Competitive Equilibrium												
w_1	.336	.336	.336	.271	.275	.325	.249	.275	.325	.271	.275	.328
w_2	.135	.135	.135	.158	.152	.130	.197	.152	.130	.158	.152	.130
y_1	.672	.672	.672	.542	.550	.65	.497	.550	.650	.542	.55	.65
y_2	.707	.707	.707	.828	.800	.682	1.036	.800	.682	.828	.800	.682
n_{11}	9	9	9	22	20.93	10.57	30	20.93	10.57	22	20.93	10.57
n_{12}	–	–	–	–	–	–	–	–	–	–	–	–
n_{13}												11.43
n_{21}	.379	.379	.379	1	1.067	11.43	1	9.07	11.43	1	1.07	.279
n_{22}	.621	.621	.621	1	1	.721	1	1	.721	1	1	.721
Union Equilibrium— Partial Wage- Employment Trade-off												
w_1	.336	.336	.384	.271	.325	.385	.266	.325	.385	.271	.319	.376
w_2	.135	.148	.175	.158	.148	.178	.165	.148	.175	.158	.138	.163
π_1	1	1	.552	1	.477	.231	.783	.350	.169	1	.529	.256
π_2	.778	.778	.387	1	.610	.295	1	.610	.295	1	.712	.344
n_{11}	9	9	9	22	22	22	30	30	30	22	22	22
n_{12}	–	–	–	–	–	–	–	–	–	–	–	–
n_{21}	.379	.285	.235	–	–	–	–	–	–	–	–	–
n_{22}	.621	.715	.765	.542	.651	.769	.532	.651	.769	.542	.637	.753
y_{11}	.672	.672	.769	–	1	1	1	1	1	1	1	1
y_{12}	–	–	–	1	1	1	1	1	1	1	1	1
y_{21}	.707	.704	.807	.828	.778	.919	.868	.778	.919	.828	.724	.855
y_{22}	.707	.778	.919									
Union Equilibrium— General wage- Employment Trade-off												
w_1	.336	.343	.406	.281	.343	.406	.281	.343	.406	.271	.332	.392
w_2	.146	.178	.211	.146	.178	.211	.146	.178	.211	.158	.155	.183
π_1	1	.874	.423	.877	.367	.177	.643	.268	.130	.995	.436	.211
π_2	9	.557	.269	.983	.411	.199	.982	.411	.199	1	.543	.263
n_{11}	9	9	9	22	22	22	30	30	30	22	22	22
n_{12}	–	–	–	–	–	–	–	–	–	–	–	–
n_{21}	.368	.259	.259	–	–	–	–	–	–	–	–	–
n_{22}	.632	.741	.741	.562	.687	.812	.562	.687	.812	.542	.664	.784
y_{11}	.672	.681	.812	1	1	1	1	1	1	1	1	1
y_{12}	–	–	–	1	1	1	1	1	1	1	1	1
y_{21}	.703	.720	.851	.766	.437	1.107	.766	.937	1.107	.826	.814	.962
y_{22}	.766	.937	1.107									

the general union equilibrium.   Moreover this occurs
without any unemployment in the competitive equilibrium.
     Table 3 shows the effects of varying the degree
of absolute and comparative advantage.   Obviously
with unemployment in the competitive equilibrium these
changes cannot affect the income of low skilled workers, but it does affect the income of high skilled
workers.   Increasing the level of absolute advantage increases the income of the high skilled workers,
and can also increase the income of low skilled
workers (cf. 19 and 20).
     In the union equilibria, however, variation in
absolute or comparative advantages have no effect on
the income of low skilled workers, or of high skilled
workers who are in the difficult job union.   The
constancy of income is probably the result of the
constant elasticity assumption used;   efficiency
wages fall to offset the increase in both absolute
and comparative advantage.   The principal effect of
changing absolute advantage is to induce some high
skilled worker to trade down into the easy job union.
This occurs in cases where the high skilled workers
who are employed in these different job unions are
worse off than in the competitive equilibria, but
those who trade down into the low skilled union and
get employment there are better off (of course a
lower proportion of them do get employed).
     Finally Table 4 illustrates the effect of diff-
erent elasticities of demand.   However, to prevent
getting extreme results it is also necessary to vary
the reservation wage across some cases, and this
makes it difficult to make strict comparisons of
wages or incomes, except for cases with common reservation wages.   We can say that lowering the partial elasticity of demand for labour in the difficult
job, lowers both wages and incomes for all groups in
all equilibria.   Variation in β seems to have ambig-
uous effects - lowering wages for both jobs in some
equilibria (cf. 22 and 28), raising them in others
(cf. 23 and 29).
     In no cases did the incomes of the lowest skilled
workers who were employed in the union equilibrium
fall.   In cases 19-21 all the low skilled workers
received wages above the reservation wage in the competitive equilibrium, and while unionisation raises
the wages of those employed, some now become unemployed, and so receive lower incomes than in the
competitive case.   For the high skilled workers the
incomes of some or all of those who remain in employment in one or both of the union equilibria are lower

Table 3:

Constant Parameters: $\alpha_{11} = 2$, $\alpha_{12} = 2.5$, $n_1 = 22$, $n_2 = 1$, $\beta = .9$, $\gamma = .2$, $\delta = .5$, $\nu = 2$, $\omega = .55$

Case No:		13	14	15	16	17	18	19	20	21
Varying Parameters	a	1.05	1.5	2	1.05	1.5	2	1.05	1.5	2
	b	1.5	1.5	1.5	2	2	2	3	3	3
Competitive Equilibrium	w_1	.275	.275	.275	.275	.275	.275	.277	.282	.281
	w_2	.192	.147	.147	1.52	.112	.110	.107	.076	.075
	y_1	.550	.550	.550	.550	.550	.550	.557	.563	.561
	y_2	.757	.826	1.102	.800	.843	1.103	.845	.861	1.124
	n_{11}	19.852	21.072	20.539	20.934	22	21.983	22	22	22
	n_{12}	–	–	–	–	–	–	–	–	–
	n_{13}	2.148	.928	1.461	1.066	–	.017	–	–	–
	n_{21}	1	.023	.268	1	1	.223	–	–	.220
	n_{22}	1	.977	.732	1	1	.777	1	1	.780
Union Equilibrium— Partial Wage— Employment Trade-off	w_1	.325	.325	.325	.325	.325	.325	.325	.325	.325
	w_2	.198	.138	.104	.148	.104	.078	.099	.069	.052
	π_1	.448	.484	.514	.477	.515	.547	.521	.563	.597
	π_2	.573	.660	.842	.610	.703	.897	.666	.768	.979
	n_{11}	22	22	22	22	22	22	22	22	22
	n_{12}	–	–	–	–	–	–	–	–	–
	n_{21}	1	.060	.209	1	.060	.209	1	.060	.209
	n_{22}	–	.940	.791	–	.940	.791	–	.940	.791
	y_{11}	.650	.650	.650	.650	.650	.650	.650	.650	.650
	y_{12}	–	–	–	–	–	–	–	–	–
	y_{21}	1	.975	1.297	1	.975	1.300	1	.975	1.300
	y_{22}	.778	.778	.778	.778	.778	.778	.778	.778	.778
Union Equilibrium— General Wage— Employment Trade-off	w_1	.343	.343	.343	.343	.343	.343	.343	.343	.343
	w_2	.238	.167	.125	.178	.125	.097	.119	.083	.062
	π_1	.344	.372	.365	.367	.396	.421	.400	.433	.459
	π_2	.386	.417	.506	.367	.944	.539	.449	.485	.588
	n_{11}	22	22	22	22	22	22	22	22	22
	n_{12}	–	–	–	–	–	–	–	–	–
	n_{21}	1	1	.117	1	1	.117	1	1	.117
	n_{22}	–	–	.883	–	–	.883	–	–	.883
	y_{11}	.687	.687	.687	.687	.687	.687	.687	.687	.687
	y_{12}	–	–	–	–	–	–	–	–	–
	y_{21}	1	1	1.371	1	1	1.371	1	1	1.371
	y_{22}	.937	.937	.937	.937	.937	.937	.937	.937	.937

Table 4:

Constant Parameters	a = 1.05, b = 2, α_{11} = 2, α_{21} = 2.4, n1 = 22, n2 = 1, ν = 2, β = .9(22·27), β = .1(28-33)											
Case No:	22	23	24	25	26	27	28	29	30	31	32	33
Varying Parameters												
ω	.25	.15	.05	.25	.15	.05	.25	.15	.05	.25	.15	.05
γ	.2	.5	.8	.2	.5	.8	.2	.5	.8	.2	.5	.8
δ	.25	.25	.25	.5	.5	.5	.25	.25	.25	.5	.5	.5
Competitive Equilibrium												
w1	.285	.075	.024	.271	.075	.025	.263	.242	.227	.125	.075	.061
w2	.228	.056	.019	.158	.049	.016	.211	.194	.181	.099	.060	.049
y1	.570	.150	.050	.542	.150	.050	.526	.484	.453	.250	.150	.123
y2	21.828	.294	.101	.828	.255	.085	1.105	1.017	.950	.520	.315	.258
n11	21.172	19.716	6.806	22	15.572	6.188	2.554	1.663	.694	1.275	.544	1.026
n12	–	1.188	.75	–	6.428	15.812	19.446	20.337	21.306	5.649	17.806	20.974
n13	–	1.096	14.438	–	–	–	–	–	–	15.649	1.65	–
n21	1	1	1	1	1	1	1	1	1	1	1	1
n22	1	1	1	1	1	1	1	1	1	1	1	1
Union Equilibrium–Partial Wage-Employment Trade-off												
w1	.285	.106	.040	.271	.106	.040	.263	.242	.227	.143	.106	.061
w2	.228	.058	.021	.158	.040	.015	.211	.194	.181	.139	.083	.049
π1	1	.394	.167	1	.362	.156	1	1	1	.283	.407	1
π2	1	1	1	1	.884	1	1	1	1	.168	.423	1
n11	21.828	22	21.783	22	22	22	2.554	1.663	.694	2.658	2.454	1.026
n12	.172	–	.217	–	–	–	19.446	20.337	21.306	19.341	19.546	20.974
n21	–	–	–	–	–	–	–	–	–	–	–	–
n22	–	–	–	–	–	–	–	–	–	–	–	–
y11	.570	.212	.081	.542	.212	.081	.526	.484	.453	.296	.212	.123
y12	.570	–	.053	–	–	–	.526	.484	.453	.347	.208	.123
y21	–	–	–	–	–	–	–	–	–	–	–	–
y22	1.196	.307	.111	.828	.212	.077	1.105	1.017	.950	.728	.437	.258
Union Equilibrium–General Wage-Employment Trade-off												
w1	.285	.109	.041	.271	.109	.040	.263	.242	.227	.211	.128	.061
w2	.228	.057	.031	.158	.049	.016	.211	.194	.181	.142	.085	.049
π1	1	.377	.203	1	.339	.153	1	1	1	.125	.308	1
π2	1	1	.211	1	.705	.895	1	1	1	.161	.399	1
n11	21.828	17.05	17.05	22	22	22	2.554	1.663	.694	3.895	2.589	1.026
n12	.172	4.95	4.95	–	–	–	19.446	20.337	21.306	18.105	19.411	20.974
n21	–	–	–	–	–	–	–	–	–	–	–	–
n22	–	–	–	–	–	–	–	–	–	–	–	–
y11	.570	.217	.081	.542	.217	.081	.526	.484	.453	.421	.255	.123
y12	.570	.079	.079	–	–	–	.526	.484	.453	.355	.213	.123
y21	–	–	–	–	–	–	–	–	–	–	–	–
y22	1.197	.300	.165	.828	.255	.085	1.105	1.017	.990	.745	.448	.258

than in the competitive equilibrium, in about half
the cases presented, demonstrating that the ability
of unionisation to improve the distribution of income is by no means a result of negligible probability.

CONCLUSIONS

In this paper we have presented a model in which we
attempt to provide a description of an economy containing many unions in which all agents can be
thought of as being in equilibrium.   The model is
thus an attempt to set out explicitly what might be
involved in the long-run general equilibrium model
of trade union Pettengill claimed to have provided
but did not, and also disproves Pettengill's claim to
have discovered a general result - that unionisation
worsens the distribution of income.
     Since this paper is as much concerned with how
to model a fully unionized economy in equilibrium as
it is with specific results, it may be useful to
elaborate on why we chose this particular model and
how it might be extended.
     Some features of our model, such as the use of
Cobb-Douglas production structure, the assumption of
a single output good, are used either to allow explicit calculation of the optimal union bargain, or
to avoid introducing numerous complexities on the
demand side that would not necessarily enlighten the
discussion of the effect of unionisation on income
distribution.   More serious questions could be
raised about the modelling of the labour markets.
     The assumption of perfect substitution between
labour of different types is clearly special.   One
could simply have allowed labour of different types
to be inputs of different degrees of substitutability
in different sectors.   However our formulation has
the merit of allowing one to still speak sensibly
about workers of different skills, while, through
comparative advantage, making the allocation of workers to jobs matter.   It also reflects a view that we
are modelling a long run equilibrium in which people
at the stage of making a choice of job are relatively
good substitutes for each other, and that it is
really substitution between jobs (or acquired skills)
that is difficult.   In any case, with an appropriate
degree of comparative advantage the range of jobs
which people with a particular set of skills need
ever, in practice, contemplate entering is going to be
very narrow.
     Let us now return to the question of the use of

a partial equilibrium versus general equilibrium wage
employment trade-off. Of course one can make the usual comments about the amount of information unions
would need to calculate the general equilibrium trade-
off, and also the fact that in general equilibrium the
partial equilibrium demand trade-offs have to be consistent with the general equilibrium. But there is
another point involved. As can be seen from studying
the general equilibrium trade-off (6) and (7), the
implication here is that unions are effectively bargaining, not against their employer, but against other
unions.   But what is it reasonable for one union to
think about the behaviour of other unions ?   A reasonable assumption might be that unions take as given
their own membership, and the wage-employment package
set by other unions. But as we can see from (6) and
(7), if that was the case, there would be nothing
left to bargain about; if W2 and L2 are fixed, say,
then (6) and (7) solve for W1 and L1.   Unions might
then take as given either the employment level selected by the other union, and recognise that in striking its own bargain it will affect the real wage of
the other union, or, equivalently, at least in equilibrium, take as given the real wage of the other
union and acknowledge that it can affect the employment of the other union through its bargain.   Taking
the price of output and the allocation of capital to
its sector as fixed is a way of not requiring unions
to think about the way their bargains interact with
each other.
    A somewhat related point concerns the question
of whether one should use efficient bargains or not.
Efficient bargains require that both sides have considerable information about each other, and it seems
unlikely that in such a context the union could fail
to be aware of the general equilibrium effects of
their bargains. But in the general equilibrium
context of this model the notion of an efficient
bargain is unclear, since all equilibria involve
firms earning zero profits, so there is nothing to
bargain against. The only way to get round this
would be to have unions bargaining against the sup-
pliers of capital; but this would first of all
require introducing some explicit modelling of the
behaviour of capitalists (we have taken a one period
model with capital supplied inelastic); but, since
capital is mobile between sectors, it would not make
sense for unions in a particular sector to bargain
only against capitalists in their sector, but rather
against all capitalists, in which case it would also
make sense to have unions acting cooperatively. This

would be simply a standard political economy model
of games between labour and capital, which raises a
rather different set of issues.   Of course in
telling a complete story of the distribution of income, rather than the distribution of earned income,
such considerations would be important.   Finally,
of course, there is the problem that if employers in
a particular sector can be treated as a monolithic
group for the purpose of bargaining with labour, it
seems inconsistent to have them acting competitively
in the output market.

Thus while there are obvious ways in which our
model can be extended, the general equilibrium considerations that we focus on place some limits on
what extensions it might be sensible to attempt.

A NEGATIVE INCOME TAX IN A PARTLY UNIONISED ECONOMY

Anthony A. Sampson

SECTION 1: INTRODUCTION

In many economies the level of unemployment pay sets
a floor to the wage rate. The interaction of the tax
and social security systems, yielding effective marginal tax rates of around 100% for some low paid workers,
eliminates the incentive to take a job at a wage less
than some critical level. If the marginal product of
labour at full employment is less than this critical
wage, unemployment will result. This unemployment is
involuntary in the sense that jobs are available at
which the marginal product of labour exceeds the marginal disutility of labour and remain unfilled because
of the tax/social security system.

Several factors could give rise to this unemployment. The simplest, considered by Meade (1961) is over-
population in the sense that at full employment of a
homogeneous labour force, the average product of labour
would exceed some conventionally defined subsistence
level, whereas the marginal product of labour would not.
Alternatively, if workers differ in their capabilities,
some workers might have a marginal value product less
than a subsistence level, and in an economy with unemployment pay those workers would never take a job.
Meade (1964) suggests that technical change, by increasing the demand for skilled labour and reducing the dem-
and for unskilled labour, is making this problem worse.

In this paper we consider a third reason for this
unemployment: labour market distortions. Specifically,
we view unemployment as occurring because trade unions
raise the wage rate and lower the level of employment
in the unionised sector. The consequent increase in
labour supply to the non-unionised sector lowers the
market clearing net of tax wage to below the level of
unemployment pay.

Since this unemployment arises because the
effective marginal tax rate is 100%, so some workers

are no better off when employed, a Negative Income
Tax (1) has been suggested (Green, 1967). This
combines a basic minimum income with a marginal tax
rate of less than 100% everywhere, and provides an
incentive to work at any positive wage rate. In
the simple model considered in this paper, it will
ensure full employment. In Section 3 of the paper
we define two tax systems: a conventional linear
tax system combined with unemployment pay, and a
Negative Income Tax system. In Section 4 we set up
a simple model with a homogeneous labour force, some
of whom are organised by a trade union, which determines the real wage and hence employment level in
the unionised sector. In consequence, the real wage
that would yield full employment in the competitive
sector is below the level of unemployment pay. We
assume that the disutility of labour is zero, hence
the net of tax wage in the competitive sector equals
the level of unemployment pay. Unemployment is
positive under a conventional tax system. We then
assume the introduction of a Negative Income Tax,
where the basic minimum income is set equal to the
level of unemployment pay, and the marginal tax rate
is set so that the net of tax income of the unionised
wage rate is unchanged at the original gross unionised wage rate. On the assumption, relaxed in
Section 5, that the unionised wage rate does not
change as a consequence of the shift to a Negative
Income Tax, we examine the budgetary consequences.
    Under the Negative Income Tax, workers have an
incentive to take a job at any wage rate, hence the
wage rate in the competitive sector falls to ensure
full employment. The net budgetary cost of the
scheme, or level of supplementary finance required,
depends on the ratio of the level of employment in
the non-unionised sector to the level of unemployment.
Each worker previously employed in the non-unionised
sector receives from the state an amount equal to his
previous net of tax income, and then pays tax on a
lower gross wage, so the cost to the state is positive.
Each previously unemployed worker now receives his
previous unemployment benefit from the state but now
pays tax on his wages. Hence, the cost to the
state is negative.
    In Section 5 we relax the assumption that the
introduction of the Negative Income Tax will have no
effect on the unionised wage rate. We view the
union as having a utility function defined over net
of tax real wage rates and employment levels, and we
adopt the utilitarian function used recently by
Oswald (1979, 1982), McDonald and Solow (1981) and

Sampson (1983).   The union sets the real wage, and
accepts the employment level determined by the profit-
maximising decisions of firms.   We find that the
effect on the unionised wage rate of the switch to a
Negative Income Tax is indeterminate.   One consseque-
nce of the switch is that the net income of workers
in the competitive sector rises, and this will increase the unionised wage rate.   Another consequence
is that the income tax structure becomes more progressive, which increases the employment cost of a
rise in the net of tax real wage, and induces the
union to lower its wage.   In this respect, the
Negative Income Tax is similar to the tax on wage
increases, proposed by Layard (1982) and Lerner (1978)
as a remedy for unemployment.   We find that if the
initial level of unemployment is high, the effect of
a Negative Income Tax on the unionised wage rate is
negative.   A low initial level of unemployment will
result in a higher unionised wage rate.   Although
unemployment still vanishes, labour market distortion may be so much worse that output falls.

SECTION 2:   NOTATION

w, N, $f(N)$	Wage, employment and output in sector A.
v, L, $g(L)$	Wage, employment and output in sector B.
U, P	Level of unemployment, working population
S	Budget surplus
$Q = f(N) + g(L)$	Output
x	Unemployment pay
y	Net of tax income per worker
$\phi(y)$	Indirect utility function
$1 - a$, $1 - c$	Marginal tax rates
b	Minimum income under negative income tax
CTS	Conventional tax and social security system
NIT	Negative Income Tax system
A	Index for unionised sector
B	Index for non-unionised sector

SECTION 3:   LINEAR TAX SYSTEMS

Each worker is assumed to supply one unit of labour
per period, hence gross of tax income is equal to
the gross of tax wage rate.   The price of output is

27

normalised at unity, hence real and nominal magnitudes are equivalent. Figures 1 and 2 sketch net of tax income per worker y, as a function of gross of tax income w, for two tax systems. Figure 1 is for a "conventional" tax system (referred to as "CTS") where the tax base is total income, and the tax rate is 1 - a. The "CTS" contains an untaxed unemployment benefit level x, regarded by the government as a basic minimum level of income below which no one shall be allowed to fall. Workers have the choice of working for a net of tax income y = aw or being unemployed and receiving unemployment pay x. We assume that workers are indifferent between working for a net of tax wage y = x and being unemployed, and so no worker will accept a job at a gross wage of less than x/a. Hence the net of tax wage (2) under the CTS is

$$y_o = \text{Max}(x, aw) \tag{1}$$

and the segment xzy in Figure 1 sketches this.

In Figure 2 we sketch a negative income tax system, referred to as "NIT": each worker receives b from the state, and then pays a marginal tax rate 1 - c on all earned income. Hence an unemployed worker receives b and an employed worker b + cw, so the net of tax wage under the NIT is

$$y_1 = b + cw \tag{2}$$

and this is sketched in Figure 2. In the paper we examine the consequences of changing from a CTS to an NIT where the NIT has two properties:

1. The basic minimum b under the NIT is the same as the level of unemployment pay x under the original CTS;
2. The model has single wage w_o in the unionised sector, and the marginal tax rate 1 - c for the NIT is chosen so that the net of tax wage in the unionised sector is unchanged at the original gross wage w_o. Hence, c is determined by

$$aw_o = x + cw_o \tag{3}$$

So we commence with a net of tax y as a function of gross income xzj under a CTS, and change to an NIT giving a net of tax function xk. In Section 4 of

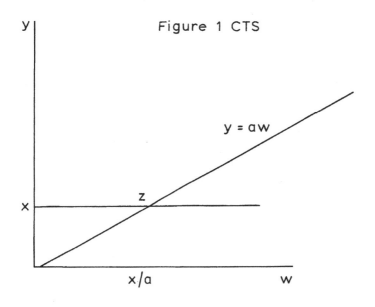

Figure 1 CTS

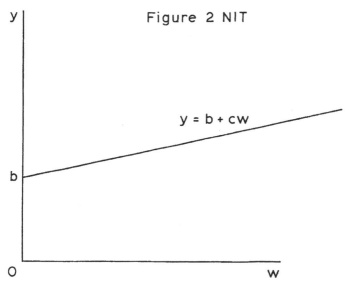

Figure 2 NIT

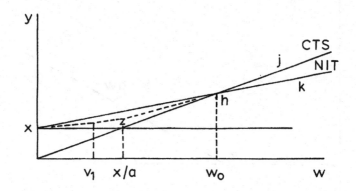

Figure 3

the paper we discuss the employment and budgetary
consequences of the change on the assumption that the
union does not change its gross wage rate.   In
Section 5 we then discuss how the union will react
to the change in the tax system.

SECTION 4:   THE LABOUR MARKET

The economy consists of two perfectly competitive
productive sectors A and B, and has a working population of P identical workers, each of whom supplies
one unit of labour.   Both sectors produce the same
commodity, with a given capital stock and state of
technology.   The only difference between the sectors is that the workers in section A are members
of a single trade union, which sets a real wage w,
whereas workers in sector B are not unionised, and
the real wage v is determined by competition.   Let
N workers in sector A produce $f(N)$ output, and let
L workers in sector B produce $g(L)$ output, where

$$f'N > 0, \quad f''(N) < 0, \quad g'(L) > 0, \quad g''(L) \leqq 0 \quad (4)$$

and national income Q is given by

$$Q = f(N) + g(L) \tag{5}$$

Firms maximise profits in each sector, and output is determined by aggregate supply (3), and will satisfy the condition that the marginal physical product of labour in each sector will equal the real wage rate:

$$f'(N) = w \qquad g'(L) = v \tag{6}$$

We will therefore have demand for labour functions $N(w)$ and $L(v)$ where (4) and (5) imply

$$N'(w) < 0 \qquad L'(v) < 0 \tag{7}$$

and our assumption that output is determined by aggregate supply implies that actual employment will be $N(w)$ and $L(v)$ in each sector respectively.

In Figure 4 the horizontal distance $O_A O_B$ represents the total working population P. The demand for labour $N(w)$ in sector A is measured to the right

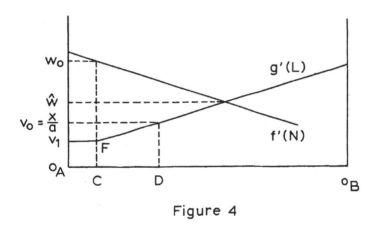

Figure 4

from O_A by the curve $f'(N)$, and the demand for labour $L(v)$ is measured to the left from O_B by the curve $g'(L)$ (4). If both labour markets were competitive, full employment would be established at a real wage $\hat{w}$. The determinants of union behaviour are discussed in Section 5 of the paper, and here

31

we now assume that the union establishes a real wage $w_0 > \hat{w}$, so that employment in Sector A, $N(w_0)$, is given by the distance $O_A C$.   If unemployment pay x were zero, the real wage in sector B would fall to v_1, which would satisfy

$$L(v_1) = P - N(w_0) \tag{8}$$

If unemployment pay x were higher than the net of tax wage av, as no workers would be willing to work for a gross wage less than x/a, the real wage in sector B would be

$$v_0 = x/a \tag{9}$$

Employment $L(v_0)$ would be the distance DO_B, and unemployment

$$U = P - N(w_0) - L(v_0) \tag{10}$$

would be measured by the distance CD in Figure 4. Since the level of unemployment pay sets a floor to the real wage v in sector B, we have

$$v = Max\{x/a, \; L^{-1} (P - N(w))\} \tag{11}$$

and we assume that in the original state, with a conventional tax system, w_0 is high enough to ensure that $v_1 < x/a$, so that some workers are unemployed.

We now envisage a shift to a negative income tax, as defined by (2) and (3), on the assumption, relaxed in Section 5, that the unionised wage rate does not change, so $w_1 = w_0$, and hence net of tax incomes in the unionised sector do not change. The net of tax income in the non-unionised sector is now given by

$$y = x + cv$$

and hence workers will be prepared to work in sector B at any positive wage rate.   As a consequence of the shift from a CTS to an NIT, the wage rate in sector B falls to v_1, and the unemployed workers take jobs in sector B.   National Income increases by the area CDEF in Figure 4.   All workers in the non-unionised sector B are better off (both the previously employed and the previously unemployed), and workers in the unionised sector A are just as well off.

We now consider the budgetary consequences of the introduction of the NIT. Using the subscripts 0 and 1 to denote values under the original CTS and NIT respectively, we define the "budget surplus" S as income tax receipts from workers less payments by the state to workers. Hence S is the government revenue available to finance other items of expenditure. Under the CTS, defined by (1),

$$S_0 = (1 - a)w_0 N_0 + (1 - a)v_0 L_0 - xU \qquad (12)$$

and under the NIT defined by (2)

$$S_1 = (1 - c)w_1 N_1 + (1 - c)v_1 L_1 - b(N_1 + L_1) \qquad (13)$$

We assume that the gross real wage in the unionised sector stays constant during the shift to the NIT, so $w_1 = w_0$, and that the basic minimum income level b in the NIT is the same as the level of unemployment pay x under the CTS. Since $w_1 = w_0$, $N_1 = N_0$, and all the unemployed workers take jobs in the non-unionised sector under the NIT, and the original net of tax wage av_0 in sector B was equal to the level of unemployment pay, we have

$$w_1 = w_0, \ N_1 = N_0, \ L_1 = L_0 + U, \ av_0 = x,$$

$$b = x \qquad (14)$$

Using (14), together with (2) which yields the NIT marginal tax rate as a function of the CTS marginal tax rate, from (12) and (13) after some manipulation,

$$S_1 - S_0 = (1 - c)v_1 U + \{(1 - c)v_1 - v_0\}L_0 \qquad (15)$$

The sign of $S_1 - S_0$ determines the net budgetary cost of the switch from the CTS to the NIT, and if $S_1 - S_0 < 0$ the switch has to be financed from other tax sources, reducing government spending elsewhere, government borrowing, or increasing the marginal tax rate $1 - c$. Since $1 - c < 1$ and $v_1 < v_0$, the coefficient on U in (15) is positive, and on L_0 is negative. Since the government was paying x to the unemployed under the CTS, and still pays them x under the NIT, the government budget improves by the income tax $(1 - c)v_1$ now paid by workers who were previously unemployed. Workers who were previously employed in sector B paid $(1 - a)v_0 = v_0 - x$ in taxes. The

33

government now pays them x and collects $(1 - c)v_1$ in taxes, hence the loss in tax for each worker previously employed in sector B is $v_0 - (1 - c)v_1 > 0$. The switch to an NIT is more likely to be "self-financing", in the sense of not requiring finance from other sources, the higher the ratio of unemployment to employment in the non-unionised sector.

One obvious source of supplementary finance for the switch from a CTS to an NIT is profits taxation. On our assumption that $w_1 = w_0$, profits in sector A remain constant. In sector B, the wage falls from v_0 to v_1, and employment increases from L_0 to $L_1 = L_0 + U$. Profits Π in sector B increase by the area FEHI in Figure 4, which can be approximated by

$$\Pi_1 - \Pi_0 = L_0(v_0 - v_1) + \tfrac{1}{2}(v_0 - v_1)U \qquad (16)$$

Using (15) and (16), if all the extra profits are available for taxation, the budgetary gain following the switch from a CTS to an NIT is

$$S_1 - S_0 + \Pi_1 - \Pi_0 = (1 - c)v_1 U - cv_1 L_0$$
$$+ \tfrac{1}{2}(v_0 - v_1)U \qquad (17)$$

Finally, we comment on a non-linear NIT. From (15) and (17), the budgetary gain following the switch to a linear NIT will be greater the higher the original level of unemployment. Both the original workers in sector B and the originally unemployed become better off, whereas the government budget only improves as a worker becomes employed. The marginal tax rate $1 - c$ was determined in the above comparison by imposing the condition that unionised workers be made no worse off by the introduction of a linear NIT. A self-financing NIT might require higher marginal tax rates than $1 - c$ discussed above. One solution might be a non-linear system with marginal tax rates $1 - c$ above for unionised workers, and a higher marginal tax rate for workers in the competitive sector.

In Figure 3 the dotted curve xh followed by the line segment hs would represent a non-linear NIT with falling marginal rates of tax. Net of tax income for workers in the non-unionised sector B would be higher than the level x under the CTS, hence the move from the CTS to the non-linear NIT schedule xhj would be a Pareto improvement.

34

SECTION 5: THE UNION WAGE RATE

The discussion so far has been on the assumption that
the wage rate set by the union in sector A does not
change as a result of the transition from a CTS to
an NIT. We now relax that assumption, and prove in
this section that the effect on the union wage rate
is a priori indeterminate. Figure 5, which is
similar to Figure 4, illustrates the importance of
the effects of the NIT on the union wage rate.

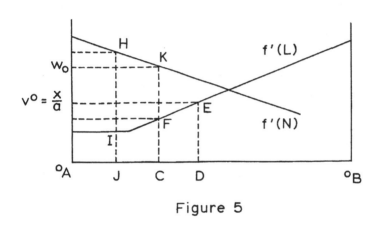

Figure 5

The original unionised wage rate was w_0, so $O_A C$
measured employment in the unionised sector, with
wage v_0 in the non-unionised sector; employment was
DO_B, hence unemployment was CD in Figure 5. At a
constant union wage rate w_0, employment in the non-
unionised sector expands to CO_B, and the gain in
national income is the area FEDC. If the union then
raises its wage to w_1, employment in sector A falls
by JC and expands in sector B by JC. This yields
a loss in national income equal to the area HFKI.
A fall in w would yield an analogous gain in output.
Hence if the introduction of the NIT led to a large
increase in the unionised wage rate, national income
could fall.
We discuss this effect by using the model of the

rational trade union.   It has a utility function
defined over the net of tax real wage rate and the
level of employment of union members.   It chooses
a gross real wage w, to maximise this utility function, in the knowledge that firms will react by setting the employment $\bar{N}(w)$.   We adopt the following
utility function

$$\Theta = N\emptyset(y) + (M - N)\emptyset(\alpha) \tag{18}$$

where M is the level of union membership, y is the
net of tax income of employed union members, and α
is the level of income that a union member who lost
his job would achieve.   The term $\emptyset(y)$ is an indirect
utility function, and we assume that

$$\emptyset'(y) > 0, \qquad \emptyset''(y) < 0 \tag{19}$$

Forms like (18) have been used by Oswald (1979, 1982a),
McDonald and Solow (1981) and Sampson (1983).   The
utility function Θ can be interpreted either as a
weighted sum of individual utilities, or as the
expected utility of a union member who has a probability N/M of having a unionised job in the forthcoming contract period.   It defines a family of
convex indifference curves in net wage-employment
space, with the property that neither the net wage
nor level of employment are inferior.
By defining net of tax real income y as

$$y = \beta + \gamma w \tag{20}$$

the union's choice of w, and hence y and N(w), will
depend on the parameters α, β and γ.   Under the CTS,
a union member who lost his job would either receive
unemployment pay x or work in the non-unionised sector for the same net of tax pay x, so $\alpha = x$ for the
CTS.   Under the NIT, such a worker would find employment in the non-unionised sector at a wage v,
hence have a net income of x + cv.   We assume for
simplicity that v is a constant.   So the values of
the parameters α, β and γ under the two tax systems
are

$$\text{CTS:} \quad \alpha = x \qquad \beta = 0 \qquad \gamma = a \tag{21}$$

$$\text{NIT:} \quad \alpha = x + cv \qquad \beta = x \qquad \gamma = c \tag{22}$$

For given (α, β, γ), first-order conditions for
utility maximisation are

$$N'(w)\{\emptyset(y) - \emptyset(\alpha)\} + \gamma N\emptyset'(y) = 0 \qquad (23)$$

so that the union balances the utility gain $\gamma\emptyset'(y)$ of a higher net of tax real wage for its N members, against the loss in utility $\emptyset(y) - \emptyset(\alpha)$ suffered by the $N'(w)$ members who lose their jobs.

The second-order conditions for utility maximisation require that

$$\Theta''(w) = N''(w)\{\emptyset(y) - \emptyset(\alpha)\} + 2\gamma\emptyset'(y)N'(w)$$

$$+ \gamma^2 N\emptyset''(y) < 0 \qquad (24)$$

hold, which we assume to be the case. Since $\emptyset(y) > 0$ and $N'(w) < 0$, $\emptyset''(y) < 0$ hold, this requires that $N''(w)$ should not be large and positive. A concave function $N(w)$ would suffice. The comparative static effects are

$$\frac{\partial w}{\partial \alpha} = N'(w)\emptyset'(\alpha)/\Theta''(w) > 0 \qquad (25)$$

$$\frac{\partial w}{\partial \beta} = -\{N'(w)\emptyset'(y) + \gamma N\emptyset''(y)\}/\Theta''(w) < 0 \qquad (26)$$

$$\frac{\partial w}{\partial \gamma} = -\{wN'(w)\emptyset'(y) + N\emptyset'(y)$$

$$+ \gamma wN\emptyset''(y)\}/\Theta''(w) \gtrless 0 \qquad (27)$$

Since the effect of a change in the marginal tax rate $1 - \gamma$ is to alter the slope of the union's opportunity locus in $y - N$ space, and y and N are both normal goods in the union's utility function, the indeterminacy of the sign of $\partial w/\partial\gamma$ arises from income and substitution effects operating in different directions.

If β and γ change in such a way that net of tax income at the original wage rate remains constant, β and γ have to satisfy

$$d\beta = -wd\gamma \qquad (28)$$

and we obtain

$$\left.\frac{\partial w}{\partial \gamma}\right|_{d\beta = -wd\gamma} = -N\emptyset'(y)/\Theta''(w) < 0 \qquad (29)$$

These effects are illustrated in Figures 6 and 7.

Let AB in Figure 6 represent the union's opportunity set in real net of tax wage-employment space, and let its indifference curve touch AB at C. The effect of a rise in α is to lower the utility loss $\emptyset(y) - \emptyset(\alpha)$ suffered by union members who lose jobs in the unionised sector. The union will therefore be prepared to trade off a larger fall in employment against a given rise in the real wage. Its indifference curve through C will now be flatter, drawn as dotted in Figure 6, and the union will choose a higher real wage.

Let AB in Figure 7 represent an original opportunity set. If γ increases and β changes according to (28), the original gross of tax real wage and level of employment yields the same net of tax real wage. A given fall in employment now yields a smaller rise in the net of tax real wage. The new budget line is therefore DE, which is flatter than AB but passes through the original choice C. The union will then choose a lower real wage and higher employment level F (5).

We can hence express the union's choice of w as a function of $w(\alpha, \beta, \gamma)$ of the parameters it faces, with partial derivatives given by (25), (26) and (27). The original CTS choice was $w_0 = w(x, 0, a)$ and the union responds to the introduction of the NIT with a choice $w_1 = w(x + cv, x, c)$, hence the change Δw is

$$\Delta w = w(x + cv, x, c) - w(x, 0, a)$$

The first term in the Taylor seris expansion of Δw is

$$\Delta w = cv \left.\frac{\partial w(x, 0, a)}{\partial \alpha}\right|_{\alpha = x} + x \left.\frac{\partial w(x, 0, a)}{\partial \beta}\right|_{\beta = 0}$$

$$+ (c - a)\left.\frac{\partial w(x, 0, a)}{\partial \gamma}\right|_{\gamma = a} \tag{30}$$

We impose the condition $aw^0 = x + cw^0$, so that $d\beta = -w_0 d\gamma$, in which case (30) simplifies to

$$\Delta w = \{(cvN'/w^0)\emptyset'(x) + xN\emptyset'(y^0)/w^0\}/\theta''(w) \tag{31}$$

Since $\theta''(w) < 0$ and $N'(w) < 0$ the first term in (31) is positive and the second term is negative. The transition to the NIT described above implies that the income of a union member priced out of a job increases by the net of tax wage cv in the competitive

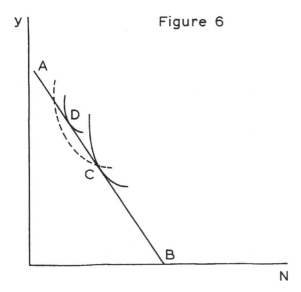

Figure 6

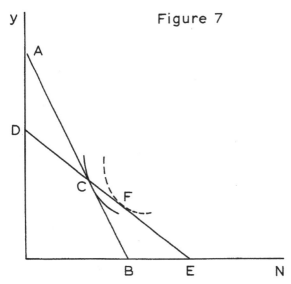

Figure 7

sector, and the effect of this is to raise the unionised wage rate. The other effect is to make a higher net of tax wage more costly in terms of lost jobs, and this alone reduces the unionised wage rate.

The crucial determinant of Δw is the wage rate v paid to workers in the non-unionised sector under the NIT in comparison with the level of unemployment pay x. From Figure 4 it is clear that the level of unemployment U in the CTS is an increasing function of $(x/a - v)$. If v is very small in relation to x/a, unemployment will be very high under the CTS. The positive term in (31) will be small, so $\Delta w < 0$ will hold and the union wage rate will fall as the NIT is introduced.

An upper limit to v is x/a, in which case unemployment will be zero in the CTS. If we use (23) to eliminate $\emptyset'(y^0)$ in (31), write $\alpha = x$ and $\gamma = z$, note that

$$c/a = (y - x)/y$$

we can evaluate (31) for $v = x/a$. This yields

$$\Delta w = \frac{xN'(w^0)\{\emptyset(y^0)(y - x) - \{\emptyset(y^0) - \emptyset(x)\}\}}{y\theta''(w)}$$

Since $\emptyset(y) = \emptyset(x) + (y - x)\emptyset'(x) + (y - x)^2\emptyset''(x)/2$ this becomes

$$\Delta w = \frac{-xN'(w^0)(y - x)^2\emptyset''(x)}{2y\theta''(w)} > 0$$

Hence we find that $\Delta w < 0$ when v is very small, and $\Delta w > 0$ when $v = x/a$. The critical value of v at which $\Delta w = 0$ cannot be found by (31) alone, since (31) is only the first term in a Taylor series expansion of $w(x + cv, x, c) - w(x, 0, a)$ around $w(x, 0, a)$ (6).

SECTION 6: CAVEATS AND CONCLUSIONS

The basic conclusion of the paper is clear. If the level of unemployment pay in the CTS is high in relation to the wage that would yield full employment, the level of unemployment will be high. The introduction of a linear NIT would result in a fall in the unionised wage rate, reducing the degree of labour market distortion, as well as yielding full employment. The government's budget would improve, so that the scheme would generate a positive net revenue.   If on the other hand, the level of unemployment pay is low in relation to the market clearing wage, so that unemployment under the CTS is low, the introduction of an NIT would lead to a higher real wage in the labour market.   Although unemployment is eliminated, national income might fall.   The scheme would require supplementary finance.   A nonlinear NIT, with decreasing marginal tax rates, would lessen the increase in the unionised wage rate, and lower the net budgetary cost.   Since workers in the non-unionised sector would still be better off than under the CTS, the only losers would be union members who lost their jobs as a result of the rise in the unionised wage rate.

The model is concerned with only two labour market distortions: the effect of a monopoly union, which leads to a divergence between the marginal products of labour in the two sectors, and the effects of unemployment pay.   Workers in the model are homogeneous, and supply one unit of labour, and choose unemployment only because they would be no better off financially.   The effect of an NIT is that all workers will always benefit financially by working, however low the net of tax wage rate.   The NIT requires a higher marginal tax rate than the CTS for income levels above unemployment pay, and the main drawback of the model is that it ignores any distortions that would arise from this higher marginal tax rate.   In models with a variable labour supply, in terms of effort on hours of work, the substitution effects of the rise in marginal tax rates will reduce labour supply.   On the assumption that leisure is non-inferior, labour supply will only rise when the wage rate is substantially higher than average.   The switch to the NIT will not change the average tax rate for workers whose gross income was around the average, hence their labour supply would fall.   For workers paid less than this, the income effect of the lump sum element in the NIT would reduce labour supply.

Similar arguments occur if the tax distortions arise because of decisions about occupational choice or education and training.   However, a Meade (1964) type argument would reinforce the case for the NIT. Technical progress may increase the demand for skilled labour at the expense of unskilled labour, and even now unemployment is heavily concentrated among the unskilled.   The unskilled are therefore unlikely to find jobs at a wage rate regarded as acceptable in terms of conventional standards, hence an NIT is the only way of inducing them to take jobs.

The unskilled wage rate would fall, and the effect of this is to increase the incentive to acquire skills, despte the higher marginal tax rate.

In conclusion, the NIT would reduce unemployment, at the possible cost of increasing distortions elsewhere, largely arising out of greater equality of post-tax incomes.   In this respect its effects are similar to the tax-based incomes policies advocated by Layard (1982) and Lerner (1978), which also operate by increasing the employment costs of higher wage rates.   As Lerner points out, these distortions might be slight in comparison with the distortion of large-scale unemployment.

NOTES

1.   As pointed out by Marshall (1978), the present U.K. tax treatment of retired people is a perfect example of Negative Income Tax.

2.   We use the subscript 0 to denote values prevailing under the CTS, and the subscript 1 to denote values prevailing under the NIT.

3.   We assume that the price level adjusts to clear the market for output, so aggregate demand for output is always equal to $f(N(w)) + g(L(v))$. The economy is therefore on the boundary of the states of Classical Unemployment and Keynesian Unemployment, as defined by Malinvaud (1977).

4.   The horizontal segment of $g'(1)$ is included for simplicity, to avoid the union having to conjecture the effects of its action on the wage in the non-unionised sector.

5.   This effect of increasing the employment cost of a higher real wage in the NIT context, is similar to the employment-creating effects of Layard's tax on wage increases (1982).

6.   The concavity of $w(\alpha, \beta, \gamma)$ depends, inter alia, on the sign of $N'''(w)$, which in turn depends inter alia on the sign of $f''''(N)$.

UNION UTILITY MAXIMISATION AND OPTIMAL CONTRACTS

Jane Black and George Bulkley

This paper analyses the type of contract which will
be chosen by a union which attempts to maximise the
sum of the utilities of its M members, subject to
the constraint that the firm must earn a profit of
at least an amount, π_0. The determination of π_0
is an important issue, a primary function of trade
unions being to secure as much of the value added by
the firm's activities for their members as possible.
However, the exact determination of π_0, through relative bargaining strengths, threats of strikes or
lock-outs, is not the focus of this paper, which is
primarily concerned with the efficiency costs resulting from the existence of the union.   These costs
will be shown to depend crucially on the type of contract chosen, where π_0 is treated as given, although
it will also be shown that in some circumstances,
depending on the type of contract, the absolute level
of π_0 may affect efficiency.
    As argued by Akerlof and Miyazaki (1980), the
firm is assumed to be indifferent between any two
contracts which yield the same level of profit. On
the other hand, the union, assuming that individual
workers have diminishing marginal utility of income,
will be concerned when choosing a contract with the
distribution of income amongst its members as well
as with total wage payments.   The level of employment and any transfer payments such as lay-off pay
are important determinants of this income distribution.
    This approach in which the union attempts to
maximise the sum of members' risk averse utility
functions subject to the firm earning a minimum level
of profits is analogous to that of implicit contract
theory, surveyed in Hart (1983), where the firm is
modelled as choosing a contract to maximise expected
utility level, u_0. Some of the results of the

analysis of implicit contract theory hold, when uncertainty is introduced into our model, where it is
the union rather than the firm which is the active
agent.
        In common with much of implicit contract theory
and models of union behaviour, efficiency is defined
with reference to the first best competitive equilibrium in which the marginal revenue product of the
marginal worker is equal to his opportunity cost.
It is recognised that this does not constitute a
complete welfare evaluation of the effects of unionisation if the union does not constitute the only
market imperfection.   For example, there is the
well known second best text book case where if the
firm is acting as a mononsist the introduction of a
union can increase Walrasian efficiency.
        Unlike implicit contract theory and conventional
analysis of wage determination, we allow for the possibility that the optimal contract may result in the
number employed, L, exceeding the number of union
members, M.   Both Oswald (1982) and McDonald and
Solow (1981) restrict attention to interior solutions
where L < M.   This rules out the interesting question, under what circumstances will the M union members allow additional, non-union employees to be
taken on ?   Consideration of who the M members of
the union are suggests that this may be a common case
in practice.   In the conventional analysis, all M
members are assumed to be in a Rawlsian 'original
position', all with an equal likelihood of employment.   However, in most bargaining situations the
unions and firm have a history so that some N members
are working and (M-N) are unemployed.   Further, with
the observation that in practice those who work in
one period have first priority for work in the subsequent period, there will be a split of interest
between the currently employed and the currently
unemployed members.   Since it is the currently employed who have the power to enforce contracts, by
strikes for example, an important case to consider is
where the M members the union represents consist only
of the N currently employed workforce.   In this case
an interior solution with L < M will be the exception
rather than the rule, especially in an expanding economy.   At the other extreme is the assumption that M
includes all those currently employed by the firm and
all those potentially employable who would otherwise
be unemployed.   The intermediate assumption is that
M consists of the currently employed plus others who
have some specific link with the firm or union but
where there is a pool of other unemployed workers

who could be employed if this was necessary for the optimal contract. It will be assumed that the union has sufficient bargaining strength for it to insist that no non-union member is employed if there is an unemployed union member.

As a starting point, the maximum utility under certainty derivable by the union will be considered. Various constraints will then be placed upon the variables which may enter into the contract and the effects upon Walrasian efficiency examined.   It will be shown that a contract incorporating agreements about redundancy and retirements could achieve both the maximum possible level of union utility and Walrasian efficiency.

Assume that the utility of an employed union member is given by $u(w_i)$ where w_i is the income he receives from employment and that the utility of an unemployed union member is given by $u(r_j+b)$ where r_j is any transfer payments he receives either from the firm or by a levy on employed members and b is the opportunity cost of working, assumed constant and the same for all workers. Ruling out managerial theories of the union where the union's utility function includes M or L as direct arguments the union's utility function is given by

$$V = \sum_{1}^{L} u(w_1) + \sum_{L+1}^{M} u(r_j+b) \qquad L \leqslant M$$

$$\text{or} \quad V = \sum_{1}^{M} u(w_i) \qquad\qquad\qquad L > M$$

The firm's costs other than labour are assumed to be fixed and profit is defined net of these. Revenue, $R(L)$, is assumed to depend only upon the amount of labour employed, where $R'(L) > 0$, $R''(L) < 0$. Define $B(L)$ as the total amount paid out by the firm in wages and transfer payments to the unemployed. The profit constraint states

$$R(L) - B(L) \geqslant \pi_o \qquad\qquad\qquad (1)$$

Assume that non-union members, if employed, are paid a wage of w_a. The total payments to union and non-union members must equal $B(L)$, giving

$$\sum_{1}^{L} w_i + \sum_{L+1}^{M} r_j = B(L) \qquad L \leqslant M \qquad (2a)$$

$$\sum_1^M w_i + w_a(L-M) = B(L) \qquad L > M. \qquad (2b)$$

The union would like to maximise V subject to constraints (1) and (2).

V will be maximised if the following conditions hold:

$$R'(L) = b \qquad (3)$$

$$w_a = b \qquad (4)$$

$$w_i = w \qquad \text{for all } i \qquad (5)$$

$$r_j = w - b \text{ for all } j \qquad (6)$$

w_a and w must also be such that condition (1) holds as an equality.

Condition (3) states that for the firm and union's joint surplus to be maximised, the marginal product of the Lth worker should be equal to his opportunity cost. Thus Walrasian efficiency results. Condition (4) states that if non-union members are employed they should be paid their minimum supply price, so leaving the maximum possible share of the wage bill to be distributed amongst union members. Conditions (5) and (6) only apply if the union members have diminishing marginal utilities of income, in which case the sum of utilities is maximised if the income of each union member is equalised, the employed receiving w and the unemployed receiving $(r+b) = w$.

In what follows we examine various possible contracts to see if the optimal level of output as characterised by (3) is produced and whether they provide for efficient distribution of income as characterised by conditions (5) and (6). The real world imposes restrictions upon what it is feasible to specify in a contract. The first restriction which we impose which is common to all the models discussed below is that wage discrimination between union and non-union members is not possible either because of a union belief in an 'equal pay for equal work' principal or because the union's bargaining power is not sufficiently great to stop the firm from taking on non-union members in preference to union members if the former are actually cheaper.

SECTION 1:   CONTRACTS DEFINED OVER w ONLY

Nickell (1983) has argued that bargaining over the quantity of labour hired is unlikely because this

violates the firm's 'right to manage'.   There would
also seem to be good reasons, based on moral hazard
arguments, for unions not to negotiate lay-off pay
for unemployed members.   If they did, then it would
be possible for one worker to join several unions and
claim lay-off pay from several firms.   In practice
workers are not perfectly homogeneous and the decision
about who is to be employed out of the pool, M, is
not random but is determined by some selection procedure.   Thus the worker intent on drawing several
lots of lay-off pay has only to ensure that the
selection procedure rejects him.   Similar objections
apply to union members themselves imposing a levy on
employed workers to subsidise the unemployed.
     Oswald (1982) has analysed the consequences of a
contract which only specifies the wage at which
workers can be hired, but our analysis differs from
his in two respects: we explicitly introduce a profit constraint and we do not limit our attention to
interior solutions.
     The profit maximising firm picks L to satisfy

$$R'(L) = w$$

where w must satisfy the condition

$$R(L) - wL = \pi_o.$$

If there is no mechanism by which the union can
transfer income from employed to unemployed members
the union's utility function is given by

$$V = u(w)L + u(b)(M-L) \qquad\qquad L \leq M$$

or

$$V = u(w)M \qquad\qquad L > M$$

     Figure 1 illustrates the possibilities.
     If $\pi_0 = \pi_1$ the union will prefer to let the firm
make profits $\pi = \pi_2$ where the indifference curve i$_3$
is tangential to $R'(L)$ giving a wage of w_3 and employment L_3.   The firm's profit constraint is not binding.   This is Oswald's (1982) case.   However, if
$\pi_0 = \pi_3$ the best the union can achieve is to set wages
at w_2 resulting in L_2 employed and $M-L_2$ unemployed
union members.   An interesting case is where $\pi_0 = \pi_4$.
Here, the union can increase the wage rate paid to
its members by allowing the firm to employ L_1-M non-
union members.   True, it would be better off if a
discriminatory wage of b could be paid to non-union
members but this has been ruled out by the 'equal

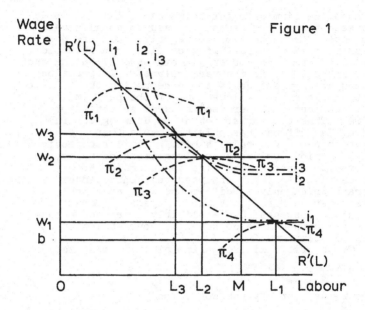

Figure 1

pay' assumption.

Although one has to be careful about drawing
aggregate conclusions from this partial equilibrium
model, a somewhat surprising implication of the model
should be noted: the higher the profit rate required
by the firm, the higher the resulting employment level.
So, for example, an increase in corporation tax in a
situation of perfect international capital mobility
would increase gross profit requirements and hence
employment.

SECTION 2:   CONTRACTS WHICH SPECIFY BOTH w AND L

It was originally pointed out by Leontieff (1947),
with a later exposition by McDonald and Solow (1982),
that the union can increase its utility by bargaining
about L as well as w.   Consider Figure 2.

If the firm must achieve profit level π_1, the
union maximises its utility at $w = w_2$, $L = L_2$ which
is the point where the iso-profit line π_1 is tangential to the indifference curve i_2.   This gives a
higher level of utility than setting the wage at w_1
and allowing the firm free choice to pick employment
level L_1.

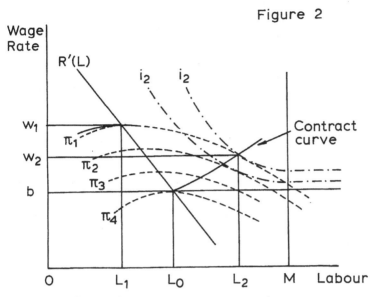

Figure 2

The slope of the contract curve, i.e. the locus
of tangencies of the iso-profit lines and the union's
indifference curves, depends upon the assumption made
about $u''(w)$.   If $u''(w) = 0$ then the union is indifferent about intra-union income distribution and
picks that contract which maximises the total value
added going to its members.   This will be achieved
if $L = L_0$ for all values of π_0 and the contract curve
will therefore be vertical.   If, however, $u''(w) < 0$,
the union will prefer to increase both wages and employment as π falls and the contract curve will slope
upwards to the north east from the point (L_0, b).
(A formal proof is given in an appendix).   Thus
unless the profit constraint is set at $\pi_0 = \pi_4$,
Walrasian over-employment will result as illustrated
in the diagram.
       The conclusion that there will be over-employment
depends not only upon the assumption that $u''(w) < 0$
but also on the assumption that $L_0 < M$.   If this
latter assumption is not valid, then Walrasian under-
employment will result.   Consider Figure 3.
       By assumption, the union is assumed indifferent
to the utility of non-members.   If $M = M_1$ its optimal strategy is to set $w = w_1$ and $L = M_1$.   However,
if $M = M_2$ the union can maximise its members' incomes

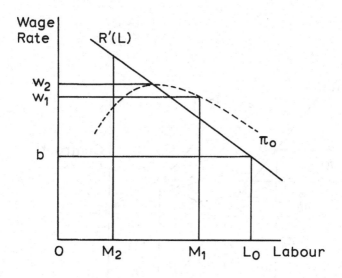

Figure 3

by setting w = w_2 and allowing the firm to take on
sufficient non-union members to equate R'(L) = w_2.
Again there is the implicit assumption that it is
not possible to pay discriminatory wages.   In both
cases there is Walrasian under-employment.

A contract specifying only w and L has been
shown to result either in over-employment or under-
employment depending upon the assumptions about M
relative to L_0.   Only if both L_0 < M and u"(w) $\leq$ 0
does the efficient outcome occur.

SECTION 3:   CONTRACTS WHICH PERMIT REDUNDANCY PAYMENTS

Once the possibility of redundancy payments is introduced the {w,L} contract discussed above is shown to
have an inherent instability.

Consider firstly a union which is interested
only in the welfare of the N workers who are currently employed.   Assume that for the Nth worker his
marginal revenue product is less than b but he is
paid wage w_1 as in Figure 4.

Redundancy payments are normally in the form of
a lump sum but r is defined here as the income flow
generated by the lump sum.   The firm could afford to

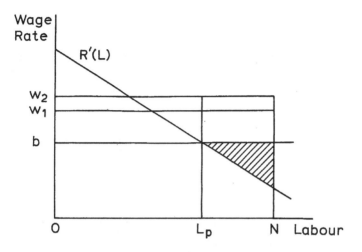

Figure 4

make redundancy payments of $r_1 = (w_1-b)$ to $(N-L_p)$ workers increasing its profits by the shaded area. However, it is assumed that the union can capture any profits in excess of π_0 and so the union can achieve a higher level of utility by negotiating a contract with

$$w = w_2, \quad r_2 = w_2-b$$

where

$$R(L_p) - w_2 L_p - r_2(N-L_p) = R(N) - w_1 N.$$

Each member of the union will now receive the same, higher, level of utility, $u(w_2)$ if employed and $u(r_2+b) = u(w_2)$ if made redundant. Note it is only necessary for the union to negotiate about two prices in this contract, w and r, a hiring and a firing price. The firm will equate $R'(L) = w-r$ and the Walrasian employment level L_p is achieved.

Now consider the outcome of a $\{w,L\}$ contract where the union is concerned with the utility of M members, $M > L_0$. It negotiates a contract with $w = w_1$, $L = L_1$ as in Figure 5.

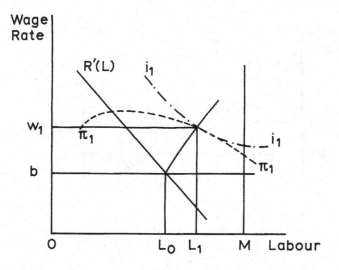

Figure 5

It now becomes apparent that it could achieve a higher level of utility for the L_1 workers by negotiating
a {w,r} contract with redundancy payments for L_1-L_0
workers and a higher wage.   However, there remain
$M-L_1$ unemployed union members who receive no redundancy payments.   The union would now consider that
it should enter into a new {w,L} contract to improve
income distribution between the employed and unemployed members and so the process would continue until
the number of union members neither employed nor
receiving redundancy payments fell to zero.

The reason for this apparently paradoxical situation in which the union would first be pressing
for higher employment and then for redundancies, is
the assumption that there is no mechanism for intra-
union transfers of income.   The redundancy payment
is being used as a very clumsy device to provide
such a mechanism.   There does, however, appear to be
a more direct instrument that the union can use.
This is discussed in the next section.

SECTION 4: CONTRACTS WHICH PERMIT BARGAININGING
ABOUT RETIREMENTS

When considering the maximum possible level of utility that the union could achieve it was noted that the solution required the conditions

$R'(L) = b$

and $w = b+r$

in the case where the optimal solution has $L < M$.

The problem for the union, therefore, is to set employment at the level L_0 where $R'(L) = b$ but at the same time find some device to transfer income to the $M-L_0$ members who will be non-employed without running into any of the moral hazard difficulties outlined earlier.

One way of ensuring that transfer payments go only to those who have a genuine connection with the firm is to pay them only to those who have been working for the firm. Redundancy payments achieve this but are very clumsy. The alternative is for the union to negotiate about retirements. The distinction between a redundancy and a retirement is that a retiring worker can be replaced by a new employee. Assume that the firm currently employs N persons so that M-N union members are unemployed. If the union negotiates a contract in which $M-L_0$ current employees retire with a pension of $r = w-b$ and at the same time insists that the firm takes on M-N new employees this will achieve the desired result in which L_0 are employed at wage w and $M-L_0$ receive transfer payments of r. The utility of all union members will be equalised and Walrasian efficiency satisfied.

Note that while redundancy pay is a price instrument, retirement pay is not, as the firm would not voluntarily retire $M-L_0$ employees and also take on the M-N unemployed workers at a wage of w. This would have to be written into the contract.

There are of course more dimensions to being employed, unemployed and retired than are allowed for in our very simple utility functions. However, the analysis in this section does suggest a rationale for why unions are more willing to discuss early retirements than redundancy policies.

SECTION 5: BARGAINS WHEN THERE IS UNCERTAINTY

The conclusions to be drawn from the earlier sections are that Walrasian efficiency and efficient
intra-union income distribution will only result
under some assumptions about the nature of M and
about what variables can be included in the bargain.
This section looks briefly at the consequences of
introducing uncertainty into the model.

It is assumed that the union has to make a bargain in advance of knowledge about the position of
the marginal revenue product curve, now defined as
$R'(L,\theta)$ where θ is a random variable representing
demand variations.   It is however assumed that the
union can observe the position of $R'(L,\theta)$ once it
has occurred so that it is not necessary for the
union to guard against the firm dissimulating about
the true state of nature.   Much of the implicit
contract literature is concerned with this last
moral hazard point but it is assumed away here.

Suppose the set M is clearly defined and is
such that for all possible values of θ, $R'(L,\theta) < b$
when evaluated at M.   A Walrasian efficient solution is for the firm to pay a wage w to those employed and lay-off pay of $\ell = w-b$ to those not employed on any one occasion.   The marginal cost to
the firm of employing an extra worker is then b and
for all values of θ the profit maximising firm will
choose that $L^*(\theta)$ which satisfies $R'(L^*,\theta) = b$.
All M union members enjoy the same level of utility
as each other and for all values of θ.   The distribution of income is therefore both efficient between
union members and intertemporally.   Grossman and
Hart (1981), however, point out that all risks are
borne by the firm and that the firm, if it also is
risk averse, could enjoy the same expected level of
utility with a lower mean rate of profit but less
variability in profit levels.   It would pay the
union, therefore, to share some of the risks with the
firm accepting a contract with lower wage and lay-off
payments in bad times and higher wage and lay-off
payments in good times.

The contract above assumes that there is a
clearly defined set of union members M who are elig-
ible for lay-off pay.   Under uncertainty, since
there is a chance of being required to work if dem-
and is high, the moral hazard objections to transfer
payments are less serious than in the certainty case
when an unscrupulous worker could avoid working and
could 'enlist' with several firms.

Another assumption in the above analysis is that

the pool of M workers exceeds the maximum number ever
required. Consider now the case where there is a body
of N workers currently employed by the firm but where
N is such that for some values of θ the marginal revenue product of the Nth worker exceeds b. Assume also
that it is the utility of these N members which enters
into the union's utility function. In the certainty
case we saw that redundancy payments could be used to
achieve Walrasian and distributional efficiency if the
marginal revenue product of the Nth worker was less than
b, but that, even with a linear utility function there
would be Walrasian under-employment if the Nth worker's
marginal revenue product exceeded b. In the case of
uncertainty, efficiency can be achieved for low marginal
revenue products by the union negotiating a lay-off
payment of ℓ = w-b. For high marginal revenue products the union would like to be able to exploit non-
union members ensuring that they were paid only the minimum supply price of b. This would increase the total
expected profits of the firm allowing a higher expected
wage to be paid. This was ruled out by the 'equal pay
for equal work' assumption. Now under uncertainty effective discrimination between union and non-union members
without discriminatory wages could be achieved by the
union entering into a contract contingent upon θ. A
contract under which if $R'(L,\theta) > b$, evaluated at N,
then a wage of b applies, but if the converse is true,
a higher wage w and lay-off pay of ℓ = w-b are paid would
result in all those employed receiving the same wage at
any one time. The wage rate would vary with θ but non-
union members would never receive more than b. This
contract would result in the paradoxical situation that
the N union members would receive higher incomes in times
when demand was low than when it was high. It would also
result in highly variable incomes for both the firm and
the N union members. If either the firm or the union
members are risk averse, then an improved contract could
be negotiated which would display Walrasian under-employment when demand was high.
      The contract described above seems highly imp-
lausible and results from the assumption that it is
not possible to discriminate against non-union labour. In practice, some discrimination can occur.
Interpret N as a core of workers established with
the firm. In many firms there are extra benefits
for years of service. These may be in the form of
rising pay scales, holiday entitlements, improved
pension benefits and levels of redundancy pay. It
is also common for LIFO to apply to redundancies.
Traditionally much of this discrimination has been
justified by reference to the usefulness of the more

experienced worker to the firm which wants to retain their services.   However, the analysis above suggests an alternative rationale: the core of long-standing employees do not wish to prevent the firm from taking on extra employees when times are good as this raises the revenue potential of the firm and hence the firm's ability to pay higher wages is increased, but, by a policy of discriminatory benefits which apply only to the longer standing employee, essentially temporary workers who are dismissed when times are bad need not be paid much more than their opportunity cost.   Such discriminatory behaviour may well result in employment being closer to Walrasian efficient levels.

CONCLUSIONS

Under certainty, if otherwise competitive workers form a union which then acts as a monopoly to maximise the utility of the M selfish workers, this does not, per se, result in deviations from Walrasian employment levels.   Under or over employment may result, but this depends entirely on the variables which are specified in the firm-union contract.   For example, if a wage can be specified for unemployed union members, and if there are more than the Walrasian number of workers in the union, then the Walrasian employment level will result under the optimal contract.   Even if union membership is smaller than this, if a lower wage, b, can be specified for non-union employees then Walrasian employment levels will result.   It has been argued that in practice, moral hazard problems rule out the first contract and the 'equal pay for equal work' principle the second.   However, if unions can bargain about other variables, specifically redundancy pay and early retirements, in addition to wages, then Walrasian employment levels may still result, providing the union membership is sufficiently large.

APPENDIX

Given $u''(w) < 0$ it can be shown that as the minimum level of profit required by the firm is reduced so the union will choose to increase both wages and employment levels subject to the constraint $L < M$.

$$\Pi = R(L) - wL$$

Holding Π constant

$$\frac{dw}{dL} = \frac{R'(L) - w}{L}$$

$$V = Lu(w) + (M-L)u(b)$$

Holding V constant

$$\frac{dw}{dL} = \frac{-(u(w)-u(b))}{Lu'(w)}$$

Equating these to find the locus of back to back tangencies of the iso-profit lines and the union's indifference curves gives:

$$R'(L) = w - \frac{(u(w)-u(b))}{u'(w)} \qquad (A1)$$

The point (b,L_0) lies on this curve where L_0 is the value of L for which $R'(L) = b$.

If $u(w) = a + cw$, i.e. the utility function is a linear relationship, (A1) reduces to:

$$R'(L) = b$$

and so $L = L_0$ the Walrasian efficient level for all values of Π_0.

More generally, however, along the contract curve

$$R''(L)dL = \frac{(u(w)-u(b))u''(w)}{u'(w)^2} \, dw$$

Given the assumptions $R''(L) < 0$ and $u''(w) < 0$, this implies that along the contract curve

$$\frac{dw}{dL} > 0.$$

Part Two

MACRO-ECONOMIC STUDIES OF TRADE UNION BEHAVIOUR

MONEY WAGE RIGIDITY IN AN ECONOMY WITH RATIONAL
TRADE UNIONS

Richard Jackman

While the evidence of nominal inertia, of the failure of money wages and prices to adjust rapidly to market-clearing levels, is everywhere about us, a convincing and generally accepted theoretical explanation of this phenomenon has yet to be developed (1). This paper offers a possible explanation, related to recent work by Phelps (1978) and Taylor (1979, 1980) on staggered (or non-synchronised) wage contracts. It has been claimed (e.g. Taylor, 1980, p. 2) that in a model with rational expectations and in which wage contracts are the only source of rigidity, the practice of non-synchronised wage setting will of itself be capable of endogenously generating inertia in money wages and, associated with it, persistent real effects following from nominal shocks. However, Taylor's model embodies a quasi-Phillips curve mechanism determining wages, which is assumed, rather than derived from any optim- ising behaviour. It could be argued, therefore, that, through the Phillips curve assumption, nominal inertia is imposed on, rather than explained by, Taylor's model.

This paper investigates a model of non-synchro- nous wage setting in which wages are determined by trade unions, each of which attempts to maximise the welfare of its own members. The paper shows that, in a model of this sort, there will be nominal inertia and nominal disturbances will have persistent real eff- ects, even though trade unions are concerned only with real variables (real wages and employment) and are as- sumed to be fully informed and to behave rationally.

The nominal inertia arises from the fact that in a model with non-synchronous wage setting, adjust- ment to a nominal shock entails transfers of real income. The magnitude of these real income trans- fers is directly related to the speed of adjustment of nominal magnitudes. Trade unions may then wish to reduce such real income transfers by embarking on a course of slow adjustment to nominal disturbances.

The main result of the paper is to show that a preference by trade unions for stability of real wages can generate nominal inertia and persistent unemployment in response to purely nominal shocks (or disturbances to aggregate demand). It is also shown that the timepath of money wages and unemployment generated by the model is consistent with the standard Phillips curve, and also with the wage equation assumed by Taylor (1980).

In a formal model of the paper we examine an economy with just two trade unions. This simplification eases the exposition very greatly. While many of the results can be shown to hold if there are many unions and the structure of the system is the same (2), the exact characterisation of the disequilibrium adjustment process cannot be determined explicitly in a model with many unions. The two union model should thus be regarded as giving some qualitative indication of the type of solution that would be obtained in the general case.

MODEL WITH TWO UNIONS

The basic institutional assumptions of the paper are, in common with those of the Phelps and Taylor models, that wage rates are governed by annual wage contracts which specify a given nominal wage, and that wage contracts are determined in different sectors of the economy at different dates in the year. While this assumption is obviously in accordance with everyday empirical observation in an economy such as that of the U.K., the theoretical rationale for wage contracts is less clear. For example, Lucas (1981, p. 564) has argued that "none of these models offers an explanation as to why people should choose to bind themselves to contracts which appear to be in no-one's self-interest". In general, however, it seems sufficient to postulate that it costs resources to change nominal wages or prices to generate a model in which it will be optimal for wage and price changes to be infrequent and in which, therefore, markets will generally not be in equilibrium (Mussa, 1981; Rotemberg 1982). It then only requires a short step to explain the existence of fixed length nominal wage contracts (3).

I assume there are two industries in the economy, each consisting of a large number of firms so that there is perfect competition in the product market. In each industry there is a single trade union to which all workers in the industry belong.

Wages in each industry are assumed to be determined by the trade union and common to all firms in the industry. For simplicity, I assume labour is the only factor of production and there are constant returns to scale. Labour is homogeneous so that, by choice of units, output in each industry can be equated with employment, and the product price in each industry with the money wage.

In each industry there are annual wage contracts, but the contract dates are not synchronised. Again for simplicity I assume the contract dates are six months apart so that the model can be analysed in terms of symmetrical half-year periods. For further symmetry, the two industries are assumed the same size in equilibrium (in terms of employment and thus of output shares).

The two industries are denoted A and B, and time periods measured in half-years. Thus the model is one of two-period overlapping contracts. The logarithm of the money wage in period t is denoted $w_{A,t}$ in industry A and $w_{B,t}$ in industry B, and the corresponding product prices as $p_{A,t}$ and $p_{B,t}$ respectively. The average money wage (w_t) and the general price level (p_t) in the economy are defined as fixed weight geometric averages of money wages and of prices in the two industries respectively:

$$w_t = \frac{1}{2} (w_{A,t} + w_{B,t}) \tag{1}$$

$$p_t = \frac{1}{2} (p_{A,t} + p_{B,t}) \tag{2}$$

Since by definition $w_{a,t} = p_{A,t}$ and $w_{B,t} = p_{B,t}$ we also have

$$w_t = p_t \tag{3}$$

We next define the product demand curve for each industry. Because the model is symmetric it is only necessary to set down equations for one industry, with exactly equivalent expressions applying to the other. We assume that the demand for the product of industry A in period t is given by

$$y_{A,t} = \bar{a} + (m_t + \bar{v} - p_t) - \gamma(p_{A,t} - p_t)$$

where all the variables are expressed in logarithms, $y_{A,t}$ is industry A output in time t, $\bar{a}$ is a constant, m_t is the nominal money stock, and $\bar{v}$ the velocity of circulation of money. The second term in the expression $(m_t - p_t - \bar{v})$ measures real aggregate demand, and the third the price elasticity of demand for the product (4). Since aggregate demand is not the focus of interest of this paper it is modelled in the simplest possible way: that is I take the velocity of circulation as constant, and further measure the money stock in units such that $\bar{a} + \bar{v} = 0$. The demand function then simplifies to

$$y_{A,t} = m_t - p_t - \gamma(p_{A,t} - p_t) \qquad (4)$$

Recalling that units have been chosen such that employment is equal to output and wages to prices, this demand relationship can be rewritten as a relationship between employment and wages:

$$\ell_{A,t} = m_t - w_t - \gamma(w_{A,t} - w_t) \qquad (5)$$

Or equivalently

$$\ell_{A,t} = (m_t - p_t) - \gamma(w_{A,t} - p_t) \qquad (6)$$

where $\ell_{A,t}(=y_{A,t})$ is employment in industry A. Employment in industry A is in this system a function of real money balances as well as of the real wage.

Using equations (1), (2) and (3), we can write the real wage $(x_{A,t})$ and employment in industry A as functions of the money stock and the money wages in the two industries:

$$x_{A,t} = \frac{1}{2}(w_{A,t} - w_{B,t}) \qquad (7)$$

$$\ell_{A,t} = m_t - \frac{1}{2}(1 + \gamma)w_{A,t} - \frac{1}{2}(1 - \gamma)w_{B,t} \qquad (8)$$

Equations (7) and (8) thus describe the constraints facing the industry A union: the level of real wages and employment it will obtain by setting any money wage $w_{A,t}$. It remains to specify the union's objective function. It is convenient to adopt a particular functional form, similar to the Stone-Geary function that has been frequently used in consumer demand analysis. Thus, let the union's utility be given by:

$$u_{A,t} = (x_{A,t} - x_0)^\theta (\ell_{A,t} - \ell_0)^{1-\theta} \qquad (9)$$

where x_0 and ℓ_0 are exogenously given minimum acceptable, "fallback" or "baseline" levels of real wages and employment. x_0, ℓ_0 and the parameter θ are assumed common to the two unions (5).

In recent work, Dertouzos and Pencavel (1981) have argued in favour of the Stone-Geary specifications on the grounds that it is less restrictive than other standard forms of union utility functions (most of which it contains as special cases) and that, in empirical work, their results rejected some of the more restrictive special cases (e.g. wage bill maximisation). The advantage of the Stone-Geary formulation in the present context is that it does not impose homotheticity on the union utility function. In particular, it allows the union, through its choice of θ, to choose whether employment or real wages are the "luxury good" with the high income elasticity so that when demand fluctuates real wages will rise or fall. By contrast if θ is low, it is employment that will adjust to changes in demand. But a low value of θ does not mean that real wages have a low weight in the union utility function, because the desired level of real wages depends also on x_0. Thus the combination of a high value of x_0 and low value of θ allows a functional representation of union preferences for a high, but stable, level of real wages (6). (From a neoclassical standpoint one might want to argue that a high level of x_0 is caused by the payment of unemployment benefits, the value of leisure or by expected earnings outside the industry.)

It is not straightforward to rationalise the apparent preference of trade unions for stability of real wages over stability of employment. In particicular in the present model we cannot make use of arguments based on efficient contracts in the presence of unemployment benefits (Feldstein, 1976) or asymmetric information (Hall and Lilien, 1979). The reason is that in the present model firms play no independent role and make no profits: they are simply the passive agents through which the unions exert their monopoly power at the expense of the consumer. One can argue that instability of wages is costly to all union members while instability of employment is costly only to the most junior employees and potential recruits to the industry. Hence unions, which are run by (and for) the more senior and established workers in the industry prefer employment instability to wage instability. But this argument does not appear to have been satisfactorily formalised.

Equilibrium is modelled by taking a constant value of the nominal money stock ($\bar{m}$), and by assuming that each union sets its wages to maximise its utility on the assumption of a given wage in the other union. Union A chooses w_A to maximise its utility function (equation (9)) subject to the constraints described by equations (7) and (8). The first-order condition is given by

$$(1+\gamma)w_A = (1+\gamma-2\theta)w_B + 2(1-\theta)(1+\gamma)x_0$$
$$+ 2\theta(\bar{m}-\ell_0) \tag{10}$$

In equilibrium, the wages in the two industries will be the same, so that, setting $w_A = w_B = w^*$,

$$w^* = \bar{m} - \ell_0 + \frac{1-\theta}{\theta}(1+\gamma)x_0 \tag{11}$$

and hence, from (6), equilibrium employment in each industry is given by

$$\ell^* = \bar{m} - w^* = \ell_0 - \frac{1-\theta}{\theta}(1+\gamma)x_0 \tag{12}$$

In equilibrium money is neutral - it affects only money wages (and prices). Employment is determined by the preferences of the trade unions and by the demand elasticity they face (the measure of their monopoly power). In interpreting equations (11) and (12) it should be noted that $x_0 < 0$, because by choice of units the logarithm of the actual real wage is zero and $x_0 < x$. Hence

$$\frac{dw^*}{d\gamma} < 0 \quad \frac{dw^*}{d\theta} > 0 \quad \text{and} \quad \ell^* > \ell_0$$

as the logic of the model requires.

THE ADJUSTMENT PROCESS

If the economy described by the above model is thrown out of equilibrium, for example by an unanticipated change in the stock of money, given the wage contract assumptions the unions cannot instantaneously restore equilibrium by equiproportionate changes in money wage rates. Further, since wage contracts are not synchronised, each union, when setting its wage, faces a trade-off between real wage stability and speed of adjustment.

To model this process, it is first convenient to assume that each union, when setting its wage at the beginning of any period t, is concerned to maximise

66

a function of the average real wage and the average
level of employment over the lifetime of the wage
contract (i.e. two periods).   Thus it maximises

$$\tilde{u}_{A,t} = (\tilde{x}_{A,t} - x_0)^{\theta} (\tilde{\ell}_{A,t} - \ell_0)^{1-\theta} \tag{13}$$

where

$$\tilde{x}_{A,t} = \frac{1}{2} (x_{A,t} + x_{A,t+1}) \tag{14}$$

and

$$\tilde{\ell}_{A,t} = \frac{1}{2} (\ell_{A,t} + \ell_{A,t+1}) \tag{15}$$

The actual values that real wages and employment take in each period of the contract depend on
the money wage union A sets, the level of nominal
aggregate demand (i.e. the stock of money) and the
level of money wages in industry B.   We take the
stock of money as given, and set equal to $\bar{m}$.   For
the first of the two periods of the contract the
industry B wage is known and pre-determined, having
been set at the beginning of the previous period.
But for the second period of the contract, the wage
in industry B will be renegotiated and thus the wage
set in industry A in period t depends on the expected wage set in industry B in period t+1.   The
wage set in industry B in t+1 will in turn depend on
the wage industry A is expected to set in period t+2
and so on.

We will want to assume that the adjustment path
has the properties of consistency, in the sense that
it is optimal for each union, given its expectations
of how the other union will behave, to set wages
consistent with the other union's expectations
(Taylor, 1979).

Specifically, consider union A setting its wage
at the beginning of period t.   The average industry
B wage expected to prevail over the period of the A
industry wage contract is defined by

$$\tilde{W}_{B,t} = \frac{1}{2} (W_{B,t-1} + W_{B,t+1}^{e}) \tag{16}$$

It then follows immediately that

$$\tilde{x}_{A,t} = \frac{1}{2} (W_{A,t} - \tilde{W}_{B,t}) \tag{17}$$

and

$$\ell_{A,t} = \bar{m} - \frac{1}{2}(1 + \gamma) w_{A,t} - \frac{1}{2}(1 - \gamma) \tilde{w}_{B,t} \quad (18)$$

Maximisation of (13) given (17) and (18) is clearly precisely analogous to the equilibrium analysis, and the solution is the counterpart of equation (10), that is

$$W_{A,t} = \frac{1+\gamma-2\theta}{1+\gamma} \tilde{W}_{B,t} + 2(1-\theta) x_0$$
$$+ \frac{2\theta(\bar{m} - \ell_0)}{1 + \gamma} \quad (19)$$

If each union sets its wage in accordance with equation (19), and if the timepath of wages to emerge is in each period consistent with expectations, then (19) can be written in the form of a difference equation that will hold in each period. Denoting W_t^s as the wage set in period t, the difference equation takes the form

$$W_{t+1}^s - 2\frac{1+\gamma}{1+\gamma-2\theta} W_t^s + W_{t-1}^s =$$
$$4\frac{(1-\theta)(1+\gamma)x_0 + (\bar{m} - \ell_0)}{1+\gamma-2\theta} \quad (20)$$

Equation (20) is a standard second order difference equation, so that the timepath of wages can be written

$$w_t^s = w^* + (w_0^s - w^*) \lambda^t \quad (21)$$

where

$$\lambda = \frac{1+\gamma}{1+\gamma-2\theta} \pm \sqrt{\left(\frac{1+\gamma}{1+\gamma-2\theta}\right)^2 - 1}$$

takes the value of the roots of the associated characteristic equation. It is apparent from (21) that the speed of adjustment of the system to equilibrium depends on the value of λ: if λ is close to one the adjustment process is long drawn out, while if it is close to zero, adjustment is very quick.

If, following standard procedure, we confine

attention to values of λ corresponding to stable roots (on the grounds that unions will not choose an adjustment path that leads them ever further away from their desired position) it is apparent that λ takes the sign of the expression $(1+\gamma-2\theta)$. If unions have a preference for real wage stability over employment stability, which appears to be the empirically relevant case, we have $\theta < 0.5$ and hence $\lambda > 0$. Even if $\theta > 0.5$, even moderate values of the demand elasticity (e.g. $\gamma = 1$) will be sufficient to ensure $\lambda > 0$. In what follows we therefore assume $\lambda > 0$ and that wages follow a timepath of monotonic convergence to equilibrium (7).

If $0 < \lambda < 1$, $\frac{\partial\lambda}{\partial\theta} < 0$ and $\frac{\partial\lambda}{\partial\gamma} > 0$. In particular as $\theta \to 0$, $\lambda \to 1$ and the timepath of adjustment becomes extremely slow (8). Because the trade unions are averse to accepting the losses of real income that result from rapid adjustment of nominal values they choose a slow path of adjustment, even though that entails persistent unemployment.

For example, if originally the system were in equilibrium with money supply m_1, and the money supply were then reduced to m_2, the cumulative losses of real wages and employment to union A, the union which adjusts first, are given by (9)

$$\sum_{t=1}^{\infty} \tilde{x}_{A,t} = -\frac{1}{4}\frac{(1-\lambda)^2}{1-\lambda^2}(\bar{m}_1 - \bar{m}_2) \qquad (22)$$

$$\sum_{t=1}^{\infty} (\overset{\sim}{\ell}_{A,t} - \ell^*) = -\frac{1}{4}\frac{(1+\lambda)^2 - \gamma(1-\lambda)^2}{1 - \lambda^2}(\bar{m}_1 - \bar{m}_2) \qquad (23)$$

Thus the more rapid the adjustment (the smaller the value of λ where $0 \leqslant \lambda \leqslant 1$) the larger the cumulative real wage loss and the smaller the cumulative employment loss.

The corresponding expressions for union B are

$$\sum_{t=1}^{\infty} \tilde{x}_{B,t} = \frac{1}{4}\frac{(1-\lambda)^2}{1-\lambda^2}(\bar{m}_1 - \bar{m}_2) \qquad (24)$$

and

$$\sum_{t=1}^{\infty} (\overset{\sim}{\ell}_{B,t} - \ell^*) = -\frac{1}{4}\frac{(1+\lambda)^2 + \gamma(1-\lambda)^2}{1 - \lambda^2}(\bar{m}_1 - \bar{m}_2) \qquad (25)$$

Aggregating over the two industries

$$\sum_{t=1}^{\infty} (\tilde{x}_{A,t} + \tilde{x}_{B,t}) = 0 \qquad (26)$$

$$\sum_{t=1}^{\infty} \left[(\mathcal{X}_{A,t} - \ell^*) + (\mathcal{X}_{B,t} - \ell^*) \right] =$$

$$-\frac{1}{2} \frac{(1+\lambda)^2}{1-\lambda^2} (\bar{m}_1 - \bar{m}_2) \qquad (27)$$

While from the standpoint of each individual union the choice of λ affects both cumulative real wages and cumulative employment, in the aggregate average real wages are unaffected by λ, whereas aggregate employment does depend on λ. The fact that real wage effects, which are of such concern to individual unions, are simply transfer payments in the context of the economy as a whole means that the outcome is socially inefficient. Neither union takes into account the effect of its decisions on the members of the other union. Before discussing the policy implications of the model, however, it is interesting to consider its relationship with empirical studies on wages and unemployment.

EMPIRICAL IMPLICATIONS

There has been much discussion of the empirical relationship between the rate of change of money wages and the level of unemployment. The model of this paper will generate a relationship between wages and unemployment consistent with the elementary Phillips curve. Assume the economy has been subjected to a nominal shock. Then denoting annual average values of variables by subscript T, we have (see Appendix)

$$\Delta W_T = W_T - W_{t-1}$$

$$= \frac{1}{4} (w_{t+1}^s + 2w_t^s + w_{t-1}^s) - \frac{1}{4} (w_{t-1}^s + 2w_{t-2}^s + w_{t-3}^s)$$

$$= -\frac{1}{4} (\bar{m}_1 - \bar{m}_2) \lambda^{t-3} (1-\lambda^2)(1+\lambda)^2 \qquad (28)$$

and $U_T = \ell^* - \ell_T$

$$= \frac{1}{4} (\bar{m}_1 - \bar{m}_2) \lambda^{t-1} (1+\lambda)^2 \qquad (29)$$

Thus the nominal shock can be substituted out from equations (28) and (29) to give

$$\Delta W_T = - \frac{1-\lambda^2}{\lambda^2} U_T \qquad (30)$$

Equation (30) represents the disequilibrium component of the Phillips Curve. When the economy is shocked, the process of restoring equilibrium will take time and we will observe both disequilibrium unemployment and wage adjustment. In this system, however, unemployment does not cause wage changes, rather both variables are the outcome of the unions' response to the nominal shock.

While the model is obviously very greatly over-simplified, it is nonetheless of some interest to examine orders of magnitude. A "consensus" estimate of the impact of unemployment on inflation is a unit coefficient. This magnitude requires that $\lambda^2 = \frac{1}{2}$ in equation (30) which in turn implies, from the definition of λ following equation (21) that $\theta = .03 (1+\gamma)$. In an economy in which there were in fact only two industries one might typically set $\gamma = 1$ so that $\theta = 0.06$, implying that there would have to be a very strong preference by unions for real wage stability in order to generate an adjustment path consistent with observed data.

The model is also consistent with the wage equation assumed by Taylor (1980) which in our notation can be written

$$w_t^s = W_T - hU_T \qquad (31)$$

Again a nominal shock will have proportionate effects on $(w_t^s - W_T)$ and U_T, with $h = (1-\lambda)^2/(1+\lambda)^2$.

POLICY IMPLICATIONS

The model suggests a number of policy issues which may be briefly noted:
1. Insofar as nominal inertia is explained by structural features of the economy rather than by incomplete information or misperceptions of macro-

economic variables, the unemployment costs of monetary deflation cannot be reduced by explicit and
public commitments by governments to particular
money strategies. In the model the slow response
of money wages to changes in nominal aggregate dem-
and arises from the preferences of trade unions for
real wage stability and not from any ignorance or
confusion regarding the stance of monetary policy.
2. In the model there is a clear role for incomes
policy, which one may represent by imposing some
exogenously given, higher value of λ in order to
speed the adjustment to the new equilibrium. If
effective, the incomes policy will succeed in reducing the cumulated total unemployment involved in
any monetary deflation (equation (27)), but at the
expense of increasing the variability of real wages
(equations (23) and (25)). The higher value of λ
is not optimal from the viewpoint of the individual
unions, which would account for union opposition to
incomes policies in the context of this model.
3. It may, however, be possible to encourage
unions to choose a higher value of λ by means of
appropriately designed fiscal instruments. If, in
the context of a monetary deflation, there were a
subsidy given for wage cuts, the real income cost to
the union of a faster rate of adjustment would be
reduced, and it would therefore choose a higher
value of λ. The effect would again be to reduce
aggregate unemployment.
4. The introduction of synchro-pay, that is to say
a common date for all pay settlements throughout the
economy, would cut through all these problems.
While such an approach is not very promising in
current circumstances in the U.K., where the trend
is towards increasingly decentralised pay bargaining,
in principle it might be seen as a means of internal-
ising the externality caused by the real income
effects of the adjustment process.

CONCLUSION

This paper has presented a model in which nominal
shocks have persistent real effects due to a combination of non-synchronised wage contracts and the
preference of trade unions for stable real wages.
The adjustment process to a nominal disturbance is
shown to have real income effects, and it is shown
that such effects can be reduced by slow adjustment
of nominal wages. Nominal wages thus behave in the
manner described by the elementary Phillips curve.

It should be stressed that, throughout the adjustment process, the trade unions behave rationally and they are fully informed. Unlike a number of recent rational expectations models, the process does not assume that people are ignorant or confused about the values of aggregate economic variables that are published in the daily newspapers. Nor does the argument rest on persistent errors in expectations. Instead, nominal inertia and the associated persistence of the real effects of nominal shocks are attributed to the combination of the rational behaviour of self-interested trade unions and to adjustment costs in the economy which rule out a uniform and co-ordinated reduction in money wages in response to a fall in aggregate demand.

APPENDIX

Derivation of equations (22) - (29)

Consider a twelve month period, consisting of periods t and t+1, where union A sets its wage at the beginning of period t and union B at the beginning of period t+1. From equations (16) and (17) we have

$$x_{A,t} = \frac{1}{2}(w_t^s - \frac{1}{2}(w_{t-1}^s + w_{t+1}^s)) \tag{A1}$$

From equation (11), equation (21) can be written in the form

$$w_t^s = w^* + (\bar{m}_1 - \bar{m}_2)\lambda^t \tag{A2}$$

Thus

$$\tilde{x}_{A,t} = -\frac{1}{4}(\bar{m}_1 - \bar{m}_2)\lambda^{t-1}(1-\lambda)^2 \tag{A3}$$

By the same reasoning

$$\tilde{x}_{A,t+2} = \lambda^2 \tilde{x}_{A,t}, \quad \tilde{x}_{A,t+4} = \lambda^4 \tilde{x}_{A,t} \text{ and so on.}$$

Hence

$$\sum_{t=1}^{\infty} \tilde{x}_{A,t} = -\frac{1}{4}(\bar{m}_1 - \bar{m}_2)\frac{(1-\lambda)^2}{1-\lambda^2} \tag{A4}$$

73

which is equation (22) of the text.   Since the real
wage in industry B in each period is simply the negative of that in industry A, as defined in equation
(7), equation (24) and (26) follow immediately.

The employment equations are derived by re-
arranging equation (18) as below

$$\ell_{A,t} = m - \frac{1}{2}(w_{A,t} + \tilde{w}_{B,t}) - \frac{1}{2}\gamma(w_{A,t} - \tilde{w}_{B,t}) \tag{A5}$$

Using (A2) and (A3)

$$\ell_{A,t} = m - w^* - \frac{1}{4}(\bar{m}_1 - \bar{m}_2)\lambda^{t-1}(1+\lambda)^2$$

$$+ \frac{1}{4}\gamma(\bar{m}_1 - \bar{m}_2)\lambda^{t-1}(1-\lambda)^2$$

From (12)

$$\ell_{A,t} - \ell^* = -\frac{1}{4}(\bar{m}_1 - \bar{m}_2)\lambda^{t-1}((1+\lambda)^2$$

$$- \gamma(1-\lambda)^2) \tag{A6}$$

and hence, by the same reasoning as with real wages

$$\sum_{t=1}^{\infty} (\ell_{A,t} - \ell^*) = -\frac{1}{4}(\bar{m}_1 - \bar{m}_2)\frac{(1+\lambda)^2 - \gamma(1-\lambda)^2}{1-\lambda^2} \tag{A7}$$

which is equation (23) of the text.

The expression for employment in union B
equivalent to equation (A5) is derived simply by
reversing the A and B subscripts.   The first and
second terms on the right hand side of (A5) are unaffected by this operation, but the sign of the
third term is reversed.   The analysis proceeds as
before leading to equation (25), and thereby
equation (27) of the text.

Equation (28) follows directly by substituting
equation (A2) into the definition of ΔW_T given in
the text.   In deriving equation (29), ℓ_T is
defined as

$$\ell_T = \frac{1}{2}\left[\frac{1}{2}(\ell_{A,t} + \ell_{A,t+1}) + \frac{1}{2}(\ell_{B,t} + \ell_{B,t+1})\right]$$

Jackman: Money Wage Rigidity

so that

$$U_T = -\frac{1}{2}\left[(\gamma_{A,t} - \ell^*) + (\gamma_{B,t} - \ell^*)\right]$$

and making use of equation (A6), and its equivalent for industry B, gives equation (29) of the text.

ACKNOWLEDGEMENT

I am grateful to the Social Science Research Council for financial support while writing this paper.

NOTES

1. For evidence on the "almost complete absence of market clearing movements of wages" in the United States, see Hall (1980). While there appears to be less nominal inertia in other countries (see Sachs 1979 or Grubb, Jackman and Layard 1983) recent experience of deflationary monetary policies in any of these countries demonstrates an evident lack of complete flexibility.
2. An earlier version of this paper (Centre for Labour Economics Working Paper No. 493) explores this case.
3. The contracts will presumably only be fixed length in the short run. No doubt there are substantial costs to altering the frequency with which wage changes are made, leading to short-run rigidities, while in the long run contract lengths will adjust to a desired level.
4. This demand function has recently been used by Rotemberg (1982).
5. It might appear more natural to write the union utility function in terms of actual values rather than logarithms. But provided that x_0 and ℓ_0 are "close to" $x_{A,t}$ and $\ell_{A,t}$ the logarithmic form can be regarded as an approximation to the conventional form of utility function.
6. The empirical results reported by Dertouzos and Pencavel (1981) are substantially consistent with this hypothesis. In our notation they found x_0 close to the actual level of the real wage and θ significantly less than 0.5.
7. If γ were very small and θ close to one, giving $\lambda < 0$, the timepath of wages would oscillate. The first union to set its wage would "overshoot" the new equilibrium, the second union would make

only a much smaller adjustment.   The two unions
would then converge on the equilibrium wage one from
above and one from below.

8.   It is also the case that as $\gamma \to \infty$, $\lambda \to 1$.
This case is similar to that discussed in recent
models by Begg (1982) and Blanchard (1982).   Each
union sets its wage an infinitesimal amount below
that of the other union, but the reduction is sufficient to restore its desired level of employment.
Demand shifts back and forth from one sector to the
other, leaving unemployment in the sector with the
higher wages.   Only as money wages gradually edge
down and the average money wage level falls, can
aggregate employment start to recover.   While these
assumptions do generate nominal intertia, they do so
only at the expense of a wholly implausible characterisation of the behaviour of unemployment.

9.   The derivation of these and subsequent
expressions is given in the Appendix.

UNION WAGE BARGAINING IN A FIXED PRICE MODEL

Christopher J. Ellis and John Fender

INTRODUCTION

It has long been a common claim in Macroeconomics that trade unions cause wages to be sticky but employment to be highly variable over the business cycle. However, union behaviour is typically modelled in an unsatisfactory way. The unions are simply assumed to defend some historically given wage rate and to pay no attention to the employment consequences of their actions. Recent work by McDonald and Solow (1981) suggests that even when firms and unions bargain over both employment and wages, relatively stable wage rates and highly variable employment levels may arise. Their analysis is suggestive but is partial equilibrium in character, as they recognise. (1)

The main aim of this paper is to examine the effects of bargaining in a complete macroeconomic model. The framework which we use is the temporary equilibrium with rationing structure developed by Barro and Grossman (1976), Malinvaud (1977) and others, to which we add a representative union. This not only facilitates an examination of bargaining but also provides a mechanism for endogenizing the wage rate.

As is generally the case in this type of Temporary Equilibrium model, there are a number of different rationing regimes. The market for the fixed price consumption good may be characterized by either excess supply or demand (2), and the labour market may also display excess supply (unemployment) or excess demand (full employment). However, the wage rate and employment level are endogenously determined by the solution to the bargaining problem; this is rather different from the exogenously fixed wage models of Barro and Grossman or Malinvaud. Further,

it is possible that the bargain will yield a level
of employment in excess of that required to produce
the output demanded.   So there is a possibility of
labour hoarding.   Bargaining changes the relationship between product market conditions and the level
of employment.
   We adopt the Nash solution to the bargaining
problem and find that our model presents us with a
much richer menu of possibilities than either Barro
and Grossman or McDonald and Solow.   Real wages may
either rise, fall, or remain constant when the exogenous variables of our model change, and this will
allow us to tell various stories about real wage
rate changes over the business cycle.   Also the
possibility of labour hoarding allows us to examine
cases where average productivity moves either pro or
counter cyclically, or is invariant over part of the
cycle.
   The plan of the rest of the paper is as follows:
in section one we present the model and discuss the
various regime possibilities.   In the second section, we derive and discuss the comparative statics
results.   In section three, we consider the circumstances under which the various regimes obtain and
the factors which lead to shifts between regimes.
In the concluding section, we consider further how
the model may be interpreted and suggest some possible
extensions.

SECTION 1:   THE BASIC MODEL

The economy to be studied consists of a labour pool
of n homogeneous workers, one representative union,
one representative firm, and the government.
   Each worker supplies one unit of labour inelastically, is paid a wage rate w when employed, and
receives unemployment benefit $\bar{w}$ from the government
when unemployed.

$$u(.) = \begin{cases} u(w) & \text{when employed} \\ u(\bar{w}) & \text{when unemployed} \end{cases} \qquad (1)$$

where u(.) is the worker's concave utility function.
There is no specific utility or disutility attached
to employment per se (3): therefore we write the
union's maximand as the sum of workers' utilities.

$$\ell u(w) + (n-\ell)u(\bar{w}) \qquad (2)$$

where n is the level of full employment and ℓ the level of employment(4).

There is one output good in the economy, the price of which is fixed and normalized to unity. If there is excess demand for this good, the union's maximand needs modification. We assume unemployed workers receive insufficient income to encounter rationing, whereas employed workers are allocated a ration c; in these circumstances, the union's maximand is (5);

$$\ell u(w,c) + (n-\ell)u(\bar{w}) \tag{3}$$

The firm is a simple profit maximizer whose maximand is written as:

$$\text{Max } \pi = y - w\ell \tag{4}$$

$$\text{s.t. } f^{-1}(y) \leq \ell \text{ where } f^{-1}(y) \text{ is the inverse}$$
$$\text{production function}$$

where y is output, which cannot exceed the level of demand exogenous to the firm, x. If $f^{-1}(y) = \ell$, all labour is used productively. However, if $f^{-1}(y) < \ell$ then there is labour hoarding ℓ^H defined as the difference between total employment ℓ and productive labour $\ell^P = f^{-1}(y)$.

The government, employed workers and the unemployed demand output as below

$$x = \alpha(w\ell + (n-\ell)\bar{w}) + g \tag{5}$$

where α is the constant marginal propensity to consume and g is government spending. When there is excess demand for goods, c is determined by the following equation:

$$c = \frac{f(\ell) - g - \alpha(n-\ell)\bar{w}}{\ell} \tag{6}$$

This assumes the government's demand g to have a prior claim on output.

Finally, to complete the model, we adopt the Nash solution to the bargaining problem. This states that the bargain maximizes the product of the difference between that which each bargainer obtains from the bargain and that which each could achieve in its absence (6). In this case, all n workers would be unemployed and the union would receive $nu(\bar{w})$ if no bargain were struck. The firm would produce no output and profit would be zero. Hence, we may write the Nash maximand (for the case where workers are unrationed) as (7):

$$MaxN = \{\ell u(w) + (n-\ell)u(\bar{w}) - nu(\bar{w})\}\{y-w\ell-0\} \quad (7)$$
$$w,\ell$$

which simplifies to

$$MaxN = \ell\{u(w) - u(\bar{w})\} \{y-w\ell\}$$
$$w,\ell$$

This is maximised subject to the following three constraints:

$$\ell \leq n \qquad x \geq y \qquad \text{and} \qquad f(\ell) \geq y.$$

Bargainers are also assumed to take the level of demand as given and not to take into account the effects of their own actions on aggregate demand (this is reasonable since we are assuming a representative firm and union). Since each constraint can hold either with equality or inequality, it might appear that there are eight possible regimes. However, the coexistence of labour hoarding with excess demand for goods is impossible (i.e. $x>y$ is incompatible with $f(\ell)>y$), since in such circumstances it would always be profitable for the firm to put the hoarded labour to work. The case where all three constraints hold with equality is a borderline case; we are hence left with five possible regimes, as illustrated in Table 1. Below we list the conditions for each regime and discuss each briefly.

Table 1:

	Full Employment ($\ell=n$)		Unemployment ($\ell<n$)	
	$\ell^H>0$	$\ell^H=0$	$\ell^H>0$	$\ell^H=0$
ESG ($x=y$)	2	*	1	3
EDG ($x>y$)	✕	4	✕	5

Notes:

1. ESG and EDG indicate excess supply and demand for goods.
2. * represents a borderline case between regimes 2 and 4.
3. We assume that the case where $x<y$ never occurs; since firms are assumed not to be able to store output, there is no point in their producing more output than can currently be sold.

Regime 1: Keynesian Unemployment and Labour Hoarding
Here output is demand determined as (5)

$$\underset{w,\ell}{\text{Max}}\ N = \ell\ \{u(w) - u(\bar{w})\}\ \{x - w\ell\} \tag{8}$$

The bargainers take demand as given and maximize (8) by choice of w and ℓ. Here we have the standard Keynesian problem; workers wish for more employment and the firm more demand. The demand would be forthcoming if employment were increased; however, since labour does not swap directly for goods, there is no mechanism for this improvement to be generated. The first order conditions are (9) and (10).

$$\frac{\partial N}{\partial \ell} = \{u(w) - u(\bar{w})\}\{x - w\ell\} - w\ell\{u(w) - u(\bar{w})\} = 0 \tag{9}$$

$$\frac{\partial N}{\partial w} = \ell u'(w)(x - w\ell) - \ell^2\{u(w) - u(\bar{w})\} = 0 \tag{10}$$

This gives rise to labour hoarding
$\ell^H = \ell - f^{-1}(x) = \ell - \ell^P.$

Regime 2: Keynesian Full Employment and Labour Hoarding.
Here output is again demand determined; however, the level of employment given by the conditions (9) and (10) exceeds full employment. Hence, the solution to the problem involves setting $\ell = n$ and choosing w to maximize (11) given demand $x = \alpha wn + g.$

$$N = n\{u(w) - u(\bar{w})\}\{x - wn\} \tag{11}$$

so the wage rate will be determined by (12):

$$\frac{\partial N}{\partial w} = n\ u'(w)\{x - wn\} - n^2\{u(w) - u(\bar{w})\} = 0 \tag{12}$$

We have labour hoarding upon this regime
$\ell^H = n - f^{-1}(x) = n - \ell^P.$

Regime 3: Classical-Keynesian Unemployment.
This regime is not a borderline case as it might first appear. This is a regime which may occur if the equations (9) and (10) selected a level of employment which was insufficient to produce the output

demanded.   In such circumstances employment will be
demand determined via the production function.   We
term this regime classical-Keynesian unemployment
since the economy is on its aggregate production
function in a demand deficient equilibrium.

Under these circumstances, demand determines
employment as (13).

$$\alpha\{w\ell + (n-\ell)\bar{w}\} + g = f(\ell) \tag{13}$$

And the Nash maximand must be reformulated to determine the wage rate as (14).

$$N = \ell\{u(w) - u(\bar{w})\}\ \{f(\ell) - w\ell\} \tag{14}$$

Hence, the wage rate is determined in (15).

$$\frac{\partial N}{\partial w} = \ell u'(w)\{f(\ell) - w\ell\} - \ell^2\{u(w) - u(\bar{w})\} = 0 \tag{15}$$

We have no labour hoarding in this regime.

Regime 4:   Repressed Inflation.   If the solution to
equations (9) and (10) implies full employment, but
even full employment output cannot meet demand, then
employed workers will face rationing as defined by
(16).

$$c = \frac{f(n) - g}{n} \tag{16}$$

Since consumption is determined by output and we have
full employment, the Nash solution involves maximizing (17) by choosing w.

$$N = n\{u(w,c) - u(\bar{w})\}\{f(n) - wn\} \tag{17}$$

differentiating w.r.t. w gives (7)

$$\frac{\partial N}{\partial w} = nu_w(w,c)\{f(n) - wn\} - n^2\{u(w,c)$$

$$- u(\bar{w})\} = 0 \tag{18}$$

Regime 5:   Classical Unemployment.   The rationale
behind this regime is somewhat similar to regime 3.
Suppose the solution defined by equations (9) and
(10) selected a level of employment which could not
satisfy demand.   In regime 3 we suggested that emp-

loyment would rise until excess demand was eliminated.   However, this may not be optimal in all cases.   A falling marginal product of labour may reduce the firm's profits making the expansion of employment necessary to meet output demand undesirable.   This case resembles Malinvaud's case of classical unemployment.   In this circumstance, employed workers will face a ration c as defined in (6).

$$c = \frac{f(\ell) - g - (n-\ell)\alpha\bar{w}}{\ell} \tag{6}$$

and the Nash maximand needs to be rewritten as (19).

$$N = \ell\{u(w,c) - u(\bar{w})\}\{f(\ell) - w\ell\} \tag{19}$$

The level of employment and wages are determined by (20) and (21).

$$\frac{\partial N}{\partial \ell} = \{u(w,c) - u(\bar{w})\}\{f(\ell) - w\ell\} + \{f'(\ell)$$

$$- w\}\ell\{u(w,c) - u(\bar{w})\} = 0 \tag{20}$$

$$\frac{\partial N}{\partial w} = \ell u_w(w,c)\{f(\ell) - w\ell\} - \ell^2\{u(w,c) - u(\bar{w})\} \tag{21}$$

SECTION 2: COMPARATIVE STATICS RESULTS

In this section we present and discuss the comparative statistics effects of changes in government expenditure and unemployment benefits on the real wage, employment, and productivity.   Our results are summarized for convenience in Table 2 at the end of the section.   The more complex derivations are given in Appendix 1.

Regime 1: Keynesian Unemployment with Labour Hoarding.
This is perhaps the most interesting of the five regimes and the one upon which McDonald and Solow's results are precisely confirmed.
     By substituting equation (9) into (10) and simplifying, we obtain

$$\frac{u(w) - u(\bar{w})}{u'(w)} = w \tag{22}$$

This is an efficiency condition (8) and a key rela-

tionship.   It states that the rate at which the firm
is prepared to exchange increases in employment for
increases in wages at a given output level is equal
to the rate at which the union is prepared to do so.
Similar conditions obtain in all five regimes.
   It follows immediately from (22) that

$$\frac{dw}{dg} = 0 \tag{23}$$

$$\frac{dw}{d\bar{w}} = \frac{-u'(\bar{w})}{wu''(w)} > 0 \tag{24}$$

Equation (23) tells us that changes in government expenditure do not effect the real wage rate.   This
result highlights the importance of the coexistence
of unemployment and labour hoarding on this regime.
The increase in demand generated by the rise in government expenditure can be met by putting hoarded
labour to work, whilst any required revenue redistribution between the bargainers can be achieved by
employing more workers.   This will not violate the
efficiency   condition. (22).   Equation (24) states
that an increase in unemployment benefits increases
the real wage.   We also have (see Appendix 1)

$$\frac{d\ell}{dg} = \frac{1}{2w - \alpha(w-\bar{w})} > 0 \tag{25}$$

and

$$\frac{d\ell}{d\bar{w}} = \frac{\alpha(n-\ell) - \ell(2-\alpha)dw/d\bar{w}}{2w - \alpha(w-\bar{w})} \tag{26}$$

Expression (25) is a multiplier showing that increases
in government expenditure raise employment.   The
sign of expression (26) is not entirely clear.   We
know $dw/d\bar{w}$ is positive;   this raises the cost of employment to the firm and hence tends to reduce employment by reducing labour hoarding.   However, since
w and $\bar{w}$ rise, demand effects raise the firm's revenue, which tends to increase employment.   There is
a strong case for arguing that the first effect will
dominate and employment will fall with an increase in
unemployment benefit (9).   This will be assumed to
be the case hereafter.
   However, demand and hence output increases with
both government spending and unemployment benefit.
We have

$$\frac{dx}{dg} = \frac{1}{1 - \alpha(w-\bar{w})/2w} > 1 \qquad (27)$$

and

$$\frac{dx}{d\bar{w}} = \frac{2\ell\alpha\bar{w}(dw/d\bar{w}) + 2w\alpha(n-\ell)}{2w - \alpha(w-\bar{w})} > 0 \qquad (28)$$

Expression (28) is again a type of multiplier (10). It is hence quite likely that output and employment move in opposite directions in response to an increase in $\bar{w}$ in this regime. Using our results (25)-(28), we can now draw some conclusions about how changes in government expenditure and unemployment benefits will affect labour hoarding and productivity.

For an increase in g we know $d\ell/dg > 0$ and $dx/dg > 0$, from equation (9) we have $x = 2w\ell$ so we may write

$$\frac{x}{\ell} = 2w \qquad (29)$$

and thus

$$\frac{d(x/\ell)}{dg} = \frac{2dw}{dg} = 0 \qquad (30)$$

Therefore, productivity is constant for changes in government expenditure. We also know that the number of workers used productively ℓ^P is determined by output sales but as usual the marginal product of labour is diminishing. We also have

$$\frac{d1^H}{dg} = \frac{d1}{dg} \left[1 - \frac{2w}{f'(1^P)} \right] \lesseqgtr 0 \text{ as } f'(1^P) < 2w \qquad (31)$$

For the case of a change in unemployment benefits, expressions (24) and (29) immediately imply

$$\frac{d(x/\ell)}{d\bar{w}} > 0 \qquad (32)$$

A rise in the unemployment benefit rate raises productivity, since it raises demand and hence output, but reduces total employment. The effect upon labour hoarding is now

$$\frac{d1^H}{d\bar{w}} = \frac{d1}{d\bar{w}} \left[1 - \frac{2w}{f'(1^P)} \right] - \frac{21}{f'(1^P)} \frac{dw}{d\bar{w}} \qquad (33)$$

which < 0 if $f'(1^p) < 2w$ and $\frac{dl}{dw} < 0$.

Regime 2: Keynesian Full Employment and Labour Hoarding.

The major difference between this regime and regime 1 is the absence of unemployment; consequently, any revenue redistribution required in the bargain must be achieved by wage rate changes.

The wage rate will be determined by (12) which may be manipulated to give the efficiency condition (34):

$$\frac{u(w) - u(\bar{w})}{u'(w)} = \frac{x - wn}{n} \tag{34}$$

where demand is simply $x = \alpha wn + g$.

From the efficiency condition and definition of demand, it is easy to show (see Appendix 1):

$$\frac{dw}{dg} > 0 \tag{35}$$

and

$$\frac{dw}{d\bar{w}} > 0 \tag{36}$$

Expression (35) tells us that the real wage rises with increased government expenditure. This occurs so as to redistribute some of the increased revenue from the firm to the union. Expression (36) is perhaps a somewhat counter-intuitive result; it tells us that a rise in unemployment benefit raises the wage rate on a full employment regime. It arises because the cost to the union of a breakdown in the bargain is reduced. This may be interpreted as raising the union's bargaining power.

On this regime, changes in g or $\bar{w}$ clearly cannot affect employment, but both clearly have demand effects. Increases in government expenditure raise demand directly, and indirectly by raising wage rates. An increase in unemployment benefit will raise demand since it raises the wage rate (equation (36)). The extra output required to satisfy demand is obtained by putting hoarded labour to work so we have:

$$\frac{d\ell^H}{dg} < 0, \quad \frac{d\ell^H}{d\bar{w}} < 0 \tag{37}$$

and

$$\frac{d(x/\ell)}{dg} > 0, \quad \frac{d(x/\ell)}{d\bar{w}} > 0 \tag{38}$$

Labour hoarding falls and productivity rises in response to an increase in either g or $\bar{w}$.

Regime 3: Classical-Keynesian Unemployment.   On this regime, the goods market is in equilibrium, employment is determined by output sales via the production function;   consequently, there is no labour hoarding.
From equation (12) we obtain the appropriate efficiency condition (39).

$$\frac{u(w) - u(\bar{w})}{u'(w)} = \frac{f(\ell) - w\ell}{\ell} \tag{39}$$

Demand is defined as in equation (8).
Here the comparative statics effects are less clear cut;   formal derivations are given in Appendix 1.
In this regime, in contrast to the two we have already considered, the real wage falls when government expenditure is increased.   This effect occurs because an increase in g raises demand and therefore employment.   This raises the union's utility surplus more than the firm's profits.   The efficiency condition then requires that the wage rate falls to achieve the appropriate redistribution.   We note that this was the classical-Keynesian view, that the real wage moves countercyclically, expressed by both Keynes and the classical economists (11).
An increase in $\bar{w}$ in this regime raises demand and hence, both output and employment (12).   Its effect upon the wage rate is somewhat problematic. There are two competing effects;   first, the employment increase tends to depress the wage rate for the same reasons as in the government expenditure case. Second, a rise in $\bar{w}$ reduces the union's utility surplus, and hence, tends to raise the wage rate. However, there does seem to be a strong case for arguing that the wage rate rises, at least when the system is near full employment (see equation (A26) in Appendix 1).   Hereafter, we will take this effect to be positive.   The effects on productivity are quite clear;   the firm is operating on the production function, increases in g and $\bar{w}$ raise employment so productivity falls in both cases.

The important point to note on this regime is that the real wage rises with increases in unemployment benefit, moves 'procyclically', but falls with increases in g, moves 'countercyclically'.

Regime 4: Repressed Inflation.

This is perhaps the least interesting of our regimes (13). Here we have full employment, and full employment output on the short side of the goods market. From (18) we obtain the efficiency condition (40).

$$\frac{u(w,c) - u(\bar{w})}{u_w(w,c)} = \frac{f(n) - wn}{n} \tag{40}$$

Consumption by the employed is determined by the rationing rule (6) with $l = n$, so $c = (f(n) - g)/n$. We can obtain comparative static effects only upon the real wage in this regime. These are as (41) and (42).

$$\frac{dw}{dg} = \frac{u_c(w,c) - \pi u_{wc}(w,c)}{n(2u_w(w,c) - \pi u_{ww}(w,c))} \tag{41}$$

where $\pi = \dfrac{f(n)}{n} - w$

$$\frac{dw}{d\bar{w}} = \frac{nu'(w)}{2nu_w(w,c) - u_{ww}(w,c)(f(n) - wn)} > 0 \tag{42}$$

$dw/dg < 0$ if $u_c(w,c) - \pi u_{wc}(w,c) < 0$. This is discussed in Appendix 3, where it is shown to be negative for small amounts of rationing. This suggests that a tightening of the goods ration lowers the marginal value of the wage to workers and the union. A cut in the wage rate lowers workers' utility less than it raises the firm's profit and the joint Nash maximand rises in value. A rise in unemployment benefit cuts the union's utility surplus and thus requires a wage rate rise to achieve a new efficient distribution of revenue.

Regime 5: Classical Unemployment.

This is the only regime where the producer is on the short side of both markets, and could both produce and sell more output if he chose. He does not do so because the Nash solution determines a level of employment such that $w > f'(l)$.

88

On this regime we have an efficiency condition
(43):

$$\frac{u(w,c) - u(\bar{w})}{u_w(w,c)} = \frac{f(\ell)}{\ell} - w \qquad (43)$$

The level of goods rationing faced by employed workers is defined by (6).

Here as in regime 3 the comparactive statics effects are complex and their formal derivation is relegated to Appendix 1 (14). We have

$$\frac{dw}{dg}, \frac{d\ell}{d\bar{w}}, \frac{dy}{d\bar{w}} < 0 \quad \text{and} \quad \frac{dw}{d\bar{w}}, \frac{d\ell}{dg}, \frac{dy}{dg} > 0$$

The variable y here is output, which is less than demand x.

The key to understanding these results is the fact that changes in g and $\bar{w}$ have no direct demand effects on output. They work only through the bargain and the rationing scheme. Consider a rise in government expenditure. This tightens the ration faced by employed workers, and reduces the marginal value of the wage to them. This tends to reduce the real wage. However, employment rises with g; whether or not this reduces or raises the ration level depends on the sign of $c - \alpha\bar{w} - f'(\ell)$; if this is positive, a newly employed worker produces less than his goods ration net of his unemployment consumption. The ration tightens, re-enforcing the direct effect of g on the ration tending to reduce the real wage. The diminishing marginal product of labour implies that productivity will decline in these circumstances. A rise in unemployment benefit raises wages but reduces employment and hence output. This occurs because the effect of a rise in $\bar{w}$ is to reduce the union's utility surplus. This dominates the effects that work through the rationing scheme, and a revenue redistribution towards the union via a rise in the wage rate is required. Employment falls to maintain the efficiency of the bargain. Falling employment, of course, implies a rise in productivity.

Perhaps the most interesting of the results obtained here was that an increase in government expenditure increased employment. This is an excess demand regime with goods rationing. This is somewhat counter-intuitive. We might have anticipated that an increase in exogenous demand would have no employment effects (15).

Table 2: Summary of Comparative Statics Effects

		REGIME				
		1	2	3	4	5
Real Wage	dw/dg	0	+	-[3]	-[4]	-[5]
	$dw/d\bar{w}$	+	+	*	+	+[5]
Employment	$d\ell/dg$	+	/	+[3]	/	+[5]
	$d\ell/d\bar{w}$	*	/	+[3]	/	-[5]
Output	dy/dg	+	+	+[3]	/	+[5]
	$dy/d\bar{w}$	+	+	+[3]	/	-[5]
Productivity	$d(y/\ell)/dg$	0	+	-[3]	0	-[5]
	$d(y/\ell)/d\bar{w}$	*	+	-[3]	0	+[5]
Labour Hoarding	$d\ell^H/dg$	-[1]	-	/	/	/
	$d\ell^H/d\bar{w}$	-[2]	-	/	/	/
Rationing	dc/dg	/	/	/	-	*
	$dc/d\bar{w}$	/	/	/	0	-[5]

Notes:

* See text and Appendix 1 for conditions for signing these expressions.
1. $f'(\ell^P) - 2w < 0$ is necessary and sufficient for this result.
2. $f'(\ell^P) - 2w < 0$ and $\frac{d1}{d\bar{w}} < 0$ are sufficient for this result.
3. $f'(\ell) > \alpha(w-\bar{w})$ is sufficient for this result.
4. $K = u_c(w,c) - \pi u_{wc}(w,c) < 0$ is necessary and sufficient for this result.
5. $K < 0$ and $c - \alpha\bar{w} < f'(\ell)$ are sufficient for this result.

SECTION 3: SHIFTS BETWEEN REGIMES

We now turn our attention to the conditions under
which each regime exists, and the possibilities for
shifts between regimes.   Figure 1 shows the values
of $\bar{w}$ and g under which each regime occurs (16).

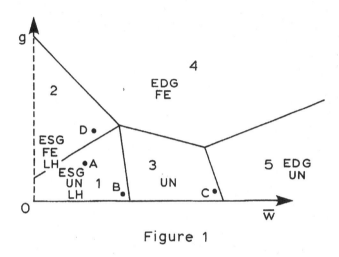

Figure 1

Figure 1 allows us to make some immediate observations.   Labour hoarding and excess supply of goods
occurs at low values of g and $\bar{w}$.   Unemployment can
occur over a wide range of unemployment benefit
levels when government expenditure is low.
     We now wish to examine the implications of
shifts between regimes.   We motivate this discussion
by describing changes in the exogenous variables g
and $\bar{w}$ as generating economic cycles.
     There has long been a debate about the behav-
iour of the real wage over the business cycle.   Empirical studies, aimed at testing for cyclical patterns
of behaviour in the real wage, have produced no clear
results (17).   Our analysis produces theoretical
reasons why the real wage may move in either direction.   This could explain the indeterminate results
obtained in the empirical studies.
     To examine the effects of shifts between regimes,
we conduct a series of exercises; starting at a given

point in ($\bar{w}$,g) space, we examine the effects upon the
real wage and productivity of an increase in either
government expenditure or unemployment benefit. Consider point A in Figure 1.   An increase in government expenditure will initially increase output and
employment and reduce labour hoarding with the real
wage rate constant and no change in productivity.
Full employment is reached before labour hoarding is
eliminated and the system switches to regime 2.
Further increases in g will increase output, reduce
labour hoarding, and increase both productivity and
the real wage.   When labour hoarding is eliminated,
the system switches to regime 4 where further government expenditure increases give a fall in the real
wage but have no effect on productivity.   Figure 2
illustrates this process.

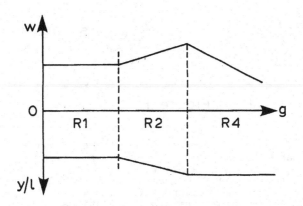

Figure 2

This story accords well with the empirical evidence.
No systematic movement of the real wage over the
business cycle occurs.   If, however, government expenditure increases at higher levels of unemployment
benefit, then counter-cyclical movements in the real
wage and productivity dominate the picture.
     Figures 3 and 4 describe an increase in govern-
ment expenditure when the economy is initially at

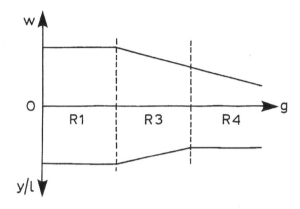

Figure 3

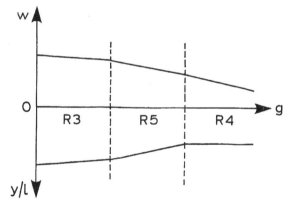

Figure 4

points B and C respectively in Figure 1. Both Figure 3 and Figure 4 show the real wage and productivity
moving counter-cyclically. This is very much in
accord with the "classical-Keynesian" view.
    The preceeding discussion motivates the analysis
of the business cycle with changes in government
expenditure. Changes in unemployment benefit can
also play a role in this process, although probably
not a major one. We illustrate the effects of an
increase in w̄ for fixed g, starting at point D on
Figure 1. The system moves through regimes 2, 1, 3,
4, and 5. The responses of the real wage and
productivity are described by Figure 5.

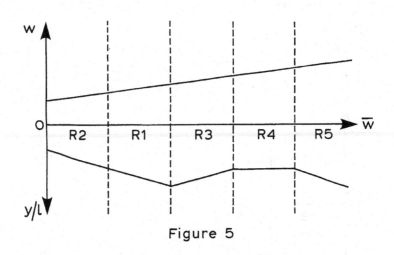

Figure 5

The diagram illustrates two interesting points.
First, increases in unemployment benefit always generate increases in the real wage (18). Second,
productivity moves counter cyclically in both R3 and
R5, where there is unemployment but no labour hoarding (19).
    We have performed these exercises for illustra-
tive purposes. There are clearly a number of others
which are possible. We leave these to the interested reader.

SECTION 4:   CONCLUDING COMMENTS

In this paper, we have constructed and analyzed a
macroeconomic model which has incorporated a wage
bargaining mechanism.   The model has a number of
interesting features;   there is the possibility of
labour hoarding, and of the coexistence of excess
demand for goods with unemployment.   It has a number of implications for the cyclical movement of
productivity and the real wage.   There are circumstances under which these could move pro-cyclically,
counter-cyclically, or be independent of the business
cycle.   Moreover, the cyclical movement of these
variables depends upon how the cycles are generated.
    There are a number of possible directions for
further research which suggest themselves:
1.   It is not certain how robust our conclusions are
with respect to changes in the way in which the bargaining process is specified.   Although the Nash
solution has a number of desirable properties, it has
been criticized and there have been a number of other
suggested resolutions of the problem.   An explanation of the implications of some of these other solutions in the type of model we have constructed
might be interesting.   Our specification of the
union's maximand, although a fairly common one,
might be criticized.   It seems to presuppose random
hiring and firing, which would be inconsistent with
the existence of seniority rules and the like.   It
might be desirable to explore alternative specifications of the union's maximand;   it might also be
desirable to analyze the implications of relaxing
the assumption that each worker supplies one unit
of labour inelastically;   so the bargain between the
union and employer would determine both the individual worker's labour supply (shift length ?) and
total employment.
2.   It might also be desirable to introduce another
sector;   this could be a non-unionized sector, in
which case the determination of the union, non-union
wage differential could be explored (20).   The
reservation wage, which we have here regarded as the
unemployment wage, could be instead interpreted as
the wage available in the non-union sector.   It
might also be desirable to consider an open economy
model in which case we might have a traded goods
sector and a non-traded goods sector.
3.   It might be desirable to dynamize the model.
The assumption of a rigid price of the good is perhaps
unsatisfactory, and it might be desirable to allow it
to change over time in response to excess supply or

demand.   This might enable the implications of trade unions and bargaining for inflation to be analyzed; this is something which has been the subject of extensive informal discussion but of little rigorous analysis (21).

Nevertheless, interesting as these extensions might be, it is first of all necessary to understand the behaviour of a fairly simple macroeconomic model with bargaining. We have presented one and analyzed it fairly extensively; we would claim that its implications are not without interest and that it seems that it can explain many stylized facts as well as, if not better than, existing models.

ACKNOWLEDGEMENT

The authors would like to thank Ken Burdett, Peter Chapman, Avinash Dixit, Andrew Oswald, Robert Solow, Makoto Yano, and participants at seminars given at Cornell University and the Economic Theory Study Group for their helpful comments and suggestions. All errors and omissions remain the sole responsibility of the authors.

NOTES

1.   "The work of embedding (wage bargaining) into a complete macroeconomic model remains to be done", McDonald and Solow (1981), p. 896.

2.   McDonald and Solow have described the case of a firm in those circumstances as "potentially important" (ibid., p. 906).

3.   This assumption is not crucial for any of our results but allows considerable expositional simplification.

4.   This union maximand has been employed frequently in the literature recently - see Oswald (1983).

5.   Naturally, u(w) = max u(w,c) when c just binds.

6.   The Nash solution has not been immune from criticism; however, it does have a number of points in its favour.
   - It can be given a game-theoretic justification.   See Harsanyi (1977).
   - It may be given a behavioural justification as in Zeuthen (1930) and Harsanyi (1956).
   - It can be given an axiomatic justification. See Nash (1950).
   - It proves to be fairly tractable; the Kalai

and Smorodinsky (1975) solution discussed in McDonald and Solow appears more complex.
- It ensures an efficient bargain.

7. It might seem that $u_w(w,c) = 0$. However, we assume that savings $w - c$ carry utility due to future consumption. This implies that money is implicit in our model in the same way as in Malinvaud's. Like Malinvaud, we do not model explicitly the expectations which determine savings behaviour.

8. This corresponds exactly to the McDonald and Solow efficiency condition when $R' = 0$ (marginal revenue = 0) - see McDonald and Solow (1981), p. 901, equation (3').

9. Clearly $d\ell/d\bar{w} < 0$ if $\alpha \to 0$ or $\ell \to n$. However, if $\alpha = 1$ and $dw/d\bar{w} \simeq w/\bar{w}$ which is true since the elasticity cannot be far from one, then $d\ell/d\bar{w}$ will again be negative if $\bar{w}(n-\ell) < w\ell$. We thank Robert Solow for this argument.

10. The magnitude of the multiplier could be larger if we allowed consumption out of profit income. We assume profits are not distributed in the short-run. This gives expositional clarity, but does not qualitatively effect any of our results.

11. See Keynes (1936), p. 17.

12. This is in contrast with the other two unemployment regimes (1 and 5) where the likely effect of an increase in $\bar{w}$ is to reduce employment.

13. Our assumption of inelastic labour supply means that there are no supply multiplier effects here.

14. We note that manipulation of equation (20) yields: $f'(\ell) + f(\ell)/\ell = 2w$, which is the same as McDonald and Solow's first order condition (p. 905, Equation (8)) with physical products replacing revenue products. This is the only regime in which such a condition holds. The regime is similar to the McDonald and Solow model in that the firm is free to move along a demand curve for its product and is not constrained by labour availability in doing so; this is the only regime in which this is true.

15. As in Malinvaud's Classical Unemployment regime (see Malinvaud (1977), p. 62). We emphasize that increases in exogenous demand affect employment through affecting the bargain via reduced availability of goods to workers. This is very different from the standard Keynesian mechanism.

16. We discuss the division of $\bar{w}$,g space in Appendix 2; the diagram embodies the most plausible assumptions about the slopes of boundaries between regimes.

17. See Dunlop (1938), Tarshis (1939), Ruggles

(1940), Kuh (1966), Bodkin (1969), Chirinko (1980), and Geary and Kennan (1982).

18.   These movements in the real wage may be described as procyclical except on regime 5 where a rise in $\bar{w}$ reduces output.

19.   The reader is reminded that an increase in $\bar{w}$ increases output and employment in R3, but reduces it in R5.

20.   See McDonald and Solow (1983) for an analysis of a wage bargaining mechanism in a two sector economy.

21.   Sometimes models of inflation incorporate a 'target' real wage, determined by a bargaining process which is often unspecified. Our analysis provides a way of determining such a target real wage, as well as of linking it to the level of unemployment. A further point is that in the unemployment regimes, an increase in unemployment due, say, to an increase in population, will, apart from the effect via aggregate demand, have no effect on the real wage.   This contrasts with what many non-union models would predict, and this may mean that increasing unemployment may not reduce inflation in a unionised economy.

APPENDIX 1: DERIVATION OF COMPARATIVE STATICS RESULTS

Regime 1
From (29) we obtain

$$dx = 2wd\ell + 2\ell dw \tag{A1}$$

and from (5) we have

$$dx = \bar{a}wd\ell + \alpha\ell dw + \alpha(n-\ell)d\bar{w} - \bar{a}wd\ell + dg \tag{A2}$$

so

$$\ell(2-\alpha)dw + \{2w - \alpha(w-\bar{w})\}d\ell = \alpha(n-\ell)d\bar{w} + dg \tag{A3}$$

If dg = 0,

$$\frac{d\ell}{d\bar{w}} = \frac{\alpha(n-\ell) - \ell(2-\alpha)\ dw/d\bar{w}}{2w - \alpha(w-\bar{w})} \tag{A4}$$

If $d\bar{w} = 0$ and using dw/dg = 0 we obtain

$$\frac{d\ell}{dg} = \frac{1}{2w - \alpha(w-\bar{w})} > 0 \tag{A5}$$

We also have (from (A1))

$$\frac{dx}{dg} = \frac{2wd\ell}{dg} + \frac{2\ell dw}{dg} = \frac{2wd\ell}{dg} \qquad (A6)$$

Thus, using (A5) and $dw/dg = 0$, we have

$$\frac{dx}{dg} = \frac{2w}{2w - \alpha(w-\overline{w})} > 1 \qquad (A7)$$

We also have, from (A1)

$$\frac{dx}{d\overline{w}} = \frac{2dw\ell}{d\overline{w}} + \frac{2wd\ell}{d\overline{w}} \qquad (A8)$$

Substituting for $d\ell/d\overline{w}$ from (A4) and manipulating

$$\frac{dx}{d\overline{w}} = \frac{2\ell\alpha\overline{w}(dw/d\overline{w}) + 2w\alpha(n-\ell)}{2w - \alpha(w-\overline{w})} > 0 \qquad (A9)$$

The effects on productivity and labour hoarding now follow directly as in the text (expressions (30)-(33)).

Regime 2

Differentiation of (34) gives

$$\{2n\ u'(w) - (x-wn)u''(w)\}dw = n\ u'(\overline{w})d\overline{w} + u'(w)dx \qquad (A10)$$

From the derivative of (5) evaluated at $\ell = n$, we have

$$dx = \alpha n dw + dg \qquad (A11)$$

Substituting (A11) into (A10) gives

$$\frac{dw}{d\overline{w}} = \frac{n\ u'(\overline{w})}{n(2-\alpha)u'(w) - (x-wn)u''(w)} > 0 \qquad (A12)$$

and

$$\frac{dw}{dg} = \frac{u'(w)}{n(2-\alpha)u'(w) - (x-wn)u''(w)} > 0 \qquad (A13)$$

From (A11), we get

$$\frac{dx}{dg} = \frac{\alpha n dw}{dg} + 1 > 0 \qquad (A14)$$

and

$$\frac{dx}{d\bar{w}} = \frac{\alpha n dw}{d\bar{w}} > 0 \tag{A15}$$

From the definition of labour hoarding (A14) and (A15), we have

$$\frac{d\ell^H}{dg} = \frac{1}{f'(\ell^P)} \frac{dx}{dg} < 0 \tag{A16}$$

$$\frac{d\ell^H}{d\bar{w}} = - \frac{1}{f'(\ell^P)} \frac{\alpha n dw}{d\bar{w}} < 0 \tag{A17}$$

also from (A14) and (A15)

$$\frac{d(x/\ell)}{dg} = \frac{\alpha dw}{dg} + \frac{1}{n} > 0 \tag{A18}$$

$$\frac{d(x/\ell)}{d\bar{w}} = \frac{\alpha dw}{d\bar{w}} > 0 \tag{A19}$$

Regime 3
Differentiation of equation (13) gives

$$\alpha \ell dw + \{\alpha(w-\bar{w}) - f'(\ell)\}d\ell = -dg - \alpha(n-\ell)d\bar{w} \tag{A20}$$

Differentiation of equation (39) and manipulation yields:

$$\{u(w) - u(\bar{w}) - u'(w) (f'(\ell) - w)\} d\ell + \{2\ell u'(w)$$
$$- u''(w)(f(\ell) - w\ell)\}dw = \ell u'(\bar{w})d\bar{w} \tag{A21}$$

So we write (A21) as

$$A d\ell + B dw = \ell u'(\bar{w})d\bar{w} \tag{A22}$$

with $A, B > 0$, we also write (A20) as

$$C d\ell + \alpha \ell dw = - \alpha(n-\ell)d\bar{w} - dg \tag{A23}$$

where $C = \alpha(w-\bar{w}) - f'(\ell)$.

Hence,

$$\begin{bmatrix} A & B \\ C & \alpha\ell \end{bmatrix} \begin{bmatrix} d\ell \\ dw \end{bmatrix} = \begin{bmatrix} \ell u'(\bar{w})d\bar{w} \\ -\alpha(n-\ell)d\bar{w} - dg \end{bmatrix}$$

$$\Delta \equiv A\alpha\ell - BC > 0 \quad \text{if} \quad C < 0$$

so

$$\frac{d\ell}{d\bar{w}} = \frac{\alpha\ell^2 u'(\bar{w}) + \alpha(n-\ell)B}{\Delta} > 0 \quad \text{if} \quad C < 0 \qquad (A24)$$

$$\frac{d\ell}{dg} = \frac{B}{\Delta} > 0 \quad \text{if} \quad C < 0 \qquad (A25)$$

$$\frac{dw}{d\bar{w}} = \frac{-c\ell u'(\bar{w}) - \alpha(n-\ell)A}{\Delta} \qquad (A26)$$

If $C < 0$ and $n \simeq \ell$ the expression will be positive. Further discussion of its interpretation is given in the text.
We also have

$$\frac{dw}{dg} = \frac{-A}{\Delta} < 0 \quad \text{if} \quad C < 0 \qquad (A27)$$

Since $y = f(\ell)$, we have

$$\frac{dy}{dg}, \frac{dy}{d\bar{w}} > 0.$$

From (A24), (A25), and the usual condition $f''(\ell) < 0$, we have

$$\frac{d(y/\ell)}{dg} , \frac{d(y/\ell)}{d\bar{w}} < 0.$$

Regime 4
Differentiation of equation (16) gives

$$dg = -n\, dc \qquad (A28)$$

and differentiation of equation (40) gives

$$\{2n\, u_w(w,c) - u_{ww}(w,c)(f(n) - wn)\}dw + \{n\, u_c(w,c)$$

$$- u_{wc}(w,c)(f(n) - wn)\}dc = n\, u'(\bar{w})d\bar{w} \qquad (A29)$$

Substituting (A28) into (A29) and manipulating, we obtain

$$\frac{dw}{d\bar{w}} = \frac{n\, u'(\bar{w})}{2n\, u_w(w,c) - u_{ww}(w,c)(f(n) - wn)} > 0 \quad (A30)$$

101

$$\frac{dw}{dg} = \frac{u_c(w,c) - \pi u_{wc}(w,c)}{n(2u_w(w,c) - \pi u_{ww}(w,c))} \tag{A31}$$

where

$$\pi = \frac{f(n)}{n} - w$$

The sign of $u_c(w,c) - \pi u_{wc}(w,c)$ is discussed in Appendix 2, where it is shown to be negative for small levels of rationing. In these circumstances, $dw/dg < 0$.

Regime 5

Simplifying (20) and differentiating, we get

$$\{\frac{\ell f'(\ell) - f(\ell) + \ell^2 f''(\ell)}{2\ell^2}\}d\ell = dw \tag{A32}$$

Since $f(\ell)/\ell > f'(\ell)$, the multiplicand of $d\ell$ is negative and so ℓ and w always move in opposite directions.

Differentiation of (A3) yields

$$\{2u_w(w,c) - \pi^* u_{ww}(w,c)\} dw + \{u_c(w,c)$$

$$- \pi^* u_{wc}(w,c)\}dc + u_w(w,c)\{\frac{\ell f'(\ell) - f(\ell)}{\ell^2}\}d\ell$$

$$= u'(\bar{w})d\bar{w} \tag{A33}$$

where

$$\pi^* = \frac{f(\ell)}{\ell} - w$$

From (6)

$$dc = \frac{-1}{\ell} \{dg + (c - f'(\ell) - \alpha\bar{w})d\ell + \alpha(n-\ell)d\bar{w}\} \tag{A34}$$

Substituting (A34) into (A30) we derive

$$\{(2u_w(w,c) - \pi^* u_{ww}(w,c))L - \frac{K}{\ell} (c - \alpha\bar{w} - f'(\ell))$$

$$+ u_w(w,c)(\frac{\ell f'(\ell) - f(\ell)}{\ell^2})\}d\ell = \{u'(\bar{w}) + (\frac{n-\ell}{\ell})\alpha\}d\bar{w}$$

$$+ \frac{K}{\ell} dy \tag{A35}$$

where

$$L = \{\frac{\ell f'(\ell) - f(\ell) + \ell^2 f''(\ell)}{2\ell^2}\} < 0$$

$$K = u_c(w,c) - \pi^* u_{wc}(w,c).$$

The first and third term in the expression multiplying $d\ell$ are both negative. Hence, $K < 0$ and $c - \alpha\bar{w} < f'(\ell)$ are sufficient conditions for the negativity of the whole expression. If we assume the expression negative, then

$$\frac{d\ell}{d\bar{w}} < 0 \text{ and } \frac{d\ell}{dg} > 0 \text{ if } K < 0.$$

Since (A33) implies w and ℓ move in opposite directions, we have

$$\frac{dw}{d\bar{w}} > 0 \text{ and } \frac{dw}{dg} < 0 \text{ if } K < 0$$

also since output moves in the same direction as labour input

$$\frac{dy}{dg} > 0 \text{ and } \frac{dy}{d\bar{w}} < 0 \text{ if } K < 0.$$

The diminishing marginal product of labour implies

$$\frac{d(y/\ell)}{dg} < 0 \text{ and } \frac{d(y/\ell)}{d\bar{w}} > 0 \text{ if } K < 0.$$

The effects upon the ration level c follow from (6)

$$\frac{dc}{d\bar{w}} = \{\frac{f'(\ell) + \alpha\bar{w} - c}{\ell}\} \frac{d\ell}{d\bar{w}} - \frac{\alpha(n-\ell)}{\ell} < 0$$

$$\text{if } K < 0 \text{ and } f'(\ell) > c - \alpha\bar{w} \qquad (A36)$$

and

$$\frac{dc}{dg} = \{\frac{f'(\ell) + \alpha\bar{w} - c}{\ell}\} \frac{d\ell}{dg} - \frac{1}{\ell} \qquad (A37)$$

This expression is difficult to sign unambiguously; however, there might be some presumption that it is negative. Positivity would seem rather perverse - it would mean that increases in government purchases of the good would increase its (rationed) consumption by employed workers.

APPENDIX 2:   DIVISION OF $\bar{w}$, g SPACE IN FIGURE 1

1.   The boundary between Regime 1 and Regime 2 is given by values of $\bar{w}$ and g which satisfy the following equations

$$\frac{u(w) - u(\bar{w})}{u'w} = w \tag{A38}$$

$$x = 2wn \tag{A39}$$

$$x = \alpha wn + g \tag{A40}$$

From (A38),

$$\frac{dw}{d\bar{w}} = \frac{u'(\bar{w})}{wu''(w)} > 0.$$

From (A39) and (A40),

$$dx = 2n\ dw = \alpha n\ dw + dg$$

so

$$n(2-\alpha)\ dw = dg$$

therefore

$$\frac{dg}{d\bar{w}} = \frac{dw}{d\bar{w}}\ n(2-\alpha) > 0$$

the boundary is upward sloping.

2.   The boundary between Regime 2 and Regime 4 is given by the values of $\bar{w}$ and g which satisfy

$$\frac{n\{u(w) - u(\bar{w})\}}{u'w} = f(n) - wn \tag{A41}$$

$$x = f(n) = \alpha wn + g \tag{A42}$$

From (A42)

$$dw = -\frac{1}{\alpha n}\ dg$$

From (A41)

$$\{2u'(w) - \pi u''(w)\}\ dw = u'(\bar{w})d\bar{w}$$

so

$$\frac{dw}{d\bar{w}} > 0$$

$$\frac{d\bar{w}}{dg} = \frac{dw}{dg}\ \frac{d\bar{w}}{dw} = -\frac{1}{\alpha n}\ \frac{d\bar{w}}{dw} < 0$$

so the boundary is downward sloping.

3.   The boundary between Regime 1 and Regime 3 is given by values of $\bar{w}$ and g which satisfy

$$\frac{u(w) - u(\bar{w})}{u'(w)} = w \tag{A43}$$

$$f(\ell) = 2w\ell \tag{A44}$$

$$f(\ell) = \alpha(w\ell + (n-\ell)\bar{w}) + g \tag{A45}$$

From (A43) we derive

$$\frac{dw}{d\bar{w}} = -\frac{u'(\bar{w})}{wu''(w)} > 0 \tag{A46}$$

From (A44)

$$\frac{d\ell}{dw} = \frac{2\ell}{f'(\ell) - 2w} < 0.$$

From (A45)

$$d\ell\ \{f'(\ell) - \alpha(w-\bar{w})\} = \alpha\ell dw + \alpha(n-\ell)d\bar{w} + dg$$

so

$$\frac{dg}{d\bar{w}} = -\alpha(n-\ell) - \alpha\ell\ \frac{dw}{d\bar{w}} + \frac{d\ell}{dw}\ \frac{dw}{d\bar{w}}\ \{f'(\ell) - \alpha(w-\bar{w})\}$$

The first two terms in the expression are negative so a sufficient condition for $dg/d\bar{w} < 0$ is

$$f'(\ell) > \alpha(w-\bar{w}).$$

(This was also the condition used in signing the comparative static effects in Regime 3.)

4.   The boundary between Regime 4 and Regime 5 is constituted by values of $\bar{w}$ and g which satisfy the following equations

$$f'(n) + \frac{f(n)}{n} = 2w \tag{A47}$$

$$nc + g = f(n) \tag{A48}$$

$$\frac{u(w,c) - u(\bar{w})}{u_w(w,c)} = \frac{f(n)}{n} - w.$$

From (A47) it follows that w is constant along the boundary.
From (A48)

$$dc = \frac{-1}{n} dg$$

(A49) yields

$$u_c(w,c)dc - u'(\bar{w})d\bar{w} = u_{wc}(w,c)\{\frac{f(n)}{n} - w\} dc$$

so

$$\frac{-1}{n} u_c(w,c)dg + \frac{1}{n}u_{wc}(w,c)\pi dg = u'(\bar{w})d\bar{w}$$

where

$$\pi = \frac{f(n)}{n} - w.$$

Therefore

$$\frac{dg}{d\bar{w}} = \frac{u'(\bar{w})}{-(u_c(w,c) - \pi u_{wc}(w,c)}$$

which is a positively sloping boundary for small amounts of rationing (see Appendix 3 for discussion of the sign of the denominator).

5.   Boundary between Regime 3 and Regime 4 is defined by values of $\bar{w}$ and g which satisfy the following equations.

$$\alpha\{w\ell + (n-\ell)\bar{w}\} + g = f(\ell) \tag{A50}$$

$$\frac{u(w) - u(\bar{w})}{u'(w)} = \frac{f(\ell)}{\ell} - w \tag{A51}$$

106

$$\ell = n. \tag{A52}$$

Using (A52) we rewrite (A50) and (A51) as

$$\alpha wn + g = f(n) \tag{A53}$$

$$\frac{u(w) - u(\bar{w})}{u'(w)} = \frac{f(n)}{n} - w. \tag{A54}$$

From (A53)

$$\alpha n \, dw + dg = 0 \tag{A55}$$

From (A54)

$$2u'(w)dw - u'(\bar{w})d\bar{w} = u''(w)\{f(n)/n - w\}dw \tag{A56}$$

so

$$\frac{dw}{d\bar{w}} = \frac{u'(\bar{w})}{2u'(w) - u''(w)\{\frac{f(n)}{n} - w\}} > 0 \tag{A57}$$

so from (A55) and (A57), we have

$$\frac{dg}{d\bar{w}} = -\alpha n \frac{dw}{d\bar{w}} < 0$$

the boundary is downward sloping.

6. The boundary between Regime 3 and Regime 5 is given by the values of $\bar{w}$ and g which satisfy the following conditions.

$$\frac{u(w) - u(\bar{w})}{u'(w)} = \frac{f(\ell)}{\ell} - w \tag{A58}$$

$$\alpha \, w\ell + (n-\ell)\bar{w} + g = f(\ell) \tag{A59}$$

$$f'(\ell) + f(\ell)/\ell = 2w \tag{A60}$$

From (A60),

$$\{\frac{\ell^2 f''(\ell) + \ell f'(\ell) - f(\ell)}{2\ell^2}\} \, d\ell = dw \tag{A61}$$

which we write as D dℓ = dw   D < 0.
From (A59)

$$d\ell\{\alpha(w-\bar{w}) - f'(\ell)\} + \alpha\ell \, dw + (n-\ell)d\bar{w} + dg = 0$$

or

$$E \, d\bar{\ell} = -\alpha(n-\ell)d\bar{w} - dg \qquad (A62)$$

where $E = \{\alpha(w-\bar{w}) - f'(\ell) + \alpha\ell D\}$, which we assume
negative.   (This assumption is weaker than the suff-
icient condition for a negative slope of the boundary
between Regime 1 and Regime 3 which is given in
Section 3.)
   Differentiation of (A58) gives

$$\{2u'(w) - \pi^*u''(w)\} \, dw = u'(\bar{w})d\bar{w}$$

$$+ \; u'(w)\{\frac{\ell f'(\ell) - f(\ell)}{\ell^2}\}d\ell$$

define $e \equiv 2u'(w) - \pi^*u''(w) > 0$

$$h \equiv -u'(w)\{\frac{\ell f'(\ell) - f(\ell)}{\ell^2}\} > 0.$$

Thus,

$$d\ell \equiv \frac{u'(\bar{w})}{(De+h)} \; d\bar{w} \qquad (A63)$$

and so (from (A62))

$$\{\frac{Eu'(\bar{w})}{(De+h)} + (n-\ell)\}d\bar{w} = -dg.$$

It is possible to show by laborious calculation that
De+h is negative, from which it follows that the
boundary is downward sloping.

APPENDIX 3

The sign of $u_c(w,c) - \pi^*u_{wc}(w,c)$ ($\equiv K$) is crucial for
some of the comparative statics results (and also for
the slope of the boundary between Regime 4 and
Regime 5).
   We show that for small levels of excess demand,
and for a Cobb-Douglas utility function, the above
term is negative.
   If a consumer maximizes

$$u = x^\alpha m^{1-\alpha}$$

subject to $m_0 + w = x + m$, where m_0 are his initial
money balances, m are his final money balances, and

x represents his consumption. His demands (in the absence of rationing) are given by

$$x = \alpha(w + m_0) \qquad m = (1-\alpha)(w + m_0) \qquad \text{(A64)}$$

If he is rationed in his consumption of x, so that he cannot consume the amount of x given in equation (A64), then x = c (where c is the ration, m is given by $m = m_0 - w - c$, and

$$u = c^{\alpha}(m_0 + w - c)^{1-\alpha}$$

This gives a worker's utility under goods rationing. Now

$$\frac{\partial u}{\partial c} = c^{\alpha-1}(m_0 + w - c)^{-\alpha}\{(m_0 + w)\ \alpha - c\}$$

This term will, in general, be positive. However, when the ration is exactly equal to the unrationed demand (i.e., the ration is just beginning to bite), $c = (m_0 + w)$ and the above term is zero. Also,

$$u_{wc}(w,c) = -\alpha c^{\alpha-1}(m_0 + w - c)^{-(\alpha+1)}$$
$$\{(m_0 + w)\ \alpha - c\} + \alpha c^{\alpha-1}(m_0 + w - c)^{-\alpha}$$

When $(m_0 + w)\ \alpha = c$ here, the first term disappears, but the second term is positive.

So, by continuity for positive π^* and for small amounts of rationing,

$$K = u_c(w,c) - \pi^* u_{wc}(w,c)$$

is negative. Similar considerations apply when π^* is replaced by π.

CAN STABILIZATION POLICY INCREASE THE EQUILIBRIUM UNEMPLOYMENT RATE ?

E. J. Driffill

INTRODUCTION

It is a notorious fact that the rate of unemployment has increased steadily - with fluctuations around a rising trend - in the U.K. over the postwar period and that most of this represents an increase in the "natural rate" of unemployment rather than being a disequilibrium phenomenon. The explanations that are offered for this increase in the natural rate include the effects of the social security system and the increased participation of workers in trade unions (Minford, 1982) and reductions in the rate of growth of productivity (Jackman and Layard, 1982). It has also been explained as a "ratchet effect" whereby unions bargain only on behalf of their (employed) members, and successive bargains reduce membership and progressively disenfranchise workers who become unemployed (Nickell, 1982).

This paper advances another argument for the increased natural rate of unemployment. It is based on a simple model of union behaviour and uses the argument that the operation of a Keynesian stabilization policy steepens unions' tradeoffs between real wages and employment and leads to a lower equilibrium level of employment and a higher real wage. It develops a model used by Calmfors (1982, 1983) to explain similar phenomena in Scandinavian countries.

The same kind of model has been used to explain how another form of government intervention - the tax-based incomes policy - has precisely the opposite effect. The tax based incomes policy flattens the unions' perceived real wage/employment trade-off and thus leads to increased employment and lower real wages.

The result offered here contrasts sharply with the now standard feature of most macroeconomic models:

110

namely, that the equilibrium rate of unemployment is independent of systematic stabilization policy as, for example, in Sargent and Wallace (1976).

SECTION 2: THE MODEL

The argument is based on the idea that the determination of employment and real wages in the economy can be modelled as the choice made by a single trade union facing a downward sloping demand for labour schedule.   This is a model developed in Oswald (1982).

In the absence of uncertainty, suppose that the demand for labour schedule can be written as

$$N = f(w) \quad , \quad f' < 0, \quad f'' < 0 \tag{1}$$

The union objective function is defined in our employment N and real wages w, and is assumed to be a quasi-concave function, increasing in both arguments:

$$u = u(N, w), \quad u_1 > 0 \tag{2}$$

$$u_2 > 0$$

This model leads to a choice of employment (N*) and real wages (w*) which are characterized by the marginal condition.

$$u_1(N^*, w^*) \cdot f'(w^*) + u_2(N^*, w^*) = 0 \tag{3}$$

which corresponds to tangency between the union indifference curve and the demand function for labour. It is convenient to work with simple functional forms which have desirable properties.   These are as follows:
1.   The demand function is linear

$$N = \alpha_o - \alpha_1 w \tag{4}$$

and fluctuations in aggregate demand affect the position (α_0) but not the slope (α_1) of the function.
2.   The utility function is linear in real wages and quadratic in the deviation of actual from full employment:

$$u = w - \beta(N - \bar{N})^2 \tag{5}$$

Under these two assumptions the marginal rate of

111

substitution in the union's preferences between employment and wages depends only on the deviation of employment from full employment. Thus the equilibrium level of employment depends only on the slope of the demand for labour schedule and is independent of the position of the curve.

With the demand function (4) and objective function (5) the optimum employment level is given by

$$N^* = \bar{N} - \frac{1}{2\alpha_1\beta} \tag{6}$$

If $\bar{N}$ corresponds to full employment, then (6) actually gives an optimal number

$$(\frac{1}{2\alpha_1\beta})$$

of persons employed, but if the objective function is modified to:

$$U = w - \frac{\beta}{\bar{N}}(N-\bar{N})^2 \tag{5'}$$

then the optimum employment is given by

$$N^* = \bar{N}(1 - \frac{1}{2\alpha_1\beta}) \tag{6'}$$

and so there is then an optimal unemployment rate

$$\frac{\bar{N} - N^*}{\bar{N}} = \frac{1}{2\alpha_1\beta} \tag{7}$$

These functional forms have the advantages that changes in the position in the demand curve (α_0) will not affect the equilibrium level of employment. In that sense, the model generates a natural rate of unemployment.

Uncertainty and Stabilization Policy

In this model of real wage and employment determination, perfectly anticipated changes in the position of the demand for labour curve facing unions would have no effect on the level of employment chosen, but only on the real wage rate. There would be no fluctuations in employment.

The existence of uncertainty could be modelled by having the unions make a real wage decision in advance of knowing the position of the demand curve. Thus the unions maximise expected utility on the demand function

$$N = \alpha_0 - \alpha_1 w + \theta \qquad (8)$$

where θ is a serially uncorrelated random variable distributed with zero mean. The unions maximise the expected value of (2) on (8) above with respect to real wages. In effect, unions set real wages in advance of knowing the state of the world, and firms are allowed to vary employment knowing what it actually is. This captures the idea of wages being set infrequently but employment being continuously varied.

The first order condition for an optimal real wage is

$$E(u_1) - \alpha_1 E(u_2(w, N)) = 0 \qquad (9)$$

The role of uncertainty in affecting the union's choice is obtained by taking a Taylor series by expansion of u_1 and u_2 around $\theta = 0$ and taking expectations. Thus:

$$u_1(w, N) = u_1(w, E(N)) + u_{12}(w, E(N))\theta$$

$$+ \tfrac{1}{2} u_{122}(w, E(N))\theta^2$$

If the third and all higher moments of θ are zero because θ is normally distributed, then

$$E(u_1) = u_1(w, E(N)) + \tfrac{1}{2}u_{122}(w, E(N)) \, \text{var} \, (\theta)$$

$$E(u_2) = u_2(w, E(N)) + \tfrac{1}{2}u_{222}(w, E(N)) \, \text{var} \, (\theta)$$

Thus, for θ normally distributed, the effect of uncertainty depends on the third order derivatives of u. It is not usually possible to say much a priori about this.

Under the assumption that the utility function is quadratic in w, N, then there is no effect of risk on the chosen real wage and the mean level of employment because the third and higher order derivatives of the utility function are all zero.

The government may wish to intervene in the
economy in order to reduce the variation in output
and employment. It is a commonplace result of
macroeconomic theory that where agents respond rationally to the available information, and are able
to make decisions on the same information as the
government, then stabilization policy cannot affect
employment. In order to be able to reduce the variance of employment, the government must be able to
act on a richer information set than that available
to private agents.

For example, in this model, it may be possible
to represent the government as being able to identify the state of the world θ which actually material-
izes, and to compensate for its effect on the demand
for labour, either reducing or completely eliminating
the variance in the demand for labour perceived by
unions. This would have the effect of reducing or
eliminating variation in employment, but not altering the mean level.

However, this desirable result depends on the
government's being able to identify the uncertainty
of θ. If the world is changing from one period to
the next, then it involves identifying the unpredict-
able change which has occurred in the position of the
demand for labour schedule and acting on that.

It is implausible to suppose that governments in
the U.K. have been doing that in the U.K. during the
period since 1945. There are three reasons:
1. Policy goals have included a high and stable
rate of employment, and stabilization policy action
has been triggered by the actual level of unemployment. The sources of shocks to employment have not
been identified in such a way that the random element
θ has been separated out and acted upon while disturbances due to inappropriate real wages have not.
2. For most of the period, the dominant model of
the economy has been one in which the level of output
is constrained by aggregate demand and not by real
wages being fixed at too high a level. Thus real
wages would never have been identified as a cause of
unemployment in that period.

The relative roles of demand and supply in the
conventional view of the determination of output and
employment have gradually shifted, so that the supply-
side view now dominates. The beginning of that
shift may be identified with the period after the
devaluation of sterling in November 1967.
3. It may be argued that the government can only
make stabilization policy contingent on the actual
employment level. The machinery available to

government may be restricted to setting tax and sub-sidy rates to provide "automatic stablizers". Thus although ex post government intervention is contin-gent on the state of nature, the government is res-tricted to operating a contingent policy rule which is predetermined ex ante, especially if changing tax and subsidy rates can be done infrequently.

Assume that the government can intervene in the economy so as to affect labour demand by an amount G so that the demand curve is now

$$N = \alpha_0 - \alpha_1 w + \theta + G \tag{10}$$

The government's intervention is contingent on the actual level of employment N, and offsets deviations from a pre-announced target value N*:

$$G = - \gamma(N - N^*), \gamma > 0 \tag{11}$$

The union then faces a modified demand curve for lab-our given by

$$N = \frac{\alpha_0}{1+\gamma} - \frac{\alpha_1}{1+\gamma} w + \frac{1}{1+\gamma} \theta + \frac{\gamma}{1+\gamma} N^* \tag{12}$$

The demand curve is made steeper by the existence of stabilization policy, but the variance of employment (for a given real wage) is reduced.

The union will choose a wage rate w to maximise E(u) as given by equation (5) subject to the const-raint (12). This implies that expected employment is given by

$$E(N) = \overline{N} - \frac{1+\gamma}{2\beta\alpha_1} \tag{13}$$

A further condition must be imposed. N* is so far undetermined. If the government is assumed to be only stabilizing and not systematically intervening to increase or decrease the demand for labour, the expected value of G must be zero and thus N* is the expected level of employment E(N): the government stabilizes employment around the mean level

$$N^* = E(N) \tag{14}$$

This determines the real value of N*.

The real wage rate chosen by the unions is given by:

$$w = \frac{\alpha_0 + \gamma N^* - (1+\gamma)\overline{N}}{\alpha_1} + \frac{(1+\gamma)^2}{2\beta\alpha_1^2} \qquad (15)$$

Solving out for N^* this gives

$$w = \frac{\alpha_0 - \overline{N}}{\alpha_1} + \frac{1 + \gamma}{2\beta\alpha_1^2} \qquad (16)$$

In the equilibrium the union is maximizing utility by choosing a real wage, given its knowledge of the demand function for labour (10) and the government's declared stabilization policy (11).

The effect of stabilization policy is shown in Figure 1. Point A shows the $(E(N), w)$ equilibrium with no intervention policy. Point B shows the effect of the intervention policy on those two variables.

The union's preferences over w and $E(N)$ are given by equation (5). Taking expectations

$$E(u) = w + \beta \, var \, (N) + \beta(E(N) - \overline{N})^2.$$

Stabilization policy will reduce $var \, (N)$, since

$$var \, (N) = \frac{var \, (\theta)}{(1+\gamma)^2}$$

for given real wages (w).

But if we are comparing two situations (1) no stabilization policy ($\gamma = 0$) and (2) stabilization policy ($\gamma > 0$), then the preference ordering over alternative $(E(N), w)$ combinations is the same under (1) and (2). But under (2) any given $(E(N), w)$ outcome has a higher level of utility attached to it than under (1), because of the reduction in uncertainty. Thus the indifference curves in Figure 1 are of

$$w + \beta(E(N) - \overline{N})^2 = constant$$

The equilibrium is a non-cooperative equilibrium in a game where in each play of the game the first move is made by the government in announcing or setting up a stabilization policy. The second move is made by the union in choosing a real wage rate. Lastly, the state of nature (θ) is revealed and a level of employment and government intervention is generated (1).

The equilibrium is clearly inferior to one in which there is cooperation or to one in which the government can make its action contingent on both

Figure 1

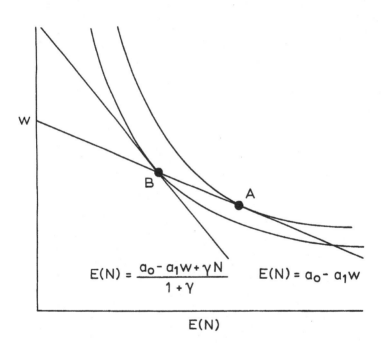

$$E(N) = \frac{a_0 - a_1 w + \gamma N}{1 + \gamma} \qquad E(N) = a_0 - a_1 w$$

employment and real wages.

In the case of cooperation, the union could agree to choose the real wage appropriate to point A in Figure 1, and the government would agree to base its stabilization policy around target level of employment equal to mean employment at point A. By choosing a sufficiently high value of γ_1 the government could reduce the variance of employment to any desired level. This is clearly superior to the non-cooperative equilibrium at B.

There is a difficulty in sustaining the cooperative equilibrium, however. If the government has to make the first move by announcing a policy rule (γ, N^*) to which it is then committed, while the union makes the second move and is unable to make a prior commitment to an agreed choice of real wage, there is always an incentive for the union to renege on any previously announced real wage choice and simply choose the real wage rate that maximizes its expected utility given the move made by the government.

This is clearly a species of "dynamic inconsistency". The possibilities for flexibility of action or precommitment for the two players are crucial in determining the possibility of sustaining the cooperative equilibrium. In the case of the government intervening contingent on both N and w, the reaction function becomes

$$G = - \gamma_1 (w - w^*) - \gamma_2 (N - N^*)$$

By setting $\gamma_1 / \gamma_2 = \alpha_1$, and letting $\gamma_1 \to \infty$, $w^* \to w_A$, and $N^* \to N_A$, the real wage/employment trade-off faced by the union approaches

$$N = \alpha_0 - \alpha_1 w$$

and the effect of this stabilization policy is just to reduce the variance of employment to zero without affecting real wage or mean employment, relative to the no-inflation position.

Variability and Utility
The variance of employment is reduced by the government intervention policy described above in equation (11).

The real wage is given by (16). And consequently the expected utility of the union is maximized at:

$$E(u) = \frac{\alpha_o - \bar{N}}{\alpha_1} + \frac{1 + \gamma}{2\beta\alpha_1^2} - \beta\left(\frac{1 + \gamma}{2\beta\alpha_1^2}\right)^2 - \frac{\beta \text{ var }(\theta)}{(1+\gamma)^2}$$

for any given value of γ.

At $\gamma = 0$, the introduction of a little stabilization policy increases the utility of the union:

$$\frac{\partial E(u)}{\partial \gamma} = \frac{-\gamma}{2\beta\alpha_1^2} + \frac{2\beta \text{ var }(\theta)}{(1+\gamma)^3}$$

At $\gamma = 0$, $\frac{\partial E(u)}{\partial \gamma} > 0$.

The optimum degree of intervention occurs where γ solves:-

$$\frac{\gamma}{2\beta\alpha_1^2} = \frac{2\beta \text{ var }(\theta)}{(1+\gamma)^3} \qquad (\gamma > 0)$$

This degree of intervention is optimal from the unions' point of view but not from the firms' point of view, since their profits are a diminishing function of the level of real wages (2).

Introducing more noise into the system
In the previous section, it was shown that if the government conditions its stabilization policy on employment alone, then both the mean level of employment and its variance are reduced. However, if the government observes G, N and w, then it can identify θ, the random shock and base G on that. In this case, the government can reduce the variance of N without affecting the mean level.

The demand function for labour is

$$N = \alpha_o - \alpha_1 w + G + \theta$$

By setting $g = -\theta$, the government removes all uncertainty about N without affecting the slope of the wages/employment trade-off faced by unions.

What would happen if the government had less than perfect information ? w is assumed here to be publicly available and correct information. Analysis of markets with incomplete and asymmetrical information usually assumes that one agent in the transaction "needs" to know some piece of information which is not communicated or publicly available (like skill or insurance risk) (3). The real wage rate is not a prime candidate for being such a variable. However, we might try to explore the consequences of assuming that the real wage rate is known to the government only with a random error.

The problem is now:

$$N = \alpha_0 - \alpha_1 w + \alpha_2 G + \Theta_1$$

where w = real wage rate, but only $\tilde{w}$ is observed, where $\tilde{w} = w + \varepsilon$.

The government can now only estimate w. The regression model for w gives an estimator of $\hat{w}$.

$$\hat{w} = a \tilde{w} + (1 - a)(\alpha_0 - N + \alpha_2 G)/\alpha_1,$$

where

$$a = (\frac{1}{\text{var } \varepsilon})/((\frac{1}{\text{var } \varepsilon}) + \frac{\alpha_1^2}{\text{var } \Theta}),$$

and an estimate of Θ, $\hat{\Theta} = \alpha_1 a \varepsilon + a\Theta$.

Now if the government responds to $\hat{\Theta}$ it can reduce var(N) to some extent, but its response to $\hat{\Theta}$ introduces noise from ε into N, at the same time as it reduces the variance coming from Θ. But this policy leaves the E(N)/w tradeoff for the union unchanged and therefore leaves its real wage decision unchanged.

What policy the government will choose is now a more open question. It can condition G on both N and $\tilde{w}$, in general. We have:

$$G = \gamma_0 - \gamma_1 N - \gamma_2 \tilde{w}$$

where $\gamma_0, \gamma_1, \gamma_2 \geqslant 0$, and $\gamma_0 = \gamma_1 E(N) + \gamma_2 E(w)$.

Substituting this into the labour demand function gives

$$N = \frac{\alpha_0 + \alpha_2\gamma_0}{1 + \alpha_2\gamma_1} - \frac{\alpha_1 + \alpha_2\gamma_2}{1 + \alpha_2\gamma_1} w + \frac{\Theta}{1 + \alpha_2\gamma_1}$$

$$- \frac{\alpha_2\gamma_2}{1 + \alpha_2\gamma_1} \varepsilon$$

for the union's wage/employment tradeoff. Responding more to N reduces var (N) but steepens the tradeoff,

thus reducing E(N). Responding more to w̃ will
flatten the tradeoff and increase E(N) but it will
also increase (var N) if var(ε) > 0. The optimum
policy depends on government preferences over E(N),
var(N), and w. The government may or may not wish
to trade lower mean N for lower variance of N.
However, it is clear that, <u>cet par</u>, more uncertainty
about w will push it in that direction, since using
w̃ to condition policy becomes then relatively less
attractive.

<u>An interpretation of postwar U.K. unemployment</u>
<u>experience</u>
If an attempt were to be made to interpret U.K. experience using the model offered in this paper, the
argument might be put as follows:

1. <u>Initial disequilibrium.</u> In the early 1950s,
governments were able to run the economy with low unemployment and relatively little inflation. This
might be interpreted as a situation when union bargaining behaviour was based on the real wage/employ-
ment tradeoffs generated by a laissez-faire macroeconomic policy (γ=0), but the government had begun
to use an interventionist policy (γ>0). This situation was clearly not an equilibrium.

2. <u>Adjustment.</u> Over the succeeding years to 1973
governments were forced to retreat from their initial view of what was "full employment" (N*) and had
to stabilize employment around successively lower
target levels, as union bargaining behaviour adjusted
to the change in the employment/real wage tradeoff
induced by stabilization policy.
     The "Barber Boom" was the last attempt by a
government to use "traditonal" Keynesian stabilization policy to achieve an unattainable target level
of employment.

3. <u>The New Equilibrium.</u> The years of the Labour
government 1974-1979 may be regarded as the new
equilibrium with stabilization policy. The equilibrium unemployment rate appeared to be in the region
of 1½ million.

4. <u>A Switch of Policy Regime.</u> The period since
May 1979 under the Conservative administration may
be regarded as a switch of regime from intervention
back to laissez-faire again. The unions' behaviour
is still based on the real wage/employment tradeoff

implied by an interventionist government policy.
Consequently a world recession has produced unemployment in excess of 3 million.   The unemployment rate
will approach an equilibrium level as "the union"
learns about the new tradeoff and adjusts its behav-
ior accordingly.   This may take some time.

CONCLUSION

This paper has outlined a model wherein the equilibrium level of unemployment is not _independent_ of
stabilization policy, as in most recent writing on
macroeconomic theory but is actually _increased_ by it.
Stabilization policy may thus appear to be counter-
productive.
    The result is generated by the interaction of
the behaviour of a union, which makes a real wage
decision in the face of uncertainty, but knowing the
form of the demand function for labour, and knowing
the government's stabilization policy rule, and a
government which announces the policy rule.
    The structure of information and the possibil-
ities for taking state-contingent action are crucial
in determining the outcome in the model.   The government has the ability to make its action contingent on the actual level of employment, but is restricted by having to respond according to a pre-
announced rule.   The union cannot make a state-
contingent wage decision, but neither can it pre-
commit itself in an agreement with the government.
    This information structure seems to represent
broad features of that in an economy such as the
U.K.   Thus the model presented here might be advanced as an explanation of the secular rise in unemployment in the U.K. since 1945.
    The argument offered in this paper formalizes
the frequently stated view that stabilization policy has changed the way unions bargain for wages
and employment causing greater militancy.   It is
an explanation of changing unemployment based on
union behaviour, but it seems more satisfactory than
the arguments about militancy which have been advanced to justify the appearance of variables like
trade union membership in empirically estimated
Phillips curves, since it is based on an explicit
model of rational behaviour by a union.
    There are, however, a number of ways in which
this hypothesis needs to be developed:
1.   The analysis should be developed for the case

where bargaining between unions and employers is explicitly modelled, as in MacDonald and Solow (1981) for example.
2. The model of the labour market as the decision of a single union is clearly unsatisfactory and it would be desirable to formalize the behaviour of an economy with many unions. This may produce a better explanation of the union side's inability to make binding agreements with governments on wages and stabilization policy.

NOTES

1. The union is therefore assumed in this analysis to be unaware of the dependence of the target employment level (N*) on its own wage setting behaviour. It acts as if N* were independent. This may seem to be an unreasonable assumption to make about the behaviour of a single decision-making entity. However, two arguments may be advanced in order to defend it. The first is an empirical argument. Calmfors' (1983) discussion of recent events in Scandinavia, where the single union model is a good representation of the structure of the economy, suggests that this assumption is reasonable. The union appears to have behaved in this way with the implied results. The second argument is theoretical, that the single union model is here being used to capture some aspects of an economy with many unions, like the U.K. While the many-union economy behaves like the single union economy in many ways, an important difference is that individual unions do not recognise a relation between their individual wage setting behaviour and the aggregate target unemployment or employment level set by the government.
2. In fact this depends on firms being risk neutral. If firms were risk averse, they might possibly be better off since the variance of profits is reduced as well as the mean. I am grateful to Monojit Chatterji for pointing this out to me.
3. Akerlof (1970), and Spence (1973) are loci classici for ideas of asymmetrical and incomplete information and their effect on market equilibria.

Part Three

EMPIRICAL ISSUES IN LABOUR MARKET ANALYSIS

EMPIRICAL APPROACHES TO LIFE CYCLE LABOUR SUPPLY

Richard Blundell and Ian Walker

SECTION 1: INTRODUCTION

The supply of labour is traditionally analysed within
the framework of static neoclassical demand theory.
This static model of labour supply is well known and
has received a considerable amount of econometric
attention. A recent survey by Heckman, Killingsworth and McCurdy (1981) provides both an excellent
guide to this literature and an extensive biblio-
graphy. Developments to the static model have for
the most part concentrated on the econometric
methodology that is required when the model is extended to incorporate household, as opposed to individual, decision making (1), the joint determination
of commodity demands and labour supply (2), and non
linearities that arise in the budget constraint due
to non linear taxes, fixed costs, rationing, etc. (3).
    These developments have all made significant
contributions to the modelling of observed labour
supply behaviour and this will be shown to remain so
even within a life cycle framework. However, the
specification of the income variable and the interpretation of the estimated coefficients within the
static model will, in general, be incorrect,with
important implications for policy analysis. Current
labour supply is, in these models, usually explained
by a combination of current wage, unearned income
and demographic characteristics. These cannot,
usually, adequately capture the way the life cycle
profile of wage and demographic variables influence
current labour supply decisions. For most households
the opportunity cost of home time (especially that of
married women) varies considerably over the life
cycle and unless households are unable to borrow or
save they will attempt to move resources between time
periods. The usual interpretation of the static

model rests on the assumption that such movements
are impossible and so, for example, the crucial distinction between anticipated and unanticipated wage
effects is never drawn.   However, provided reason-
ably simple forms for intertemporal preferences are
assumed, life cycle consistent alternatives to the
static model of labour supply, with little or no
more data requirements, can be derived.   The development and examination of such models provides the
motivation for this paper.
     Despite the great attention received by the life
cycle consumption hypothesis originally due to
Modigliani and Brumberg (1954)(4), until the work of
Ghez and Becker (1977), Heckman (1974a), Heckman and
MaCurdy (1980), MaCurdy (1981), and Smith (1977),
very little research effort had been directed towards
life cycle labour supply.   The theory of life cycle
labour supply is a relatively simple extension of
the life cycle consumption model with exogenous
income (5).   Thus, when labour supply is endogenous,
optimality considerations suggest that labour supply
is greatest when the opportunity cost of home time
is lowest.   That is, there should be an unambiguouss
positive correlation between changes in real wages
over the life cycle and changes in hours of work.
Thus, ceteris paribus, if an individual's life cycle
real wage profile has, as human capital theory
suggests, an inverted U shape then so will the life
cycle labour supply profile.   Moreover, children
have a significant impact on the opportunity cost of
female time for the years in the life cycle when the
children are young, providing important incentives to
concentrate labour supply outside those periods.   The
labour supply of those women that expect to have
children may be quite different to those that do not.
     In addition to the variation in the opportunity
cost of an individual's time over his life cycle
providing a motive for concentrating work effort at
one point rather than another, as in the usual life
cycle consumption model, there is an incentive to
shift resources from one point in the life cycle to
another in response to the difference between the
market real rate of interest and the individual's
subjective rate of time preference.   Thus, if, for
example, the interest rate exceeds the rate of time
preference then the individual has an incentive to
work harder earlier in his life cycle and less hard
later on since the interest on extra earnings com-
pensates for incurring the extra effort earlier
rather than later.   In this case the peak in the
labour supply profile will precede the peak in the

wage profile, and vice versa if the interest rate is
less than the rate of time preference.

Current labour supply is determined by the
whole life cycle profile of wages, taxes and demographic characteristics.   Hence, while the theory
is relatively straightforward, its empirical implementation would appear to require data on the whole
of the individual's past and his future expectations.
Since such data are never available to the researcher
a number of attempts at empirical implementation
have either averaged over individuals in the same age
groups to form synthetic cohorts from a single cross
section, or, adopted sufficient intertemporal separability assumptions that allow the definition of a
single summary statistic which captures the effects
of all historic and future variables.   In this later
approach current labour supplies become a function
of current observable variables and the summary
statistics which can be eliminated from the estimating equation for each individual by differencing or
substitution for some observable quantity.

The synthetic cohort approach due to Ghez and
Becker (1977) and Smith (1977) suffers from the
problem that it confounds cohort effects with true
life cycle effects and for that reason we confine
our attention to variants of the second alternative.
These have been developed in the work of Heckman and
MaCurdy (1980), MaCurdy (1981), Browning, Deaton and
Irish (1982), Altonji (1982) and Barmby, Blundell
and Walker (1983).   In Section 2 we present a
simple life cycle model, couched in continuous time,
and draw out the implications for labour supply
profiles.   In Section 3 we give a graphical exposition of the model, detail the alternative estimation approaches, outline the impact of uncertainty
and reconsider the interpretation of the static
model in the life cycle framework.   In Section 4
we discuss what implications the life cycle model
has for policy analysis and how policy analysis can
be conducted in a life cycle context.   In Section 5
we summarise the arguments and make some suggestions
for further life cycle research.

SECTION 2:   LIFE CYCLE LABOUR SUPPLY

Since, at this stage, we only wish to present the
main implications of taking a life cycle view of
labour supply we restrict our attention to a one
person model under perfect foresight (6).   We assume
that the individual has a strictly concave twice

differentiable utility function, $U(c,h)$, which is age invariant, where c denotes consumption and h hours at work. Allowing for time preference at rate ρ, an individual who earns a real wage w, and has a lifetime utility function which is intertemporally separable, Weiss (1972) for example, has shown that the time path of hours at work can be described by

$$\dot{h} = \frac{1}{D} \left[(\rho - r + \dot{w}/w)U_h U_{cc} - (\rho - r)U_c U_{ch} \right] \quad (1)$$

where $D = U_{cc}U_{hh} - U_{ch}^2 > 0$ and r is the real rate of interest at which the individual can borrow and lend. Equation (1) gives the life cycle profile of hours of work. If $U_{ch}U_c < U_{cc}U_h$ (which corresponds in the static model to assuming that leisure is a normal good) and if $\dot{w}=0$ then (1) indicates that labour supply increases over the life cycle if $\rho > r$ and vice versa. Similarly, if $\dot{w}\neq 0$ and $\rho=r$ then the path of hours mirrors the path of wages. If, on the other hand, $\rho < r$ and the wage profile is peaked then the peak in hours precedes the peak in wages and vice versa for $\rho > r$. In addition to (1), the first order conditions generate a similar expression for c, the time path of consumption. This shows that $\dot{c}$ and $\dot{h}$ tend to take on the same sign if $U_{ch} > 0$ and opposite signs if $U_{ch} < 0$. In view of the close correlation between wages and consumption it would appear that consumption and leisure are likely to be substitutes, that is $U_{ch} > 0$. Only if $U_{ch} = 0$ would consumption be independent of wages and the standard life cycle consumption model with exogenous income remain intact. Moreover, only if $\dot{w}=0$ and $\rho=r$ do we get that $\dot{h}=0$. In these circumstances assets are held constant over the life cycle so that savings are zero and unearned income is the appropriate explanatory variable and the static model of labour supply holds. The only other circumstances under which the static model holds occur when the capital market is sufficiently imperfect that no asset changes take place.

SECTION 3: ALTERNATIVE ESTIMATION APPROACHES

3.1 Life Cycle Labour Supply with Intertemporal Separability and Perfect Foresight
In order to show how the theory can be turned into a model that can be estimated it is useful to begin with the simplest possible framework of a single

individual who lives and works for two periods, faces
no uncertainty over his future wages and has no
initial assets and hence no asset income in the first
period.   The individual's preferences are assumed,
as in equation (1), to be intertemporally separable.
This model is illustrated in Figure 1 where w_t
denotes the real wage in period t, h_t denotes labour
supply, c_t denotes consumption, and s_t denotes
saving.   In the absence of any credit market to
allow borrowing and lending, the individual's real
wage profile yields an initial endowment in the
first quadrant of Figure 1 at point E.   The slope
of the indifference curve at E is the marginal rate
of substitution of income in period 1 for income
in period 0.   This can be written as the ratio of
the marginal utility of money in period 1 discounted
by the rate of time preference to the marginal utility of money in period 0.   Letting λ_t denote the
marginal utility of money in period t, the slope of
the indifference curve at E is then $\lambda_1/\lambda_0(1+\rho)$,
where ρ is the rate of time preference.
   Point E corresponds to perfectly imperfect
credit markets and h_0^s, h_1^s are the hours of work that
would result.   Notice that these hours are precisely
those that would have been predicted by the static
model.   That is, the static model is correct if
there are no opportunities for borrowing or lending.
Opening a perfect credit market where the individual is allowed to borrow and lend at the real risk-
less rate of interest r, shows that E is no longer
optimal since given the wage profile the individual
would be better off transferring resources from
period 1 to period 0 by moving to point F.   Notice
that at F the marginal rate of substitution $\lambda_1/\lambda_0(1+\rho)$
equals the slope of the credit market constraint,
$1/(1+r)$.   Thus the optimal intertemporal allocation of full lifetime wealth is characterised by the
condition that

$$\lambda_0 = \lambda_1(\frac{1+r}{1+\rho}) \qquad (2)$$

This condition indicates that the individual chooses
a savings profile such that the marginal utility of
money in period t equals the discounted value of
next period's marginal utility of money, where the
discount rate is one plus the real market interest
rate over one plus the individual's rate of time
preference.   That is, the marginal utility of money,
suitably discounted, should be held constant over
the life cycle to ensure an optimal intertemporal

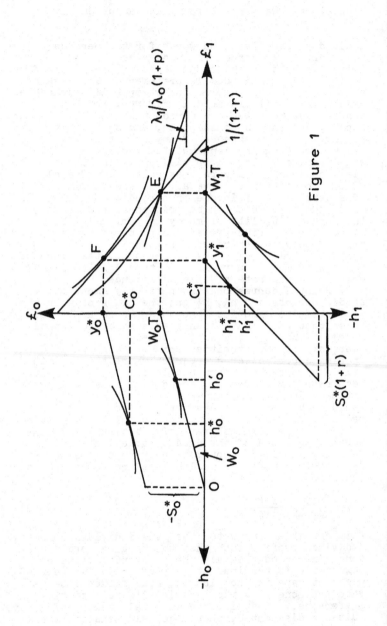

Figure 1

allocation of lifetime resources.

The optimal intertemporal allocation determines the position of the budget constraints in quadrants II and IV of Figure 1 which are relevant to how each period's resources are allocated between non-market time and consumption. Hence, the individual in Figure 1 allocates y_0^* of lifetime full wealth to period 0 and hence saves - s_0^* in order to keep λ constant after suitable discounting. Given this decision he consumes $T-h_0^*$ hours of non market time and c_0^* of the composite commodity according to the period 0 real wage. Similarly to period 1, he allocates y_1^* of lifetime wealth and hence repays $(1+r)s_0^*$. Given this allocation which keeps λ constant, he consumes $T-h_1^*$ of non-market time and c_1^* of the composite commodity according to the period 1 real wage. Thus, we can describe life cycle labour supply and consumption behaviour by the functions

$$c_t = g(w_t, \lambda_t)$$

$$h_t = h(w_t, \lambda_t) \tag{3}$$

These functions decompose consumption and labour supply decisions at a point in the life cycle into: a life cycle component given by λ_t that summarises the effects of all historic and future information and a current period component which determines, given λ_t, the allocation of the current period's income between consumption and non-market time.

The life cycle component of (3), λ_t, plays the same role in this model as permanent income does in the life cycle consumption model with exogenous income. That is, it is a sufficient statistic for all historic and future information that is relevant to the individual's choices of current hours and consumption. Since (2) characterises the time path of λ_t, and (3) characterises the time paths of consumption and labour supply, we can substitute (2) into (3) to provide a complete description of the individual's decision making as

$$c_t = g\left[w_t, \lambda_0 \left(\frac{1+\rho}{1+r}\right)^t\right]$$

$$h_t = h\left[w_t, \lambda_0 \left(\frac{1+\rho}{1+r}\right)^t\right] \tag{4}$$

Written in this form they are known as 'λ_0 constant'
or 'Frisch' functions (7). λ_0 is itself dependent
on initial assets and the whole life cycle of real
wages.   Changes in initial assets or in the lifetime wage profile affect labour supply and consumption only through λ_0.   For example, an increase in
initial wealth decreases λ_0, because of diminishing
marginal utility of money, increases consumption
and decreases labour supply at all ages.   Given λ_0
the individual needs only to keep track of time, in
order to compute the discount factor, and inspect w_t
to decide on his c_t and h_t.   Thus, two individuals
can be of the same age and face the same current
wage but differ in their labour supply decisions
because they have different λ_0's, either because they
started life with different initial assets or because one has a wage profile which is on average
higher than the other's.   In contrast, the static
model would predict that they have identical labour
supplies.   The life cycle model would only give the
same prediction if the two individuals had identical
λ_0's which would require identical initial assets
and identical wage profiles.   In addition, if these
individuals were not of the same age, the two models
would only give the same predictions if $\rho=r$ and the
wage profiles are flat in addition to requiring
identical initial assets.

3.2   A λ Constant Estimation Approach
Writing labour supply as a function of the current
wage and λ_t, as in (3), considerably reduces the
missing data problem that the whole life cycle wage
profile is unobservable.   However, it does not over-
come it altogether since λ_t is itself unobservable.
Nevertheless, (2) shows that λ_t evolves in a systematic fashion over the life cycle.   In effect λ_t is,
after suitable discounting, an individual specific
constant or fixed effect over an individual's life
cycle.   This turns out to be an extremely useful
property when it comes to estimation.   For example,
if we can write the labour supply function in (3)
as (8)

$$h_{it} = \left[\frac{\delta}{1+\delta} w_{it}\lambda_{it}\right]^{-\delta} = \left[\frac{\delta}{1+\delta} w_{it}\lambda_{io}\left(\frac{1+\rho}{1+r}\right)^{t_i}\right]^{-\delta}$$

where the i subscript indicates individual i, then
we obtain on taking logs

$$\ln h_{it} = \delta \ln w_{it} + \delta t_i \ln \left(\frac{1+\rho}{1+r}\right) + \delta \ln \lambda_{io}$$

$$+ \ln \left(\frac{\delta}{1+\delta}\right) \tag{5}$$

where λ_{io} is a constant for individual i or a fixed effect.   If we have a panel of repeated observations on a sample of individuals then (5) can be estimated directly since λ_{io} can be identified by the repeated observations on i.   Alternatively, we could first difference (5) to get

$$\Delta \ln h_{it} = \delta \Delta \ln w_{it} + \delta \ln \left(\frac{1+\rho}{1+r}\right) \tag{6}$$

since $\Delta t_i = 1$ and $\Delta \ln \lambda_{io} = 0$, which requires repeated observations in order to perform the differencing.
It is important to realise that the interpretation of the estimated wage coefficient in (5) or (6) gives the responsiveness of labour supply to evolutionary changes in the wage along the life cycle profile.   That is, this procedure explains why an individual's labour supply differs across his life cycle, but it does not explain why one individual's labour supply differs from another's since it does not explain the determinants of each individual's λ_{io}.   In other words, different individuals have different histories and different futures and hence have different labour supplies even if they face the same current wage.
Thus, to predict the responsiveness of hours of work to differences in wages across individuals, that is to parameteric changes in wages, we require the parameters of the function which determines λ_{io}. Since λ_{io} is a complicated function of unobservable variables such as the lifetime wage profile and initial assets it would seem that the missing data problem has resurfaced.   It is for this reason that Heckman and MaCurdy (1980) acknowledge that the λ constant estimation approach produces a 'clean' solution to the estimation of δ, the elasticity of labour supply to evolutionary wage changes, but estimates 'less cleanly' the parameters of λ_{io} required to discover the elasticity of labour supply to parametric wage changes.   Their approach and that in MaCurdy (1981), is to use observable variables such as age, education, experience, etc. to predict each individual's wage at each point in his life cycle from an auxiliary wage equation; and to predict each individual's initial assets from an auxiliary

property income equation with the same sort of explanatory variables.   These predictions are then used in a regression to determine the variation in the estimated fixed effects across individuals from (5), albeit one which involves the use of inherently arbitrary assumptions.

The ability of the λ constant estimation approach to separate parametric changes from evolutionary changes derives from the assumptions of a perfect credit market, so that λ_t evolves in a systematic fashion; and intertemporal separability, so that current labour supply can be written as a function of a life cycle component and a current period component.   An alternative approach to the estimation of the life cycle labour supply function exploits the intertemporal separability assumption more directly by using it to invoke two stage budgeting.

3.3 A Life Cycle Consistent Estimation Approach Under Two Stage Budgeting

This alternative approach to the estimation of life cycle responses is available even in the absence of the repeated observations from a panel of data providing the data contains information on either current saving or current consumption.   The intuition behind this approach is that current consumption or savings behaviour reveals how the individual feels about the future and hence it serves as an observable sufficient statistic to replace the unobservable λ_{it}.   Inspection of Figure 1 reveals that h_t^* can be thought as a function of the current real wage and 'income', where 'income' is defined as y_t^*, the allocation of full life cycle wealth to period t. A knowledge of either current full income plus saving or of consumption plus earnings is sufficient to pin down the position of the period by period budget constraint.

This approach exploits the intertemporal separability assumption through the use of the two stage budgeting and price aggregation results of Anderson (1979), Blackorby et al (1978), and Gorman (1968) to generate equivalent alternatives to the Frisch or λ constant labour supply function.   In order to discuss this approach, consider the individual's problem at time t in his lifetime of length L.   The current period allocation of full life cycle wealth is given by

$$y_t = w_t T - s_t = c_t + w_t(T - h_t), \qquad (7)$$

so that the life cycle budget constraint and asset accumulation constraint can be written as

$$\sum_{s=1}^{L} \frac{1}{(1+r)^s} y_s = (1+r)A_{t-1} + \sum_{s=t}^{L} \frac{1}{(1+r)^s} w_s T \equiv W_t$$

$$A_t = (1+r)A_{t-1} - s_t \tag{8}$$

where A_{t-1} is the individual's asset position at the start of period t. Maximising the intertemporally separable function

$$U(c_t,h_t) + \frac{1}{(1+\rho)} U(c_{t+1},h_{t+1}) + \ldots + \frac{1}{(1+\rho)^{L-t}}$$

$$U(c_L,h_L)$$

subject to the life cycle constraints yields, at the first stage, a time profile of s_t to equalise the marginal utility of income across the life cycle and which in turn implies a time profile of y_t through equation (7) as

$$y_t = w_t T - s_t = y(w_t,\ldots,w_L,W_t).$$

At the second stage, this level of y_t is taken as given and we obtain the labour supply function which is conditioned on y_t rather than on λ_t as

$$h_t = f(w_t,y_t) \tag{9}$$

It is clear that this specification is analogous to the traditional static model except that 'income' is no longer measured by $w_t T + m_t$, where $m_t = rA_{t-1}$ is unearned or property income. Rather, 'income' is now defined as $w_t T - s_t$. Inspection of the asset accumulation constraint in (8) reveals that $s_t = -m_t$, so that the static model is the correct specification, only when $A_t = A_{t-1}$. This only occurs under the same conditions that give h=0 in Section 2; that is, constant real wages and r=ρ. Notice that this method relies on separability to permit two stage budgeting but, since y_t is observable, we do not require such strong assumptions about credit markets since y_t may already reflect credit market imperfections.
    We can go further than this if we are prepared

to restrict intraperiod preferences.   In particular, if we assume that the indirect utility function for each period is given by the quasi-homothetic form

$$V_t = (y_t - a_t)/b_t, \qquad\qquad (10)$$

where a_t and b_t are linear homogenous functions of the period t wages, then we can solve for the relationship (9) between λ_t and y_t as

$$\lambda_t = (y_t - a_t)^{-1}.$$

Preferences of the form given by (10) are particularly useful for the life cycle analysis of labour supply and have been employed by Ashenfelter (1980), Blundell (1980), Blundell and Walker (1982), Barmby, Blundell and Walker (1983) and Browning, Deaton and Irish (1983).
    Thus, for certain preferences it is possible to write a labour supply equation conditional on the observable y_t corresponding to the Frisch labour supply function that conditions on the unobservable λ_t.   Estimates of the former provide the parameters of the latter and hence give an estimate of the responsiveness of labour supply to evolutionary wage changes.   Given the direct correspondence between this approach and the constant λ approach it should come as no surprise that again it is possible to derive only the responsiveness to evolutionary wage changes, and that the responsiveness to parametric wage changes, that is to differences across individuals, requires an explanation of y_t for each individual.
    Estimates of the life cycle consistent labour supply equation (9) are provided by Ashenfelter (1980), Blundell (1980), Blundell and Walker (1982), Barmby, Blundell and Walker (1983), and MaCurdy (1983). Ashenfelter (1980) estimates a Linear Expenditure System using time series data and notes that, given his definition of income, it is consistent with life cycle decision making.   Blundell (1980) and Blundell and Walker (1982) estimate generalisations of the LES with cross section data and use the same definition of income.   Barmby, Blundell and Walker (1983) and MaCurdy (1983) both make explicit the fact that the estimates are to be interpreted as the responsiveness of labour supply to evolutionary wage changes, although MaCurdy does compare his estimate to those

from previous work on the static model. In addition
to estimating an equation of the form (9), which he
refers to as a 'pseudo' labour supply function,
MaCurdy (1983) also estimates the first order conditions of the utility maximising problem directly
to provide alternative parameter estimates. Finally,
Altonji (1982) estimates an equation which is similar to (9) but which is conditioned on c_t rather
than on y_t. His equation is derived from noting
that in addition to the Frisch labour supply function in (4) there is a corresponding Frisch consumption function and that if the consumption function
can be solved for λ_t in terms of c_t and w_t then this
solution can be substituted into the Frisch labour
supply function to give current labour supply as a
function of the current wage and current consumption.

3.4 Reinterpreting the Static Model in a Life Cycle Context

In comparison to the life cycle specifications that
condition on λ_{it} or y_{it} the traditional static model
conditions on current unearned income m_{it}. It is
clear that this is a misspecification since m_{it}
cannot capture the profile of future (expected) wages.
Moreover, it is difficult to give any meaningful
interpretation to the wage coefficients in such models.
The essence of the problem is that wages vary across
individuals for two reasons. First, different individuals have different ages and hence are at different points on their respective wage profiles.
Secondly, individuals have different average lifetime
wages because they have different education and family backgrounds. Thus, the estimated wage coefficient in the static cross section specification confounds the effects of evolutionary wage changes over
individuals' wage profiles with the effects of parametric wage changes due to shifts in wage profiles
across individuals.

Nevertheless, it is useful to consider the reinterpretation of the wage and income coefficients of
static models in the light of life cycle decision
making. If we write a typical cross section specification of the static model as:

$$\ln h_{it} = \alpha_o + \alpha_1 \ln w_{it} + \alpha_2 m_{it} \tag{11}$$

and contrast it with the life cycle specification

$$\ln h_{it} = \delta \ln w_{it} + \delta \ln \lambda_{it}$$

$$+ \delta \ln \left(\frac{\delta}{1+\delta}\right) \tag{12}$$

then the interpretation of α_1 and α_2 will depend on how $\ln \lambda_{it}$ relates to w_{it} and m_{it}.

Since $\ln \lambda_{it}$ is a function of current assets, current wage and (expected) future wages α_1 will not estimate δ. However, as MaCurdy (1982) points out in a useful recent paper, including variables that control for future evolutionary wage changes will allow an interpretation of α_1 in (11). In particular, if a polynomial in age is sufficient to explain such changes then its inclusion in (11) would allow the wage coefficient to identify the response of labour supply to parametric shifts in the wage profile. This relies, additionally, on the unearned income variable m_{it} capturing accurately the influence of current assets.

An alternative form for (12) which conditions on λ_{io} rather than λ_{it} is given by:

$$\ln h_{it} = \delta \ln w_{it} + \delta t_i(\rho - r) + \delta \ln \lambda_{io}$$

$$+ \delta \ln \left(\frac{\delta}{1+\delta}\right) \tag{13}$$

where we have approximated

$$\ln \left(\frac{1+\rho}{1+r}\right)$$

by $(\rho - r)$. This also provides an alternative interpretation of the static model. That is, if the static model omits unearned income and enters family background and education variables that accurately control for initial assets and wage expectations contained in λ_{io} then the wage coefficient α_1 will measure δ, the intertemporal elasticity of substitution. As can be seen from (13) if ρ differs from r, age should also enter in this regression.

In general, unless these appropriate controlling factors are included, the static model coefficients will not have any meaningful interpretation. Notice also that the interpretation changes as the controlling factors are altered. It also is the case that the above reinterpretation of the static model coefficients rests on fairly strong assumptions concerning the evolution of wages over the life cycle.

140

In addition, unearned income, a variable that is often subject to severe measurement error, is being used to measure the level of assets.

3.5 Relaxing the Perfect Foresight and Intertemporal Separability Assumptions

The perfect foresight assumption, which is in the background of most of the analysis of previous sections, implies that all expectations are realised. This is an unnecessarily strong assumption which is relatively easy to relax within the life cycle structure developed in this paper. The intertemporal separability assumption is crucial here since it allows the separation of all future expectations into a single summary statistic or conditioning variable. Current decisions are made conditional on a set of expectations which, in the two stage budgeting framework described in Section 3.3, will only enter the equation through y_{it}, the current period allocation of wealth. As this is observable the labour supply decisions remain identical in form and interpretation, it is only the equation determining y_{it} that becomes a function of the expectation formation process. A similar line of reasoning follows for the λ-constant specification although, because λ_{it} is unobserved, estimation has to take account of its stochastic generating process. Once the perfect foresight assumption is relaxed, the distinction between evolutionary and parametric wage changes made in the previous sections becomes less clear cut since an individual can experience unanticipated wage changes which are equivalent to parametric shifts as well as evolutionary anticipated changes. For tax/benefit policy purposes it is precisely the response to a parametric (unanticipated) change that is required.

The variables for which an individual or household may be uncertain contain the after tax wage, price, transfer payment, interest rate and taste variables. The intertemporal problem in period t is assumed to be the maximisation of the following expected utility function given information received up to and including that period:

$$E_t\left\{ U_t(c_t,h_t) + \frac{1}{(1+\rho)} \, U_{t+1}(c_{t+1},h_{t+1}) + \cdots \right.$$

$$\left. + \frac{1}{(1+\rho)^{L-t}} \, U_L(c_L,h_L)\right\} \tag{14}$$

subject to the life cycle budget constraint which now becomes a function of uncertain variables. Expected utility maximisation assumes explicit additive separability under uncertainty which allows the maximum value of (14) to be written as

$$J_t = \max_{c_t, h_t} U_t(c_t, h_t) + \frac{1}{(1+\rho)} J_{t+1} \qquad (15)$$

where J_{t+1} represents the maximum attainable expected utility in period t+1 given the information received through period t.   From (15) it is clear that the life cycle allocation problem can be decentralised following the two stage budgeting framework outlined in Section 3.3.   The only difference being that the conditioning variable y_{it} will depend on the parameters of the distribution of the uncertain variables and may well be updated through time.   Nevertheless, consumption data can still be used to measure y_{it} so that within period estimation of labour supply may proceed as before.

The λ constant or Frisch labour supplies that condition on the unobservable λ_{it} require a knowledge of its evolution for estimation.   Provided that the household exploits all information rationally, Hall (1978) and MaCurdy (1981) have shown that:

$$\lambda_{it} = (\frac{1+\rho}{1+r}) \lambda_{it-1} + \varepsilon_{it}$$

where $E_{t-1}(\varepsilon_{it}) = 0$.   So that, with regard to the information set described above, ε_{it} is an innovation process.   It is independent of all past values of that information.   For specifications of the λ constant model where λ_{io} (or log λ_{io}) enters through the intercept term the innovation becomes part of the error process in estimation.   Since ε_{it} is not independent of current (uncertain) variables, suitable consistent estimation techniques have to be adopted to estimate the λ constant models under uncertainty.   In particular, instrumental variables are required for wage (and other) variables over which expectations are formed.   Notice that in the two stage budgeting model which conditions on y_{it} rather than λ_{io} no such problem arises.   The convenient stochastic structure for the evolution of λ_{it} has been exploited in a number of empirical studies, for example, Browning, Deaton and Irish (1983), Ham (1983), Heckman and MaCurdy (1980) and MaCurdy (1981). However, whether estimation uses first differences or levels the dependence of the innovation ε_{it} and included explanatory variables remains.

It may be argued that if the two stage budgeting model is adopted, so that y_{it} is used as an explanatory variable, then it should not be considered exogenous for estimation pruposes. Although y_{it} is a choice variable over the life cycle this does not imply that it cannot be treated as (weakly) exogenous in the estimation of period t allocations. Such weak exogeneity would occur if the stochastic structure of the disturbances over the life cycle was intertemporally separable in the same way as the observable structure (10). In this case, for second stage allocations, y_{it} could be considered as predetermined. There may, of course, be alternative reasons why y_{it} or indeed other explanatory variables such as the wage rate should be considered endogenous In particular, if the current period budget constraint is non linear due to progressive taxation, then both y_{it} and w_{it} become endogenous. In this case full maximum likelihood estimation, akin to that of Burtless and Hausman (1978) or Hausman (1980) could be used. Alternatively, suitable instrumental variables for y_{it} and w_{it} may be available, in which case consistent, but not efficient, estimation could proceed. If interest lies in the first stage allocation then the regression describing this allocation would provide suitable instruments for use at the estimation of the second stage allocation.

The interpretation of the static model described in Section 3.4 is also affected by the introduction of uncertainty. The regression that omits unearned income and approximates λ_{io} by background and education variables now includes an error term that contains the cumulation of innovation errors up to period t. As described above, these will not be independent of the current wage rate so that the reinterpretation of the static model discussed in Section 3.4 is only valid if a suitable instrumental variable regression is used to purge the wage rate of unobserved innovations. A polynomial of age variables is an obvious choice. To summarise; provided suitable care is taken of the stochastic dependence between error term and included explanatory variables over which expectations may be formed, relaxation of the perfect foresight assumption does very little to affect the structure of the second stage allocation since this depends on a single summary statistic which captures the effects of uncertainty. The first stage regressions that determine these summary statistics will depend on the process under which expectations are formed and the parameters of the distribution of uncertain variables. Nevertheless, examination of this first stage is of particular importance, especially for measuring the impact of unanticipated or parametric changes which are crucial for the analysis of tax changes considered in the next section.

These generalisations which take account of uncertainty clearly rest on strong assumptions concerning intertemporal separability.   It is difficult to see how these could be relaxed but it is quite clear that they rule out both habit formation and adjustment costs.   Since labour markets are likely to be influenced by such dynamics, caution should be exercised when interpreting the empirical results from applying the methodology described above.   It may be true, however, that behaviour under uncertainty may appear to follow the same form of dynamics as that predicted from habit formation and adjustment cost models.

SECTION 4:   POLICY IMPLICATIONS OF THE LIFE CYCLE MODEL

A major motivation for estimating labour supply responses is to evaluate the effects and welfare implications of reforms to taxes and benefits.   Within the framework of the static model many important developments have appeared in recent literature: for example, Burtless and Hausman (1978), Hausman (1980) and Zabalza (1983).   These contributions have concentrated on the non linearities of the budget constraint that occur under non linear income taxes and the techniques development that can be applied with little alteration to the life cycle framework. However, given the analysis described in Section 3, the wage coefficient of the static model does not, in general, reflect the labour supply response to an unanticipated tax reform.   Since most tax reforms are of this kind, the ability of the life cycle models to distinguish between unanticipated and evolutionary wage effects allows the correct measurement of such responses.

For the measurement of an unanticipated tax reform the λ constant wage derivative is also clearly not the appropriate measure of labour supply response since λ itself will change with unanticipated marginal wage changes.   If we consider the two stage budgeting framework, tax policy analysis requires knowledge of precisely how y_{it} is affected by unanticipated changes as well as the direct effect on labour supply through the current marginal wage variable w_{it}. Following the framework developed in Section 3.3, the labour supply of individual i in time t may be written

$$h_{it} = f(w_{it}, y_{it}) \tag{16}$$

and y_{it}, the allocation of lifetime wealth, as:

$$y_{it} = y(w_{it}, w_{it+1}, \ldots, w_{iL}, W) \tag{17}$$

The response of h_{it} to an unanticipated (and permanent) change in the marginal tax rate τ has the following two components:

$$\frac{\partial h_{it}}{\delta\tau} = \frac{\delta f}{\delta w_{it}} \cdot \frac{\partial w_{it}}{\delta\tau} + \frac{\delta f}{\partial y_{it}} \cdot \frac{\partial y_{it}}{\delta\tau} . \tag{18}$$

The first term in (18) is the usual uncompensated (or Marshallian) own substitution effect, while the second term measures the effect of current and future marginal wage change on the life cycle allocation of resources.   A transitory unanticipated tax change will require a similar analysis.

For the simulation of tax reforms, (18) is the appropriate function to evaluate and (17) indicates that this in turn requires an understanding of the formation of future marginal wage expectations. Moreover, the magnitude of

$$\frac{\partial y_{it}}{\delta\tau}$$

will depend on each individual's age and therefore the effect on average hours will depend on the complete age distribution.   In comparison, the static model, by confounding both parametric and evolutionary wage responses, does not allow the partitioning of effects described above.   Inevitably the static model will produce misleading simulations of the labour supply response to tax reforms.

SECTION 5:   SUMMARY AND CONCLUSIONS

Throughout this paper we have attempted to emphasise

the advantages of modelling labour supply in a life cycle framework.   Provided care is taken to specify life cycle consistent models along the lines described in Section 3, very little additional data requirements are imposed over those traditionally used in static models.   By cleanly separating the impact of evolutionary and parametric wage changes the life cycle models were shown to be an ideal vehicle for analysing the labour supply response to unanticipated tax reform and uncertainty.   Although certain specifications of the static model were shown to have an interpretation in a life cycle framework, in general, they condition on inappropriate variables and have no meaningful interpretation.

The arguments for taking account of life cycle optimising behaviour are extremely compelling once the strong assumptions needed to invoke the traditional static model are considered.   The principal error in the static model is to condition on unearned (or property) income which cannot capture future expectations.   However, in this paper we have shown that a proper use of two stage budgeting theory suggests an alternative conditioning variable that can be observed if consumption expenditure data is recorded.   Such data is available and in Barmby, Blundell and Walker (1983), such a two stage budgeting model for family labour supply is applied to households in the Family Expenditure Survey.

In this paper we have tried to draw comparisons to similar alternative procedures that have been developed in the recent literature.   For example, it is possible to derive the fully anticipated elasticities that Heckman and MaCurdy (1980) pay much attention to in their development of the λ constant approach life cycle behaviour.   Indeed, the λ constant procedure is shown to be directly equivalent, resting on precisely the same specification of life cycle preferences.   The two stage budgeting procedure 'looks' very similar to the static model and yet provides a life cycle consistent framework provided intertemporal separability can be assumed. The resulting model can be estimated using techniques already developed for the static model.   It is only the interpretation, simulation and policy implications of the model that differ.

This excursion into life cycle modelling has pointed to many areas that are distinctly in need of further research.   In particular, the impact of uncertainty, the generation of expectations and the simulation of tax reform, all seem worthy of further

146

consideration. Given the limited nature of most data sets, in that they are short panels or single cross sections, there seems little hope of relaxing the intertemporal separability assumptions but it is worth noting that the new and popular consumption models, of, for example, Hall (1978), rest on similar assumptions.

ACKNOWLEDGEMENT

This work was supported by SSRC Research Grant D0023 0004. We would like to thank Martin Browning, John Ham and the participants at the Hull Conference of the SSRC Labour Study Group for their comments on an earlier draft. All errors remain ours.

NOTES

1. See, for example, Ashenfelter and Heckman (1974) and the survey by Marjorie McElroy in the appendix to Killingsworth (1981).
2. See, for example, Atkinson and Stern (1980) and Blundell and Walker (1982).
3. See, for example, Burtless and Hausman (1978), and Zabalza (1983) on non-linearities induced by taxation; Cogan (1980) and Hausman (1980) on non linearities induced by fixed costs of work; Heckman (1974c) and Barton, Layard and Zabalza (1980) on the non linearity implicit in female non participation; and Ham (1982) and Lundberg (1982) on the non linearities induced by rationing.
4. For a recent survey see Modigliani (1975), and for a life cycle approach to consumption that is similar to what follows for labour supply see Hall (1978).
5. See, for example, Weiss (1972), Heckman (1974a) and Blinder (1974).
6. These implications are quite robust and survive generalisations to include learning by doing, endogenous human capital formation, endogenous retirement and uncertainty.
7. Heckman and MaCurdy (1980) refer to them as λ_0 constant functions. Browning, Deaton and Irish (1983) refer to them as Frisch functions since Frisch (1932) used additive preferences to measure the marginal utility of money.
8. This specification is used by Heckman and MaCurdy and MaCurdy (1981, 1983) where it is derived from a particular utility function.

147

9.   For example, for the Stone Geary function $U_t = b_c \ln(c_t - a_c) + (1-b_c) \ln(T-h_t-a_\ell)$ where a_c and a_ℓ are subsistence consumption and non market time, and b_c is the marginal propensity to consume, the form of (4) is

$$c_t = a_c + b_c \lambda_t^{-1}$$

$$h_t = (T - a_\ell) + (1 - b_c)w_t^{-1}\lambda_t^{-1}$$

Then substituting the above into (7) yields

$$y_t = a_c + w_t(T - a\ell) + \lambda_t^{-1}$$

and hence $\lambda_t = (y_t - a_t)^{-1}$ where $a_t = a_c + w_t(T - a_\ell)$.

10.   For the definition of weak exogeneity used here see Engle, Hendry and Richard (1983).   See Deaton (1980) for a description of the type of error separability required to produce weak exogeneity.

LONG RUN EQUILIBRIUM AND THE U.K. LABOUR MARKET

G. H. Makepeace

INTRODUCTION

Much macroeconomic modelling assumes that the labour market can be simply described. The "New Classical Macroeconomists" argue that the labour market is in equilibrium except for (small) random fluctuations reflecting unanticipated events, while the traditional monetarist view is that the labour market moves to its equilibrium position (very quickly) over time. These arguments contrast strongly with the Keynesian vision of a labour market dominated by sticky wages and short side trading. This cursory survey suggests three hypotheses concerning the operations of the labour market which are worth exploring. These may be defined as the "full equilibrium", the "equilibriating" and the "full disequilibrium" hypotheses, according to whether the labour market is assumed to be continuously in equilibrium, tending towards equilibrium or in disequilibrium with no tendency to move towards equilibrium.

There have been several attempts in recent years to estimate disequilibrium aggregate labour market models for the United Kingdom and the United States (1). These models are typically formulated as disequilibrium models, but many implicitly test the assumption of equilibrium and find it wanting. However full equilibrium is generally tested against full disequilibrium and the equilibriating hypothesis is ignored. This neglect may be important if real wages move to clear the labour market. The present paper examines the equilibriating hypothesis for real wages and employment under the assumption of an underlying growth in each over time.

The adjustment of real wages to their equilibrium value is modelled as a stochastic difference equation. A family of disequilibrium models is defined by the

restrictions required to ensure that the steady state
solution equals the equilibrium real wage.   The most
constrained member of this family is the equilibriating model and the most general member is, for want
of a better description, the general disequilibrium
model.   Although all the equilibriating restrictions
cannot be tested, a less constrained model can be
estimated, thus providing a partial test of the equilibriating model.   Estimates of the real wage models
based on U.K. data are presented in sections 4 and 5
of the paper.   The full equilibrium and equilibriating models are both rejected.   The empirical analysis is applied to employment data in section 6 with
similar results.   The main inference drawn is that
neither the "new Classical" nor the traditional
Monetarist explanations of behaviour in the labour
market are satisfactory.

SECTION 2:   LONG RUN EQUILIBRIUM CONCEPTS

Let the equilibrium real wage at time t be w_t^* (2)
and the actual real wage w_t.   Consider the price
adjustment mechanism;

$$w_t - \sum_{i=1}^{k} \delta_i w_{t-i} = \sum_{j=0}^{m} \theta_j w_{t-j}^* + u_t \qquad (1)$$

where the u's are independently and normally distributed random variables with means zero and the
same variance, σ^2, and where the lower case letter
denotes the natural logarithm of the variable
concerned (3).
        Equation (1) is of general interest because it
contains the price adjustment mechanisms used in most
disequilibrium models as special cases.   In Bowden's
PAMEQ model (4), the partial adjustment restrictions
$k = 1$, $m = 0$ and $\delta_1 = 1-\theta_0$ are imposed, but a more
general version is obtained if $k = 1+m$, $\delta_1 = 1-\theta_0$ and
$\delta_i = 1-\theta_0$ and $\delta_i = -\theta_{j-1}$ $i = j$, $i = 2,...,k$. (5)
Equation (1) may then be written as;

$$w_t - w_{t-1} = \sum_{j=0}^{k} \theta_j (w_{t-j}^* - w_{t-1-j}) + u_t \qquad (2)$$

The generalised PAMEQ equation (2) makes the plausible
assumption that the current change in real wages is a
linear function of previous disequilibria.   With an
appropriate specification for the demand and supply

150

curves, the right-hand side of (2) can be written as a linear function of the past excess demands for labour.   Price adjustment mechanisms of this form are a common feature in econometric disequilibrium models (6).   Equation (1) may be written as an error correction mechanism equation (7)(8).   The rationale for such equations is that the current change in real wages should equal the current change in equilibrium real wages plus some measure of previous disequilibria (the error correction mechanism).   One example of this form can be obtained by letting $k = 1+m$, $\delta_1 = 2-\theta_0$, $\delta_2 = -1-\theta_1$ and $\delta_i = -\theta_{j-1}$ $i = j$, $i = 3$, ...,k to give

$$w_t - w_{t-1} = w_t^* - w_{t-1}^* + (\theta_0 - 1)(w_t^* - w_{t-1}) +$$

$$(\theta_1 + 1)(w_{t-1}^* - w_{t-2}) +$$

$$\sum_{j=2}^{m} \theta_j (w_{t-j}^* - w_{t-1-j}) + u_t \qquad (3)$$

The hypotheses identified as being of interest in the introduction make the following assumptions about (1)
1.   full equilibrium where $\delta_i = 0$ $\forall i$, $\theta_0 = 1$ and $\theta_j = 0$ $\forall j \geq 1$.
2.   equilibriating where $\lim_{t \to \infty} w_t = w_t^*$ and not all of the restrictions in (i) hold.
3.   full disequilibrium where $\lim_{t \to \infty} w_t \neq w_t^*$ and not all of the restrictions in (i) hold.
The equilibrium real wage cannot be directly observed, so that the full equilibrium hypothesis cannot be tested directly.   However, if the equilibrium real wage is a loglinear function of some predetermined variables (for example, the exogeneous factors affecting the demand for and supply of labour), then this function may be substituted into (1) to obtain an estimating equation.   The full equilibrium hypothesis will not be testable but the joint significance of the δ's can be tested.   If the equilibrium hypothesis is rejected, it is important to examine whether the real wage tends to its equilibrium value over time.
Whether or not the real wage tends to its equilibrium value will depend on the stability of the equation and the relationship between the steady state or particular solution of (1) and the equilibrium value.   The stability of the difference equation is a widely discussed topic but stability alone

151

will not guarantee long run equilibrium.   Since the importance of the particular solution has, until recently, received less attention than the stability of the equation, the present paper will examine in some detail the implications for the model of requiring the real wage to equal its equilibrium value in the long run.   The approach described by Currie (1981) is used.

The general solution (1) consists of a complementary solution, w_{ct}, which is a solution of

$$w_t - \sum_{i=1}^{k} \delta_i w_{t-1} = 0$$

and a particular solution, w_{pt}, which is a solution of (1).   If the solution is stable $\lim_{t \to \infty} w_{ct} = 0$ and long run equilibrium requires $w_{pt} = w_t^*$.   The conditions under which this occurs depend on the assumptions made about the time path of w^*.   Neoclassical growth theory plus empirical observation indicate that real wages grow steadily over time, suggesting that;

$$w_t^* = \alpha' + \beta t \tag{4}$$

where w^* is not observable, t is time and β is the rate of technical progress (9).

Equation (4) is the simplest realistic assumption that can be made about the growth path of equilibrium real wages.   The basic points at issue below continue to apply when a higher order polynomial is used, but the algebra is unnecessarily complicated and the resulting restrictions (see equations (6a) and (6b)) are more complex.

The particular solution of (1) when (4) applies is given by;

$$w_{pt} = \frac{\sum_j \theta_j}{(1-\sum_i \delta_i)} w_t^* - \frac{\beta \sum_j \theta_j}{(1-\sum_i \delta_i)^2} \times$$

$$\left\{ \frac{(\sum_j \theta_j j)(1-\sum_i \delta_i)}{\sum_j \theta_j} + \sum_i \delta_i i \right\} \tag{5}$$

where the summations are from 0 to m for j and 1 to k for i.

152

Long run equilibrium, therefore, requires that,

$$\sum_j \theta_j = (1 - \Sigma \delta_i) \tag{6a}$$

and since $\beta \neq 0$,

$$(\sum_j \theta_j j)(1 - \sum_i \delta_i) = - \sum_j \theta_j \sum_i \delta_i i \tag{6b}$$

Conditions (6a) and (6b) define a family of models (10), There is the equilibriating model, in which both conditions hold, and three full disequilibrium models.   The full disequilibrium models may be described as; the "proportional" disequilibrium model, in which (6b) holds but not (6a), the "additive" disequilibrium model, in which (6a) holds but not (6b) and the "general" disequilibrium model, in which neither condition holds.   The nomenclature is based on whether a long run tendency for excess demand or supply to emerge can be attributed (1) to real wages being a fraction or multiple of the equilibrium real wage, (2) to real wages being equal to the equilibrium real wage minus or plus a constant, or (3) to a mixture of both.

Different adjustment mechanisms have different steady state properties but one special case studied below is, what may be called, the "fixed m period lag" model.   This model imposes the constraints $\theta_j = 0$ j < m and has the particular solution(11);

$$w_{pt} = \frac{\theta_m}{1 - \Sigma \delta_i} w_t^* - \frac{\beta \, \theta_m}{(1 - \Sigma \delta_i)^2} (m(1 - \Sigma \delta_i) + \Sigma \delta_i i) \tag{7}$$

The simple partial adjustment model (which is, of course, a PAMEQ model) is a possible fixed one period lag model with a particular solution;

$$w_{pt} = w_t^* - \frac{\beta}{\theta_1} \tag{8}$$

Unless $\beta = 0$, the partial adjustment mechanism, and hence the PAMEQ model, is, by assumption, an additive disequilibrium model.   One class of fixed m period lag models, which automatically satisfy the equilibriating restrictions are (12);

153

$$\Delta^k w_t = \theta_k (w^*_{t-k} - w_{t-k})$$

where

$$\Delta^k w_t = \Delta^1 (\Delta^{k-1} w_t) \text{ and } \Delta^i w_t = w_t - w_{t-1}.$$

The motivation for the development of error correction mechanisms (ECM's) was to specify adjustment equations which ensure that long run equilibrium is achieved. If one's interest is solely in equilibrating models, the proportional model can be ruled out by imposing (6a) and attention focused on (6b). From (6b), the most obvious ECM with automatic equilibrating properties is obtained by letting $k = m$, $\theta_0 = 1$ and $\theta_j = \delta_i$ $i = j$, $i = 1,\ldots,k$ (13). However, considerable care must be exercised in specifying an ECM because long run equilibrium is not guaranteed. For example, equation (3) above requires $\Sigma \theta_i = 0$ for steady state equilibrium. Further, some ECM's lose their intuitive appeal when long run equilibrium restrictions are imposed.

SECTION 3: A PARTIAL TEST FOR THE EQUILIBRATING MODEL

Unfortunately, the typology given by (6a) and (6b) cannot be tested directly at this stage because of the difficulty in identifying the θ's. (14) Nonetheless, the validity of the restriction (6b) can be tested in a fixed m period lag model, giving a direct test of the proportional disequilibrium model and, through the nesting of the models, a partial test of the equilibrating model. (15) The test is based on the likelihood ratio.

The estimating equation for the general, fixed m period lag, disequilibrium model (in which the remaining models are nested) is;

$$w_t = \theta_m \alpha + \theta_m \beta t + \sum_i^k \delta_i w_{t-i} + u_t$$

$$t = k+1,\ldots,n \tag{9}$$

where $u \sim IN(0,\sigma^2)$ and $\alpha = \alpha' - \beta m$.

The general model places no constraints on (9) and, although θ_m, α' and β are not identified, maximum likelihood estimates of $\theta_m \alpha$, $\theta_m \beta$ and the δ's can be obtained. The log likelihood is, except for a constant, given by;

$$\ln L(H_{gdm}) = -\frac{n-k}{2} \ln \hat{\sigma}^2_{gdm} \qquad (10)$$

where

$$\hat{\sigma}^2_{gdm} = \frac{1}{n-k} \sum_t (w_t - (\theta_m \hat{\alpha}) - (\theta_m \hat{\beta})t - \sum_i \hat{\delta}_i w_{t-1})^2$$

and the cap denotes the maximum likelihood estimate of the parameter.

The proportional disequilibrium model imposes the constraint (6b), which may be written as

$$\delta_1 = \frac{m}{m-1} - \sum_2^k \frac{(m-i)}{(m-1)} \delta_i$$

when the fixed m period lag is considered. Substituting this expression into (9) one obtains;

$$w_t - (\frac{m}{m-1})w_{t-1} = \theta_m\alpha + \theta_m\beta t + \sum_{i=2}^k \delta_i y_{t-i} + u_t \qquad (11)$$

where

$$y_{t-i} = w_{t-i} - (\frac{m-i}{m-1})w_{t-1}.$$

The concentrated log likelihood for (11) is, except for the same constant as (10);

$$\ln L(H_{pdm}) = -\frac{n-k}{2}\ln \hat{\sigma}^2_{pdm} \qquad (12)$$

where

$$\hat{\sigma}^2_{pdm} = \frac{1}{n-k} \sum_t (w_t - (\frac{m}{m-1})w_{t-1} - (\theta_m\hat{\alpha})$$

$$- (\theta_m\hat{\beta})t - \sum_2^k \hat{\delta}_i y_{t-i})^2$$

If RSS_{gdm} is the residual sum of squares from the regression equation (9) and RSS_{pdm} is the residual sum of squares from the regression equation (11), then the likelihood ratio statistic, LR, can be

155

written as a function of RSS_{gdm} and RSS_{pdm}. The vailidity of the constraint imposed by the proportional disequilibrium model can then be tested using the fact that

$$-2 \ln LR = (n-k) \ln \frac{RSS_{pdm}}{RSS_{gdm}}$$

has a chi-squared distribution with one degree of freedom.

SECTION 4: RESULTS FOR REAL WAGE ADJUSTMENT EQUATIONS

The empirical results are based on the fixed m period lag model, which has the following adjustment equation;

$$w_t = \theta_m w^*_{t-m} + \sum_i^k \delta_i w_{t-i} + u_t \qquad (13)$$

The full equilibrium hypothesis can be tested by the joint significance of the δ's. This partial test is sufficient in the present context to reject the full equilibrium hypothesis. The proportional disequilibrium model can be tested using the likelihood ratio statistic defined in section 3. Values of $m = 0$ and $m = k$ were used. The estimating equations, when the proportional disequilibrium is appropriate, may be written as;

(for $m = 0$)

$$w_t = \theta_o w^*_t + \sum_i \delta_i (w_{t-i} - i w_{t-1}) + u_t \qquad (14)$$

(for $m = k$)

$$w_t - k w_{t-k+1} = \theta_k w^*_{t-k} + \sum_i \delta_i (-(k-i) w_{t-k+1} + w_{t-i})$$

$$+ \delta_k w_{t-k} + u_t \qquad (15)$$

Equations (13) to (15) were estimated using two specifications for the equilibrium real wage. The first employed the time trend model defined in (4), namely $w^*_t = \alpha' + \beta t$, while the second included a number of variables suggested by previous studies of

the aggregate labour market.   Throughout the paper,
the real wage is the weekly wage rate deflated by the
GDP deflator (16) and the data is U.K. seasonally unadjusted data for the period 1956(i) to 1981(i).   The
use of seasonally unadjusted data indicates that a
value for k of at least four should be considered,
while a value of eight seemed a plausible maximum
value for k.   In practice the restrictions implied
by setting k equal to two were acceptable at the 5%
level so results for this value are also reported.
     The results for the time trend model are dis-
played in tables 1 and 2.   Columns (1A), (1B) and
(1C) present the estimates of (13), columns (1D), (1E)
and (1F) the estimates of (14) and (2A) and (2B) the
estimates of (15).   When the joint significance of
the coefficients of the lagged real wage terms in (1A),
(1B) and (1C) is tested, the "F" statistic is invariably significant at the 5% level so the full equilibrium hypothesis can be rejected immediately.
Otherwise, the various statistics indicate that equations (1A), (1B) and (1C) all describe the data
adequately (17).   When the test of the long run equilibrating condition is considered, the likelihood
ratio statistic for the restriction on (1A) contained
in (1D) is 11.90.   The corresponding statistics for
the fourth order lag (1E) compared with (1B) is 16.15
and for the second order lag 52.74.   Thus the null
hypothesis of a proportional, fixed zero period lag
model is rejected at all reasonable significance
levels.   Similar comments can be made for the proportional fixed four period lag model.   The likelihood ratio statistics for both (2A) and (2B) are
both well over 20, showing that the restrictions are
unacceptable.   Rather surprisingly, the results for
the equilibrating models, taken in isolation, are
rather encouraging although there is a strong hint of
some misspecification in the Lagrange multiplier
statistic.
     Previous studies have explicitly specified the
main factors thought to affect the demand and supply
curves for labour (and hence the equilibrium real wage)
(18).   In keeping with this tradition, linear forms
of the following demand and supply equations were
employed.

$$D_t = F(GDP_t, w_t, LC_t, Time) \qquad (16a)$$

$$S_t = G(w_t, BEN_t, TAX_t, Time) \qquad (16b)$$

where D is the demand for labour, GDP real domestic

Table 1: Estimates of the General Disequilibrium Model (I3) and the Restricted Disequilibrium Model (14) (using the Time Trend Model)

Regressor	(1A)	(1B)	(1C)	Regressor	(1D)	(1E)	(1F)
w_{t-1}	0.64 (5.42)	0.66 (5.78)	0.65 (5.85)	$w_{t-2}-2w_{t-1}$	0.29 (1.98)	0.32 (2.17)	-0.58 (9.41)
w_{t-2}	0.30 (2.17)	0.27 (1.99)	0.22 (2.07)	$w_{t-3}-3w_{t-1}$	-0.11 (0.73)	-0.15 (1.03)	
w_{t-3}	-0.06 (0.45)	-0.08 (0.59)		$w_{t-4}-4w_{t-1}$	0.06 (0.37)	-0.26 (2.64)	
w_{t-4}	0.05 (0.34)	0.01 (0.07)		$w_{t-5}-5w_{t-1}$	-0.24 (1.41)		
w_{t-5}	-0.25 (1.56)			$w_{t-6}-6w_{t-1}$	-0.01 (0.04)		
w_{t-6}	-0.05 (0.28)			$w_{t-7}-7w_{t-2}$	0.23 (1.37)		
w_{t-7}	0.24 (1.54)			$w_{t-8}-8w_{t-1}$	-0.20 (1.66)		
w_{t-8}	0.01 (0.07)						
Time	0.00 (2.27)	0.00 (2.47)	0.00 (2.47)	Time	0.00 (3.45)	0.00 (4.16)	0.00 (6.44)
Constant	0.03 (1.90)	0.03 (2.11)	0.03 (2.11)	Constant	0.05 (3.12)	0.06 (3.89)	0.10 (6.26)
R^2	0.98	0.98	0.98		0.98	0.98	0.97
$10^3 \times RSS$	17.67	19.09	19.21		20.33	23.00	37.72
F(PSS)	1.25	1.04	1.07		0.79	0.90	0.69
LM(10)	6.76	12.34	10.87		17.77	21.12	39.52

The dependent variable is w_t in all the results reported in this Table. Equations (1A), (1B) and (1C) are estimates of (13) for k equal to 8, 4 and 2 respectively, while equations (1D), (1E) and (1F) are the corresponding estimates of (14). For (1A), (1B) and (1C) the trend coefficient was between 0.0006 and 0.0007.

Notes for all tables
The variables used are defined in Appendix 2. The equations were estimated using U.K. seasonally unadjusted data for 1956(i) to 1981(i). All equations included seasonal dummies. The tables present the O.L.S. estimates of the parameters and their "t" values. RSS is the residual sum of squares. F(PSS) is the F test for the stability of the coefficients when the sample size is increased by eight. It has an F distribution with 8, (82-k) where k is the number of regressors listed in the table. LM(10) is a lagrange multiplier statistic which is distributed as an χ^2 with 10 degrees of freedom under the null hypothesis that the error does not follow a tenth order autoregressive or moving average scheme. The 5% significance points are $F_{60}^8 = 2.10$, $F_{80}^8 = 2.05$, $\chi_{10}^2 = 18.31$.

Table 2:   Estimates of the Restricted Disequilibrium Model (15)
Using the Time Trend Model

Dependent Variable	$w_t - 8w_{t-7}$		$w_t - 3w_{t-3}$
Regressors	(2A)	Regressors	(2B)
$w_{t-1} - 7w_{t-7}$	0.96 (8.47)	$w_{t-1} - 3w_{t-3}$	1.12 (10.51)
$w_{t-2} - 6w_{t-7}$	0.34 (2.17)	$w_{t-2} - 2w_{t-3}$	0.41 (2.49)
$w_{t-3} - 5w_{t-7}$	-0.13 (0.80)	w_{t-4}	-0.31 (2.61)
$w_{t-4} - 4w_{t-7}$	0.06 (0.35)		
$w_{t-5} - 3w_{t-7}$	-0.23 (1.24)		
$w_{t-6} - 2w_{t-7}$	0.04 (0.24)		
w_{t-8}	-0.24 (1.77)		
Time	-0.00	Trend	-0.00 (0.54)
Constant	-0.01	Constant	-0.01 (0.69)
R^2	1.00	R^2	1.00
$10^3 \times RSS$	23.63	$10^3 \times RSS$	28.73
F(PSS)	0.63	F(PSS)	0.84
LM(6)	20.44	LM(6)	23.36

product, LC labour costs which are paid in addition
to wages, S the supply of labour, BEN real unemployment benefits, TAX the direct tax rate and all variables are in natural logarithms.

Without LC, equation (16a) is a standard employment function used, for example, by Rosen and Quandt
(1978), Beenstock and Warburton (1982) and Smyth
(1983). The inclusion of labour costs provides a
more accurate measure of the true costs of employment
to employers and appears, for example, in the study
by Lewis and Makepeace (1981).

The possible influence of TAX and BEN on the
supply of labour are fairly clear. The benefits
variable first appeared in applied macroeconomics as
a determinant of the rate of unemployment, although
the context implied that its effects were on the supply of labour (see Spindler and Maki (1979) and
Benjamin and Kochin (1979)). Where explicit market
models have been used, it enters as a determinant of
the labour supply (see Lewis and Makepeace (1981(b))
and Smyth (1983)). The role of taxation and benefits
is discussed in Beenstock and Warburton (1982). The
time trend may be interpreted as measuring the contribution of technical progress and population
growth. The equilibrium real wage is given by the
solution to (16a) and (16b) and substituted into (13)
to (15).

The results for the fixed zero period lag model
are shown in Table 3. The results for the fixed
fourth and eighth period lag models are discussed
briefly in footnote (19) but, since they add little
or nothing to the discussion, they are not displayed.
The results for the general disequilibrium model are
given by (3A), (3B) and (3C). It is quite apparent
that the results are not improved by the inclusion of
the "economic" variables and, indeed, the four extra
variables (GDP, LC, TAX and BEN) are jointly insignificant in equations (3A), (3B) and (3C). When
the long run equilibrating condition is considered,
the equilibrating condition is rejected for the
three cases listed at the 5% significance levels.
Once again, the hypothesis of a proportional, fixed
zero period lag model is rejected. In contrast to
previous work, the contribution of output and the
three other "economic" variables is almost negligible
and these variables are invariably insignificant and
often wrongly signed.

The discussion suggests that (1C) provides the
most satisfactory results. The shorter lag structure
and the exclusion of GDP, LC, TAX and BEN are acceptable restrictions (20) while the equilibrating

160

Table 3:   Estimates of the General Disequilibrium Model (13) and the Restricted Disequilibrium Model (14) when the Determinants of the Equilibrium Real Wage are specified

Regressor	(3A)	(3B)	(3C)	Regressor	(3D)	(3E)	(3F)
w_{t-1}	0.65 (5.34)	0.68 (5.81)	0.65 (5.77)				
w_{t-2}	0.33 (2.32)	0.30 (2.17)	0.23 (1.94)	$w_{t-2}-2w_{t-1}$	0.30 (2.10)	0.32 (2.22)	-0.48 (7.37)
w_{t-3}	-0.08 (0.56)	-0.13 (0.89)		$w_{t-3}-3w_{t-1}$	-0.13 (0.86)	-0.17 (1.18)	
w_{t-4}	0.03 (0.22)	-0.00 (0.04)		$w_{t-4}-4w_{t-1}$	0.07 (0.45)	-0.22 (2.35)	
w_{t-5}	-0.22 (1.30)			$w_{t-5}-5w_{t-1}$	-0.25 (1.45)		
w_{t-6}	-0.06 (0.34)			$w_{t-6}-6w_{t-1}$	-0.04 (0.26)		
w_{t-7}	0.25 (1.55)			$w_{t-7}-7w_{t-1}$	0.21 (1.29)		
w_{t-8}	0.04 (0.26)			$w_{t-8}-8w_{t-1}$	-0.15 (1.26)		
GDP_t	-0.09 (0.82)	-0.15 (1.47)	-0.12 (1.24)	GDP_t	-0.19 (1.78)	-0.21 (1.98)	-0.11 (0.89)
LC_t	-0.07 (1.11)	-0.04 (0.79)	-0.05 (0.87)	LC_t	-0.00 (0.01)	0.00 (0.02)	0.07 (1.16)
TAX_t	0.01 (0.25)	-0.01 (0.22)	-0.00 (0.20)	TAX_t	0.00 (0.02)	0.01 (0.24)	0.01 (0.39)
BEN_t	0.01 (0.51)	0.00 (0.16)	0.00 (0.20)	BEN_t	-0.01 (0.61)	-0.01 (0.60)	-0.03 (1.50)
Time	0.00 (1.21)	0.00 (2.20)	0.00 (2.01)	Time	0.00 (2.76)	0.00 (3.00)	0.00 (2.37)
Constant	-0.19 (1.01)	-0.14 (0.82)	-0.14 (0.87)	Constant	0.00 (0.00)	0.02 (0.01)	0.30 (1.57)
R^2	0.98	0.98	0.98		0.98	0.98	0.97
10^3xRSS	17.24	18.43	18.72		18.18	20.23	30.37
F(PSS)	1.08	1.22	1.14		1.44	1.55	0.96
LM(10)	5.61	11.84	13.17		3.54	11.90	36.23

The time dependent variable is w_t. The variables used are defined in Appendix 2. The time trend takes the values 0.0014, 0.0021 and 0.0020 for (3A), (3B) and (3C) respectively.

restriction on the coefficients is not.   The solution for real wages implied by (1C) is

$$w_t = 7.61\theta_0 w_t^* - 63.25\theta_0 \beta + A_1(0.89)^t$$

$$+ A_2(-0.25)^t \qquad\qquad (17)$$

where the values for A_1 and A_2 are determined by the
initial conditions.

The solution is clearly stable although the high
value for the dominant root suggests that convergence
might be rather slow.   In the steady state solution,
the effect of the additive disequilibrium component
($-63.25\theta_0\beta$) is to cause real wages to be below their
equilibrium value if θ_0 is positive.   There is one
argument in favour of a positive value for θ_0.   Since
equilibrium real wages grow at a constant rate, β,
over time, the proportional disequilibrium component
($7.61\theta_0 w_t^*$) will eventually dominate the additive component ($-63.25\theta_0\beta$).   If β is positive, then a negative value θ_0 would imply that real wages are falling
in the long run and this is clearly unrealistic. ·The
alternative of a negative value for β coupled with a
positive growth in real wages seems equally implausible.

In the steady state, the additive component will
probably be negative while the proportional component
is positive.   The possibility of real wages being
lower than their equilibrium value arises and this
will certainly be the case if the customary assump-
tion that $\theta_0 = 1-\Sigma\delta_i$ is imposed.   When θ_0 is set
equal to $1-\Sigma\delta_i$, $w_t = 0.964 w_t^*$, which suggests that
real wages would be quite substantially below their
equilibrium value in the long run.   However, it seems
somewhat arbitrary in the present context to impose
the untestable condition that $\theta_0 = 1-\Sigma\delta_i$ and to
assume away one type of disequilibrium (21).   Since
this condition has to be imposed if any further analysis is to be undertaken, the discussion ends on this
rather inconclusive note.

SECTION 5:   FURTHER RESULTS FOR THE REAL WAGE

ADJUSTMENT EQUATIONS

The results quoted above apparently show that economic factors have little or no explicit role to play
in the determination of real wages.   The purpose of

this section is to demonstrate that this conclusion
is too pessimistic.   This is achieved by reconsid-
ering the neoclassical growth model which underlies
the linear trend model and by examining the relationship between the general economic model and an alternative bargaining model.   However the fundamental
conclusion that the equilibriating assumption is
rejected remains unchanged.

In a one sector neoclassical growth model, the
real wage will grow at a constant rate equal to the
rate of technical progress.   This provides one rationale for measuring the long run equilibrium wage by a
linear trend model.   Intuitively the rate of technical progress will be related to the rate of productivity growth suggesting that productivity changes
might give a more obviously economic determinant of
real wage changes.   More formally, if the production
function is Cobb-Douglas with constant returns to
scale, the equilibrium real wage (the total wage bill
divided by the number of workers) is proportional to
the level of output per worker.   Thus,

$$w_t^* = a + PROD_t \qquad\qquad (18a)$$

$$PROD_t = GDP_t - EMP_t \qquad\qquad (18b)$$

where PROD is productivity and EMP employment.   If
this interpretation is correct, productivity can be
substituted for the trend in the previous time series
equations.

The relationship between wages and productivity
may be obtained in other ways.   One alternative,
based on McCallum's (1974) wage inflation model, provides a link between the time series and market
models.   McCallum assumed that the demand and supply
curves were of the form;

$$D_t - GDP_t = a_o - a_1 w_t \qquad\qquad (19a)$$

$$S_t - N_t = b_o + b_1 w \qquad\qquad (19b)$$

where N is the working population.

The solution of these equations gives the equilibrium real wage as a function of productivity although productivity is expressed as output per employee in the growth model and as output per member of
the working population in the McCallum model.   In
practice, the correlation between the two productivity measures employed here was extremely high and

163

the results were not markedly different.   For this
reason, only the results for the conventional measure are reported below.

The productivity measure of relevance in this
context is the steady state value.   To obtain a
productivity measure free from short run cyclical
and seasonal factors, a four year moving average of
the quarterly values was taken.   Not surprisingly,
this was highly correlated with the trend, confirm-
ing the impression that the trend may have been
measuring the productivity changes (22).

The results obtained when the equilibrium real
wage is given by the productivity model are shown in
Table 4.   The residual sums of squares for equations
(4A) and (4B) are similar to those for the time
series model, indicating that nothing is lost by the
change in specification.   The coefficients of w_{t-1},
w_{t-2} and PROD are well determined.   The model per-
forms adequately (23) although the equilibriating
condition is rejected again.

Since the coefficient of (the log of) productivity is specified to be one, all the parameters of
the Cobb Douglas model are identified and the con-
dition $\theta = 1 - \Sigma \delta_i$ can be tested.   Equations (4C)
and (4D) report the results obtained from estimating
the model with this restriction imposed.   The condition is accepted for both orders of lag considered,
although the condition $\Sigma i\delta_i$ is rejected with likelihood ratio statistics of 28.9 and 78.6 respectively.
The preferred specification on a likelihood ratio
test is therefore (4D).   The solution of (4D) is:

$$W_t = w_t^* - 19.56\beta + A_1(0.76)^t + A_2(-0.09)^t \quad (20)$$

where β is the growth rate of productivity.

The solution is stable but the steady state value for the log of real wages differs from the equilibrium value by a constant amount.   If the Cobb Douglas interpretation is accepted, then this means that,
in the steady state, real wages equal a constant proportion of the level of per capita output.   Although
this is far from being a striking result in itself,
it is important to stress the role of the short term
adjustment mechanism, summarised by the additive disequilibrium component, in determining the solution.

The poor performance of the economic variables
in the models presented earlier may be due in part to
the dynamic specification adopted.   To test this
hypothesis, a more general dynamic form was estimated
and a search for sensible, data admissible simplifi-

Table 4:   Estimates of the Disequilibrium Model when the Equilibrium
Real Wage Depends on Productivity

Dependent Variable	w_t			$w_t - PROD_t$	
Regressor	(4A)	(4B)		(4C)	(4D)
w_{t-1}	0.66 (5.80)	0.65 (5.90)	$w_{t-1} - PROD_t$	0.68 (6.02)	0.67 (6.22)
w_{t-2}	0.27 (1.99)	0.24 (2.32)	$w_{t-2} - PROD_t$	0.28 (2.03)	0.27 (2.54)
w_{t-3}	-0.07 (0.55)	–	$w_{t-3} - PROD_t$	-0.08 (0.53)	–
w_{t-4}	0.02 (0.21)	–	$w_{t-4} - PROD_t$	0.05 (0.43)	–
$PROD_t$	0.09 (2.52)	0.09 (2.55)	Constant	0.03 (0.27)	0.03 (0.44)
Constant	0.06 (0.54)	0.06 (0.88)			
R^2	0.98	0.98		0.97	0.97
$10^3 \times RSS$	19.03	19.11		19.45	19.53
LM(10)	17.90	13.35		14.82	13.09
LM(4)	5.03	0.30		3.73	0.73

cations was undertaken. The results were still not favourable to the market model outlined, but a bargaining type of equation was found to be satisfactory.

The most general dynamic form considered was a regression of w_t on its first four lagged values, the trend, the current and first four lagged values of GDP, the retention ratio (RR), labour costs, and benefits and the seasonal dummies. The retention ratio, defined as 1-TAX, was employed instead of TAX because it is the variable most frequently used in bargaining models. The restrictions implied by setting the maximum lags on each regressor to one, two and three quarters and by imposing a fourth order autoregressive scheme were all rejected. A close examination of these equations reveals that only lagged values of w, GDP and RR have any consistent influence on wages, although GDP was also wrongly signed.

An estimating equation, emphasising the role of the retention ratio, is reminiscent of many bargaining models (see Henry et al (1976) and Dawson (1983)). Bargaining models employ a variety of estimating equations, but at the heart of many formulations is the following type of adjustment equation:

$$w_t - w_{t-1} = \beta(nw_t^* - nw_{t-1}) \tag{21}$$

where nw* is the desired net real wage, nw the actual net real wage and β is positive.

Thus it is argued that the rate of real wage inflation is determined by the difference between the net real wage desired by workers and the previous level of net real wages. Writing net real wages as the product of the retention ratio and the wage rate, then equation (21) can be written as:

$$w_t - (1-\beta)w_{t-1} = \beta(nw_t^* - RR_{t-1}) \tag{22}$$

The model is completed by assuming that desired net real wages grow at a constant rate. This type of model can be accommodated within the structure discussed earlier by interpreting $nw_t^* - RR_{t-1}$ as the equilibrium or, more aptly, the target real wage.

The contribution of the retention ratio to real wage inflation in the present formulation is given by $\beta(RR_t^* - RR_{t-1})$. Hence, expectations of a fall in real wage inflation because the desired net real wage is automatically lowered relative to the actual real wage. Yet it could be argued with at least equal force that the pressure on real wages in such a situation is actually greater. If workers are interested in net real wages then they will react to falls in the retention ratio with increased militancy (see Jackson et al (1975)). This suggests a wage equation of the following form:

$$w_t - w_{t-1} = \beta(z_t^* - w_{t-1}) - \alpha(RR_t^* - RR_{t-1}) \qquad (23)$$

where z_t^* is desired gross real wages.

RR* is normally incorporated within the target real wage term and the target net wage is assumed to grow at a constant rate. This treatment is entirely plausible if RR* is the steady state value for the retention ratio, in which case RR_t may be viewed as a measure of the anticipated current value and replaced by a distributed lag in the retention ratio.

Bargaining equations often include a proxy for the excess demand for labour as a measure of the union's bargaining strength. The perceived excess demand for labour will depend on the ratio of the full employment or steady state value of GDP to the predicted current value (defined, in logs, as GDP* and GDP^1. The term $\gamma(GDP^* - GDP_t^l)$, where $\gamma < 0$ and $GDP_t^l = \Sigma \beta_i GDP_{t-i}$, is therefore added to equation (23).

The most general form of the bargaining equation is given by:

$$w_t - \Sigma \delta_i w_{t-i} = \theta w_t^* \qquad (24)$$

where

$$w_t^* = Z_t^* + \delta_o RR_t^* + \delta_1 GDP_t^* + \Sigma \alpha_i RR_{t-1}$$

$$+ \Sigma \beta_i GDP_{t-i} \qquad (25)$$

It is customary to assume that z* follows a linear time trend and a similar assumption is made for GDP*. In the steady state, the retention ratio must be a constant so that a linear time trend model will adequately summarise the steady state values of z, RR and GDP.

The analysis began with a regression of w_t on the trend, GDP_t, RR_t and the first four lagged values of w, GDP and RR. An investigation of various restricted forms of this equation revealed that all specifications involving GDP had incorrect signs for GDP and a poor post sample stability record. For this reason, the preferred equations do not contain

167

GDP terms.

The final results of this exercise are given in Table 5. Table 5 reports results for the general fourth lag model involving wages and the retention ratio and two restricted forms. Both impose restrictions which are acceptable at the 5% level on a standard "F" test. Equation (B) restricts the maximum lag to 2 quarters and the equation (C) retains only the significant variables from (B). The appropriate autoregressive restrictions on (5A) and (5B) were both rejected at the 5% level using a likelihood ratio test. Equation (C) is the preferred specification (and indeed would emerge as such if the alternative strategy were followed of only retaining the significant variables in (A)). Further, it is just acceptable at the 5% level on an "F" test against the alternative general fourth order lag equation which adds $GDP_t, ..., GDP_{t-4}$ to (A). Equation (C) gives a satisfactory fit but the equilibriating assumption is rejected (with a test statistic of 59.52).

To summarise, the time trend in the previous results was reflecting the path of productivity. Further work on the alternative demand and supply model did not improve the results markedly, although a restricted form, which could be interpreted as a bargaining equation, did perform satisfactorily. We would favour the productivity model, but, in both cases, the equilibriating assumption was rejected.

SECTION 6: RESULTS FOR THE EMPLOYMENT ADJUSTMENT

EQUATIONS

The analysis of the previous sections may, of course, be applied directly to employment. The previous regressions were, therefore, repeated with employees in employment (EMP) used instead of real wages. The fixed zero period and k period lag models were estimated with lags of 2, 4 and 8 on the employment terms. The equilibriating restriction implied by the k period lag model was invariably rejected so that no further mention of this model will be made. The fixed zero period lag model is given, in general disequilibrium and equilibriating form respectively, by:

$$EMP_t = \theta_o EMP_t^* + \sum_{i}^{k} \delta_i EMP_{t-i} + u_t \qquad (26)$$

Table 5: Estimates of the Bargaining Model

Regressor	(5(A))	(5(B))	(5(C))
w_{t-1}	0.65 (5.55)	0.64 (5.72)	0.63 (5.91)
w_{t-2}	0.31 (2.23)	0.26 (2.35)	0.28 (2.62)
w_{t-3}	-0.10 (0.71)	-	-
w_{t-4}	0.03 (0.26)	-	-
RR_t	-0.08 (0.93)	-0.05 (0.55)	-
RR_{t-1}	0.26 (2.76)	0.21 (2.52)	0.16 (2.52)
RR_{t-2}	-0.10 (0.99)	-0.04 (0.44)	-
RR_{t-3}	-0.11 (1.13)	-	-
RR_{t-4}	0.18 (2.07)	-	-
Time	0.0010 (3.06)	0.0009 (2.98)	0.0010 (3.43)
Constant	0.05 (2.29)	0.04 (2.66)	0.05 (3.20)
R^2	0.98	0.98	-
$10^3 \times RSS$	16.44	17.53	17.73
F(PSS)	1.46	1.39	1.85
LM(10)	13.39	12.04	12.81

$$EMP_t = \theta_0 EMP_t^* + \sum_{i=2}^{k} \delta_i(EMP_{t-i} - iEMP_{t-1}) + u_t \tag{27}$$

Following the previous approach, EMP_t^*, was assumed, firstly, to follow the linear time path;

$$EMP_t^* = \gamma + \mu t \tag{28}$$

and, secondly, to be determined by GDP_t, LC_t, TAX_t and BEN_t.

The results for the general disequilibrium models are shown in Table 6. The lagged employment terms are invariably jointly significant at the 5% level, showing that the full equilibrium model is inappropriate. The "F" statistics for the joint significance of the variables GDP, LC, TAX and BEN show that these variables are not significant at the 5% level for the eight period lag model, but are significant for the four and two period lag models. Therefore, to simplify the presentation only the results which include the economic variables are presented.

One interesting feature of these results compared with the earlier results for real wages is the improved performance of the economic variables. GDP, LC and BEN are all correctly signed and GDP and BEN are significant. "F" tests show that the restrictions implied by the second order lag equation (6C) are acceptable at the 5% level when (6C) is compared with either the fourth order (6B) or eighth order (6A) lag equations. All three equations have no sign of any autocorrelation but the post sample stability statistic indicates some instability in the second order lag equation. In some respects, this is entirely plausible because the last two years of the sample (from 1979 (ii) to 1981 (i)) cover an unusual period for employment and unemployment. Given the quite remarkable scale of the recession during those years, it may be unreasonable to expect accurate predictions from equations fitted to the more normal post-war data.

The time trend is insignificant in all three equations, throwing some doubt on the need to examine the restrictions discussed earlier. However, equation (6D) shows that employment is trended and, since GDP is also trended, it seems important to enquire whether employment tends to an equilibrium level which is growing consistently over time. The likelihood ratio statistic for the restriction on (26)

Table 6: Estimates of the General Disequilibrium Model (26)

Regressor	6A	6B	6C	6D
EMP_{t-1}	0.87 (6.81)	0.87 (6.96)	0.86 (6.91)	
EMP_{t-2}	0.18 (0.11)	0.17 (1.09)	0.05 (0.40)	
EMP_{t-3}	-0.14 (0.86)	-0.14 (0.87)		
EMP_{t-4}	0.10 (0.59)	-0.01 (0.06)		
EMP_{t-5}	-0.03 (0.21)			
EMP_{t-6}	-0.17 (1.02)			
EMP_{t-7}	0.02 (0.12)			
EMP_{t-8}	0.07 (0.55)			
GDP_t	0.08 (2.02)	0.09 (2.45)	0.09 (2.60)	
LC_t	-0.00 (0.18)	-0.00 (0.24)	-0.01 (0.41)	
TAX_t	0.01 (0.94)	0.01 (1.02)	0.01 (0.93)	
BEN_t	-0.01 (2.07)	-0.02 (2.68)	-0.02 (3.24)	
Time	-0.00 (1.29)	-0.00 (1.51)	-0.00 (1.44)	0.0003 (4.41)
Constant	0.03 (0.55)	0.03 (0.60)	0.02 (0.42)	0.01 (1.80)
R^2	0.93	0.93	0.93	0.21
$10^3 \times RSS$	18.13	18.68	19.08	216.02
F(PSS)	1.55	1.78	2.51	3.11
LM(10)	9.50	10.08	7.39	76.91

implied by (27) is significant at the 5% level for all three orders of lag considered (in (6A), (6B) and (6C)). The hypothesis of a proportional or equilibriating disequilibrium model is therefore rejected and the model is not considered further.

The solution to equation (6C) is

$$EMPt = 11.11\theta_o EMP_t^* - 118.52\theta_o\mu + A_1(0.92)^t$$

$$+ A_2(-0.05)^t \tag{29}$$

where A_1 and A_2 reflect the initial conditions.

The equation is stable, but once again the dominant root is rather large. Of more interest is the steady state solution. In the long run, the effect of the additive disequilibrium component ($118.52\theta_o\mu$) is to lower employment if θ_o is positive. There is no way of signing θ_o', (although the argument presented above suggests that θ_o' is positive).

CONCLUSION

The analysis is based on the assumption that the time path of an endogenous variable can be modelled as a stochastic difference equation, involving the equilibrium value of the endogenous variable. If, for example, w is the natural log of the real wage and w* is the log of the equilibrium real wage, the simplest form for the difference equation relating w to w* is the fixed, zero period lag model.

$$w_t - \sum_{i=1}^{k} \delta_i w_{t-i} = \theta_o w_t^* + u_t \tag{30}$$

If the equilibrium real wage grows at the constant rate, β, over time, the particular solution of (26) is

$$w_{pt} = \frac{\theta_o}{1-\Sigma\delta_i} \cdot w_t^* - \frac{\theta_o\beta}{(1-\Sigma\delta_i)^2} (\Sigma_i i\delta_i) \tag{31}$$

Assuming that the solution is stable, long run equilibrium, in the sense that $w_t = w_t^*$, requires the untestable condition, $\theta_o = 1-\Sigma\delta_i$, and the testable condition, $\Sigma i\delta_i = 0$. Whether $\Sigma i\delta_i$ is zero can be tested using the likelihood ratio statistic so a

partial te st of long run equilibrium is available.
If $\Sigma i\delta_i$ is not zero, the traditional monetarist argument of long run equilibrium can be rejected.   If
one is willing to follow the standard practice and
assume that $\theta = 1-\Sigma\delta_i$, this procedure would also
give a full test of the equilibriating hypothesis.

Using equations like (30), it is possible to
test the hypothesis of full and continuous equilibrium and to carry out a partial check on the validity
of the traditional equilibriating hypothesis.   An
application of the methods advocated to U.K. real
wage and employment data for the period 1956(i) -
1981(i) yielded some interesting results.   A simple time series model, containing two lagged values
of real wages, a time trend and seasonal dummies,
provided an adequate explanation of the data.   Although a standard demand and supply model performed
rather poorly, two alternative economic models gave
satisfactory results.   However, whatever the model
specification, the full equilibrium and equilibriating
hypotheses were rejected so that real wages are not
determined by the equilibrium real wage in either
the short or the long run.

A slightly different set of results were obtained for employment.   The economic variables,
particularly GDP and benefits, make a significant
contribution to the explanation of employment growth.
The full equilibrium hypothesis is rejected and the
equilibriating restriction, $\Sigma i\delta_i = 0$, is rejected,
showing that employment has a long run tendency to
differ from its equilibrium value.   Unfortunately
the difference between the equilibrium level and the
actual level of unemployment cannot be signed, although a Keynesian (and indeed commonsense) view
would probably be that employment is lower than its
equilibrium value.   What is not at issue is that,
if the equilibrium level of employment is growing
over time, the employment will not equal its equilibrium value even in the long run.   Taking both
sets of results together, it appears that the steady
state solution of the aggregate labour market is
non-Walrasian in character with real wages and
employment differing from their equilibrium values.

APPENDIX 1:   ON ERROR CORRECTION MECHANISMS

It may be argued, as Beenstock and Warburton (1982)
do, that the dynamic adjustment equation (1) should
be written as a general function of the factors determining the real wage rather than the real wage itself.

To the author, this appears to involve an arbitrary
and asymetrical treatment of the determinants of the
equilibrium real wage.   The fundamental arguments
presented above are not altered, but, since there
are contexts in which it is natural to consider this
approach and since there are one or two extra points
of interest, this case is discussed below.
    Let

$$w_t^* = a + b \, x_t + c \, z_t \tag{A1}$$

where x and z are two factors determining the equilibrium real wage and

$$x_t = \alpha_o + \beta_o \, t \tag{A2}$$

$$z_t = \alpha_1 + \beta_1 \, t \tag{A3}$$

Consider the dynamic adjustment equation;

$$w_t - \sum_{i=1}^{k} \delta_i x_{t-i} = \mu + \sum_{j=0}^{m} \theta_j x_{t-j} + \sum_{j=0}^{m} \lambda_j z_{t-j} \tag{A4}$$

The particular solution of (A4) is;

$$w_{pt} = \frac{\sum \theta_j}{(1-\Sigma\delta_i)} x_t + \frac{\sum \lambda_j}{(1-\Sigma\delta_i)} z_t - \left\{ - \frac{\mu}{(1-\Sigma\delta_i)} \right.$$

$$+ \frac{\beta_o \Sigma \theta_j}{(1-\Sigma\delta_i)^2} \left[\frac{\Sigma \theta_j j}{\Sigma \theta_j} (1-\Sigma\delta_i) + \Sigma\delta_i i \right] +$$

$$\left. \frac{\beta_1 \Sigma \lambda_j}{(1-\Sigma\delta_i)^2} \left[\frac{\Sigma \lambda_j j}{\Sigma \lambda_j} (1-\Sigma\delta_i) + \Sigma\delta_i i \right] \right\} \tag{A5}$$

    Equation (A5) raises the same issues as previous-
ly but further discussion of these points is not
particularly informative and the reader is referred
to Currie (1981) for the details.   Instead the implications of (A5) for two particular error correction
mechanisms are examined.   The first mechanism is of
interest because it solves the problem of how to
incorporate previous disequilibria into the model and
because it may enable progress to be made in estimating the equilibriating model.   The second illustrates for the importance of (A5), by investigating
the properties of an ECM used in a recent study of

the aggregate labour market.

The case for error correction mechanisms (ECM's) rests on their desirable long run properties but they have an appealing intuitive interpretation. The actual change in real wages is decomposed into two components, reflecting the change in the equilibrium values and any previous disequilibria. Thus a typical ECM may be,

$$w_t - w_{t-1} = b(x_t - x_{t-1}) + c(z_t - z_{t-1}) + DAM_t \quad \text{(A6)}$$

where the disequilibrium adjustment mechanism (DAM) reflects the impact of any previous disequilibria.

The question immediately arises of how best to measure the impact of previous disequilibria when more than one independent variable is involved. One answer is to employ the DAM

$$DAM_t = \sum_i^k d_i(w^*_{t-i} - w_{t-i}) \quad \text{(A7)}$$

The adjustment equation implied by (A6) and (A7) is;

$$w_t - (1-d_1)w_{t-1} + \sum_{i=2}^k d_i w_{t-i} = a\sum_1 d_i + bx_t$$

$$- b(1-d_1)x_{t-1} + b\sum_2 d_i x_{t-i} + cz_t$$

$$- c(1-d_1)z_{t-1} + c\sum_2 d_i z_{t-i} \quad \text{(A8)}$$

If $\rho_1 = (1-d_1)$ and $\rho_i = -d_i$ $i = 2,\dots,k$, then (A8) may be written as

$$w_t = a + bx_t + cz_t + v_t \quad \text{(A9a)}$$

$$v_t = \sum_1^k \rho_i v_{t-i} \quad \text{(A9b)}$$

For reasons which are now apparent, the adjustment mechanism defined in (A8) is referred to as the "autocorrelation" ECM. Returning to the question of long run equilibrium, it is obvious from the form of (A6) and (A7) that the particular solution is $w_{pt} = w^*_t$. However, the terms relevant for (A5) are;

$$\delta_1 = (1-d_1) \quad , \quad \delta_i = -d_i \quad i = 2,\ldots,k$$

$$k = m \quad , \quad \mu = a\Sigma d_i \quad ,$$

$$\theta_o = b \quad , \quad \theta_1 = -b(1-d_1), \quad \theta_j = bd_j$$

$$j = 2,\ldots,k$$

$$\lambda_o = c \quad , \quad \lambda_1 = -c(1-d_1), \quad \lambda_j = cd_j$$

$$j = 2,\ldots,k$$

Substituting into equation (A5) one obtains the result that $w_{pt} = w_t^*$.

The natural candidate for the disequilibrium form of the autocorrelation ECM is the unrestricted reduced form;

$$w_t - \sum_{i=1}^{k} \delta_i w_{t-i} = \alpha + \sum_{i=0}^{k} \beta_i x_{t-i} + \sum_{i=0}^{k} \gamma_i z_{t-i} + u_t$$

$$(A10)$$

where $\beta_0 = b$ and $\gamma_0 = c$.

The equilibriating model imposes the constraints,

$$\frac{\beta_i}{\beta_o} = \frac{\gamma_i}{\gamma_o} = \delta_i \quad i = 1,\ldots,k. \tag{A11}$$

and the full equilibrium hypothesis the extra constraints,

$$\delta_i = 0 \qquad i = 1,\ldots,k . \tag{A12}$$

Equation (A10) was estimated with employment and real wages as dependent variables, using GDP, LC, TAX and BEN and TIME as regressors.   The likelihood ratio statistics for the restrictions implied by a fourth order autoregressive scheme were 32.6 and 39.4 for employment and real wages respectively.   The equilibriating hypothesis was therefore rejected at the 5% level for both sets of results.

The neatness of the argument for the "autocorrelation" ECM should not conceal the difficulties of specifying a reasonable form for the disequilibrium adjustment mechanism.   Apparently reasonable functions may not have desirable long run properties. As an example of the problems consider the mechanism given by Beenstock and Warburton (1982) in their equation (10) (p. 257).

The adjustment mechanism is (using d for their δ);

$$\delta_1 = 1-d_{13}, \quad \delta_i = 0 \quad i = 2,\ldots,k, \quad \mu = d_{10}$$

$$\theta_0 = d_{11}, \quad \theta_1 = -d_{11}-d_{15} \quad \theta_j = 0 \quad j = 2,\ldots,m$$

$$\lambda_0 = d_{12}, \quad \lambda_1 = -d_{12}+d_{13}+d_{14}. \quad \lambda_j = 0 \quad j = 2,\ldots,m$$

Substituting into (A5), one obtains;

$$w_{pt} = \frac{d_{10}}{d_{13}} - \frac{d_{15}}{d_{13}} x_t + \frac{d_{13}+d_{14}}{d_{13}} z_t - \frac{(d_{11}d_{13}+d_{15})}{d_{13}^2} \cdot \beta_0$$

$$- \frac{(d_{13}(1-d_{12})+d_{14})}{d_{13}^2} \beta_1. \qquad (A13)$$

Beenstock and Warburton assume that

$$a = \frac{d_{10}}{d_{13}}, \quad b = \frac{d_{15}}{d_{13}} \quad \text{and} \quad c = \frac{d_{13}+d_{14}}{d_{13}}$$

(equivalent to assuming that the first of the equilibriating restrictions - (6a) - holds). However, if equilibrium real wages are growing over time, then this is not sufficient to ensure steady state equilibrium and the resulting specification may lead to an additive disequilibrium model. Under the equilibriating hypotheses, with $d_{11}d_{13}+d_{15} = d_{13}(1-d_{12}) +d_{14} = 0$, the model becomes;

$$w_t = a + bx_t + cz_t + u_t$$

$$u_t = (1-d_1)u_{t-1} + v_t$$

The Beenstock and Warburton equation is therefore one possible disequilibrium equation for an autocorrelation ECM. The interpretation of their results as estimates of a "disequilibrium" model appears to undermine the tenor of their conclusion (see ".... wage rates tend to adjust to clear the market for labour", p. 272). In the present context auto-

correlation is not merely a simplifying assumption
but an economically meaninful assumption.

APPENDIX 2:   DATA SOURCES

The following variables and data sources were used
in the present study.   All data is for the U.K.
1.   Taxes on Income (Personal Sector) Economic
      Trends, October 1967, 1972, 1975 and 1981.
2.   Total Insurance Contributions (employees) as 1.
3.   Total Insurance Contributions (employers) as 1.
4.   Wages and Salaries as 1.
5.   G.D.P. (market prices, current prices) Economic
      Trends Annual Supplement 1982.
6.   G.D.P. (factor cost, current prices) as 5.
7.   G.D.P. (factor cost, 1975 prices) as 5.
8.   Consumer's Expenditure (market prices) as 5.
9.   Employees in Employment as 5.
10.   Basic Weekly Wage Rates (Manual Workers), All
      Industries and Services as 5.
11.   Benefits Index Annual Abstract of Statistics,
      1956, 1963, 1970, 1977 and 1981, Social Security
      Statistics 1977, 1981.

The price level is given by

$$P \equiv (6)/(7).$$
$$W \equiv (10)/P$$
$$GDP \equiv 7$$
$$LC = \frac{3}{4+3}$$
$$TAX = \frac{1+2}{4}$$

BEN = B/P, where B is the benefits index obtained
      as the total benefit of a married couple
      with two children (including earnings rel-
      ated benefit calculated for a man earning
      average earnings).

FLOWS TO AND FROM UNEMPLOYMENT: IS THE REGISTER BIMODAL ?

P. R. Hughes

The number of people employed on the day of a count will depend on how many have joined the ranks of the unemployed since the time of the previous count and on how many have left unemployment either for jobs or because they abandon economic activity. That is, the behaviour of the stock of the employed will depend on the behaviour of inflows and outflows.

This paper is concerned with the flows and, in particular, with the prospects of leaving the register of people who are unemployed. The paper will suggest that a large proportion of a cohort of persons flowing onto the register during a particular week are likely to remain unemployed for a relatively short time and a smaller proportion for a relatively long time. The proportions with the poor prospects of escape would appear to have increased quite sharply in Great Britain over the period 1963 to 1981; and this observation, coupled with the rise in durations of those with the better prospects of leaving the register, offers an explanation of how the increases in unemployment over the past twenty years have been duration dominated rather than inflows dominated.

Distinguishing between the relative contributions of duration and inflow changes to movements in the stock is important both for understanding developments in the labour market and for policy. If the turnover among the unemployed is rapid and the rise in the stock occurs because more people are experiencing brief spells of unemployment, then the costs of unemployment are presumably less than in the case where turnover is sluggish and the burden of unemployment is borne disproportionately by people whose characteristics may predispose them to long term unemployment (1).

The results reported here are evidence for the

179

view that the flows and the stock are bimodal. They
support the hypothesis that the inflow cohort (and
hence the stock) can be split into two segments: one
segment with favourable labour market characteristics
(younger, skilled) and a higher probability of leaving the register; the other with less favourable
characteristics (older, unskilled) and a lower probability of escape (2). However, they do not prove
bi-modality; proof would require a theoretical prediction, possibly rooted in utility maximizing behaviour and this does not, at present, exist.

Nevertheless, there are various precedents for
thinking along these lines. Fowler (1968) in his
work with stationary registers (3) deduced that the
inflow cohort contained a large proportion of persons
who would remain unemployed for a short time and a
smaller proportion who would stay unemployed for a
long time. But this hypothesis was not explicitly
built into the functions he used. Cripps and
Tarling (1974) have modelled the inflow characteristics of stationary registers over the period 1932-
1973 and obtained results that pointed to a bi-modal
distribution. In effect they specified an expression for the stationary stock with durations greater
than t that allowed for an infinity of segments among
the inflow, each with a different constant probability
of exit. The implied continuous inflow density
function, typical of each of the 16 registers that
were studied, was found to be bi-modal (see the graph
on p. 304 of Cripps and Tarling (1974)).

Other researchers have also used the concept of
bi-modality among the flows. For instance, Forbes
and Leicester (1976) have fitted various models,
based on assumptions about the inflow distribution,
to estimated duration distributions over the period
second quarter 1966 to third quarter 1973. Their
results neither confirmed nor denied bi-modality, although they thought it would be worthwhile to further
explore the possible existence of bi-modality.

Creedy and Disney (1981) have set out a stylised
model of unemployment flows which they use to simu-
late the effect of a rise in aggregate male unemployment on the proportions who are long term unemployed.
The model, which is concerned with the operation of
the unemployment benefit regime, assumes bi-modality
in inflows and outflows. Bowers (1982) in his analysis of the duration of unemployment by age and sex
refers to the Department of Employment's periodic
surveys of the characteristics of the unemployed and
notes that "Employment Exchange Managers apparently
experiencing no difficulty in classifying their

registrants into those who should and should not
experience difficulty in finding employment". Thus
the concept of a bi-modal inflow finds support at
operational levels within Benefit Offices.
    There are essentially two approaches to model-
ling duration of unemployment and the prospects of
leaving the register. The approach used by Fowler,
Forbes and Leicester, Cripps and Tarling and in this
paper is of the curve-fitting type. This approach
takes aggregate data on the distribution of uncompleted spells and infers from the aggregate data the
exit profile of the cohort. Given the characteristics of the stationary cohort, completed duration
and probabilities of leaving the register can then
be predicted.
    The other and more recent approach - see Nickell
(1979b); Lancaster (1979); Lancaster and Nickell
(1980); Narendranathan, Nickell and Stern (1982) -
uses cross-section/cohort samples of the unemployed
in order to predict the conditional probability of
leaving the register based on the characteristics of
the unemployed person (e.g., age, health, family
composition, educational qualifications), uncompleted
duration and other variables which affect the reservation wage. This approach, which is rooted in job
search theory and which uses a micro data set of
unemployed individuals, is inherently richer than the
curve-fitting approach. However, the drawback of
the characteristics approach is that its focus on the
individual rather than the group fails to reveal the
aggregate pattern of duration and flows. In this
respect, the two approaches are complementary rather
than substitutes.
    A further difficulty with the micro data set
approach is the problem of omitted variables. Nickell
(1979b) has estimated the probability of leaving unemployment of a sample of unemployed males from the
GHS 1972. He tests for possible omitted variables
by assuming that there are two different types of
individual. The individuals are different but we
cannot observe the distinction in terms of characteristics and spell duration. One group, however,
has better prospects of escape than the other. The
results show that 35% of the sample had prospects
of a shorter duration and 65% of a longer duration
after controlling for measured characteristics, spell
length and the replacement ratio.
    The above are a selection of precedents which
justify an analysis in terms of a bi-modal flow.
Other, a priori, justifications can be found in dual
labour market theory and from the observed trend in

flows and durations. Hughes (1982) has pointed to
the high level of flows relative to the size of the
stock and to the rise in durations. A segmented
register would be a way of explaining this behaviour
if it showed that the bulk of inflows came from the
short duration, favoured group (predominantly voluntary quitters) and the rise in duration from a growing
stock of people with the less favoured characteristics and little or no scope for leaving the register
(the involuntary quitters).

THE BI-MODAL FUNCTION APPLIED TO A STATIONARY REGISTER

Figure 1 illustrates a stylised example of a stationary register, where R(t), the proportion on the
register for more than t weeks, is plotted on the
vertical axis and duration on the register on the
horizontal axis.

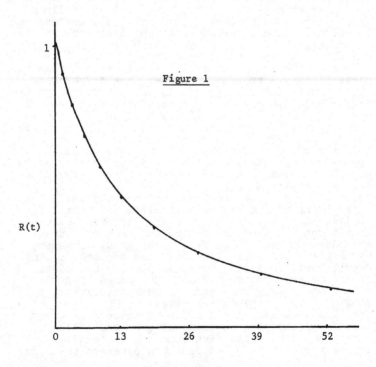

Figure 1

t weeks

R(t) is the cumulative frequency distribution of uncompleted spells, available from published sources. It is by fitting a function to this distribution that statements can be made about completed durations and the nature of the flow.
The model is assumed to have the following form:

$$R(t) = X.e^{-P_1.t} + (1 - X).e^{-P_2.t}$$

where R(t) is the ratio of numbers on the register for more than t weeks to the total stock of unemployed. P_1 is the weekly probability of exit from the register of those members of the inflow cohort who have a high probability of escape; P_2 is the weekly probability of exit of those with a low probability of escape; X is the proportion among the <u>stock</u> with probability P_1; t is duration on the register measured in weeks.
The expression for R(t) is readily derivable from first principles on condition that we can write down a form for the density function of completed durations f(t). Following Bartholomew (1978), let

$$f(t) = Z.P_1.e^{-P_1.t} + (1 - Z).P_2.e^{-P_2.t}$$

where Z is the proportion among the <u>cohort</u> with exit probability P_1.
P(t), the proportion of the inflow cohort who are still on the register after t weeks, is then:

$$P(t) = {_t}\int^{\infty} f(t) \, dt$$

and

$$R(t) = {_t}\int^{\infty} P(t) \, dt \quad / \int_0^{\infty} P(t) \, dt$$

We can also note that the hazard function, that is, the conditional probability of leaving the register, is obtainable as:

$$f(t) \quad / \quad P(t)$$

The latter result is helpful because it is a bridge with the work of Nickell (1979b), Lancaster (1979). Lancaster and Nickell (1980) and Narendranathan,

Nickell and Stern (1982) who model the hazard function directly.

COMPARISON WITH FOWLER'S RESULTS FOR A STATIONARY REGISTER

Before applying the model to more recent British data, Fowler's results for a stationary register over the period 1961 to 1965 are compared with results obtained using the bi-modal form for R(t). Fowler obtained a stationary register by averaging the frequency distributions of a series of registers of the wholly unemployed. This was done for the period 1961 to 1965 by taking eight representative registers. The average register and the ratio R(t) that he obtained are given in Table 1. He did not find it practicable to obtain a function that would fit the whole of the cumulative frequency distribution and therefore split the problem into two parts. For durations of 9 weeks and above, he fitted a log normal distribution; for durations of less than 9 weeks he used ad hoc methods.

Table 1 compares the results obtained by Fowler with the results of the bi-modal model. The model was fitted using a quasi-Newton algorithm for finding the minimum of a non-linear function subject to fixed upper and lower bounds on parameter values. The routine is referenced as EO4JAF and is available from the National Algorithms Group (NAG) Library.

It can be seen that the bi-modal results are similar but not identical to Fowler's. In particular, the implied rate of inflow is less (48000 per week) than Fowler's estimate (57000). Fortunately, it is possible to obtain a check on the actual rate of flow using the D.H.S.S. records of claims to unemployment benefit. These records show an average flow of 53000 per week over the 8 registers.

The results reported in Table 1 are not conclusive in any way; but do indicate that the bimodal model may be helpful in indicating the properties of a stationary register. For information, the parameters of the bi-modal model for Fowler's register are as follows:

$$R(t) = 0.42e^{-0.25t} + 0.58e^{-0.03t}$$

Some 42% of the stock would appear to have a good prospect of escape from the register (25% per

Table 1: Fowler's Stationary Register (1): Males and Females, 1961 to 1965

Weeks	No's.	R(t)	Bimodal R(t)	Fowler P(t)	Fowler Cohort No's.	Bimodal P(t)	Bimodal Cohort No's.
Total	398,454	1.0000	1.0000	1.0000	56857	1.0000	47906
1	350,361	0.8787	0.8919	0.7340	41733	0.8061	38619
2	314,858	0.7902	0.8045	0.5391	30652	0.6540	31331
4	269,800	0.6771	0.6749	0.3151	17916	0.4405	21103
6	238,346	0.5982	0.5862	0.2481	14108	0.3080	14755
8	213,673	0.5338	0.5229	0.2018	11476	0.2251	10782
13	165,802	0.4161	0.4226	0.1207	6860	0.1262	6045
26	108,596	0.2725	0.2862	0.0512	2912	0.0655	3137
39	79,551	0.1997	0.2010	0.0288	1639	0.0452	2164
52	61,195	0.1536	0.1416	0.0186	1055	0.0318	1522

Further Characteristics of the Register

		Fowler	Bimodal	Actual
Duration Cohort	(Weeks)	7.00	8.32	N.A.
Duration Stock	(Weeks) (2)	N.A.	46.12	N.A.
Inflow	(thous/Wk)	56.9	47.9	53.1 (3)
Residual sum of Squares		N.A.	0.0010	N.A.

Notes:

1. Composed of 8 registers: Dec. 1961, July 1962, Jan. 1963, July 1963, Jan. 1964, July 1964, Jan. 1965, July 1965.
2. Defined as $2\int_0^\infty R(t)\,dt$, that is twice the remaining average duration of all those on the register on the day of the count (see MAIN 1981).
3. D.H.S.S. claims to Unemployment Benefit: Average of 8 months.

185

week); 58% have a poor prospect (under 3% per week).
Among the cohort the proportion with the good prospects is 87% (4). Expected duration is about 8
weeks averaged over members of the cohort; among
the stock, that is averaging completed duration of
those who compose the stationary register, expected
duration is much greater (46 weeks) (5).

RESULTS FOR GREAT BRITAIN 1963 TO 1981

A principal difficulty in extending the model to
British data (6) over the period 1963 to 1981 concerns the assumption of stationarity. Fowler's
method and the fit of the bimodal model operates on
the assumption that the registers are stationary,
this assumption being necessary in order to obtain
measures of completed duration and estimates of the
flow.
    The results reported here do not rely on an
observed stationarity, but instead impose conditions
of stationarity on an averaged register which is held
to be representative of the cycle. The unemployment
experience of males and females separately over each
of four consecutive economic cycles is summarized in
terms of a single representative or stationary register. The cycles are taken from the C.S.O.'s
coincident cyclical indicator series; from trough
to trough, they are as follows:

        Jan 1963   to   Jan 1967
        April 1967   to   Oct 1971
        Jan 1972   to   Jul 1975
        Oct 1975   to   Jan 1981

    The representative registers are obtained by
averaging over each cycle the quarterly cumulative
distributions of unemployment by duration. For each
register the ratio R(t) is obtained at values of t
of 0, 1, 2, 4, 6, 7, 13, 26, 39 and 52 weeks. It is
to these values of R(t) that the bi-modal function is
then fitted.
    We expect the probabilities of exit to change
as economic conditions fluctuate, as will the proportions with the more favourable and the less favourable characteristics among the representative
cohort and the representative stock. The weights
alter because more or less of the younger, older,
skilled, unskilled among the economically active
enter or leave unemployment. Their prospects of
leaving the register also change. If labour demand

is buoyant, job offers become more plentiful, also
job search becomes less costly, the net effect is
captured in the estimated probability of leaving the
register.   Buoyant supply and a faltering in labour
demand will have different net effects so that a
person with fixed characteristics can expect to experience a change in exit probability.   It is the
outcome of these forces that is summarized in the
parameter values estimated from the bi-modal model.
    The results for the four cycles are set out in
Tables 2 and 3.   In Table 2 we observe that duration for the segment with the better prospects of
escape is between 4 and 5 weeks for males and 3 to
4 weeks for females over the first three cycles,
rising to 10 weeks and 8 weeks respectively in the
1975-1981 cycle.   For the segment with the poorer
prospects, the level is about 40 weeks for males and
25 weeks for females over the first three cyles,
rising to 55 weeks and 32 weeks in the latest cycle.
Moreover, the proportions among the cohort with the
more favourable characteristics dip sharply, particularly between the 1972-1975 cycle and the 1975-
1981 cycle.
    The greater change in parameter values between
the 1972-1975 cycle and the 1975-1981 cycle than in
the three previous cycles is reflected in the aggregate cohort duration.   For instance, cohort duration rises from 8 weeks to 12 weeks for males between
1963-1967 and 1972-1975 and then jumps to 21 weeks
in 1975-1981.   For females, the equivalent figures
are 7 weeks, 7 weeks and 16 weeks.
    The changes between the earliest and latest
cycle are picked out in Table 3 for detailed comparison.   Taking a 20 year span highlights the
differences; but it should be emphasized that the
progression is not a smooth one: most of the adjustment has occurred since the 1972-1975 cycle.
    What does Table 3 show ?   First, we observe
that the unemployed with the less favourable characteristics have become an increasing proportion of the
representative cohort.   In the early 1960s, over
85% of people flowing onto the register had good
prospects of escape; twenty years later this had
fallen to three-quarters for males and two-thirds
for females.
    The next thing we observe is that duration has
risen much more markedly for the segment with the
favoured characteristics (up from 4 weeks to 10 weeks
for males and 3 weeks to 8 weeks for females) than
for the segment with the less favourable characteristics whose duration has risen from 39 to 55 weeks

Table 2A: Representative Registers, Males and Females, Great Britain, 1963 to 1981

		Jan.63/ Jan 67	Apr.67/ Oct 71	Jan 72/ Jul 75	Oct 75/ Jan 81
MALES	RSS	(1.1 E-3)	(6.1 E-4)	(3.6 E-4)	(4.1 E-5)
P_1 (High probability of escape)	% week	26.4	21.3	20.0	9.6
Duration (= $1/P_1$)	weeks	3.8	4.7	5.0	10.4
P_2 (Low probability of escape)	% week	2.5	2.6	2.2	1.8
Duration (= $1/P_2$)	weeks	39.3	37.9	44.8	55.2
P (Weighted average of P_1 and P_2)	% week	11.9	9.5	8.2	4.9
Duration of Cohort (= 1/P)(1)	weeks	8.4	10.5	12.2	20.5
Stock	Thous	297.1	493.4	633.2	1044.6
Duration of Stock (2)	weeks	50.8	51.3	63.0	75.4
Est. Flow (3)	thous/wk	35.3	46.9	51.9	50.8
Act. Flow (4)	thous/wk	43.6	51.2	49.5	61.2
Cohort proportion with high probability of escape (= Z)	%	87.0	82.5	81.9	77.3
Stock proportion with high probability of escape (= X)	%	39.1	36.8	33.4	39.1

Notes:

1. Cohort Duration: $_0\int^\infty p(t)\ dt$
2. Stock Duration: $2\int_0^\infty R(t)\ dt$
3. Est. Flow = Stock/Cohort Duration.
4. Source: D.H.S.S. See Appendix.

Table 2B:

		Jan 63/ Jan 67	Apr 67/ Oct 71	Jan 72/ Jul 75	Oct 75/ Jan 81
FEMALES	RSS	(1.4 E-3)	(1.2 E-3)	(5.8 E-4)	(1.1 E-4)
P_1 (High probability of escape)	% week	29.8	29.0	28.0	13.3
Duration (= $1/P_1$)	weeks	3.4	3.5	3.6	7.5
P_2 (Low probability of escape)	% week	4.0	3.8	3.6	3.1
Duration (= $1/P_2$)	weeks	25.3	26.4	28.1	31.9
P (Weighted average of P_1 and P_2)	% week	15.0	15.0	14.3	6.3
Duration of Cohort (= 1/P)(1)	weeks	6.7	6.7	7.0	15.9
Stock	Thous	92.4	94.0	135.4	422.0
Duration of Stock (2)	weeks	31.8	32.4	34.6	48.6
Est. Flow (3)	thous/wk	13.9	14.1	19.4	26.6
Act. Flow (4)	thous/wk	10.3	10.8	12.8	27.4
Cohort proportion with high probability of escape (= Z)	%	84.9	85.9	86.1	65.7
Stock proportion with high probability of escape (= X)	%	42.7	44.4	44.1	31.2

Notes:

1. Cohort Duration: $\int_0^\infty p(t)\,dt$
2. Stock Duration: $2\int_0^\infty R(t)\,dt$

3. Est. Flow = Stock/Cohort Duration.
4. Source: D.H.S.S. See Appendix.

Table 3: Changes in Flow and Duration: Mid 1960s to early 1980s (G.B.)

	Jan 63/ Jan 67		Oct 75/ Jan 81		Relative Change: (ii)/(i)
Males	(i)	(%)	(ii)	(%)	
P1:					
Inflow	30.7	(87.0)	39.3	(77.3)	1.28
Duration	3.8		10.4		2.74
Stock	116.3	(39.1)	408.0	(39.1)	3.51
P2:					
Inflow	4.6	(13.0)	11.5	(22.7)	2.51
Duration	39.3		55.2		1.40
Stock	180.8	(60.9)	636.6	(60.9)	3.52
Total:					
Inflow	35.3	(100.0)	50.8	(100.0)	1.44
Duration	8.4		20.5		2.44
Stock	297.1	(100.0)	1044.6	(100.0)	3.52
Females					
P1:					
Inflow	11.8	(84.9)	17.5	(65.7)	1.48
Duration	3.4		7.5		2.25
Stock	39.4	(42.7)	131.5	(31.2)	3.33
P2:					
Inflow	2.1	(15.1)	9.1	(34.3)	4.35
Duration	25.3		31.9		1.26
Stock	53.0	(57.3)	290.6	(68.8)	5.49
Total:					
Inflow	13.9	(100.0)	26.6	(100.0)	1.92
Duration	6.7		15.9		2.38
Stock	92.4	(100.0)	422.0	(100.0)	4.57
Males and Females					
P1:					
Inflow	42.4	(86.4)	56.8	(73.3)	1.34
Duration	3.7		9.5		2.59
Stock	155.7	(40.0)	539.5	(36.8)	3.46
P2:					
Inflow	6.7	(13.6)	20.6	(26.7)	3.09
Duration	34.9		44.9		1.29
Stock	233.8	(60.0)	927.2	(63.2)	3.97
Total:					
Inflow	49.1	(100.0)	77.4	(100.0)	1.58
Duration	7.9		18.9		2.39
Stock	389.5	(100.0)	1466.7	(100.0)	3.77

for males and 25 to 32 weeks for females. Duration
has more than doubled for those with a high probability of escape but has increased by much less than
half for those with the less favourable characteristics.

The effect of these two influences on the shape
of the representative cohort is shown in Figures 1
and 2. It is clear from these graphs that over
the past twenty years the register has become more
uniform. The proportions with good prospects and
those with poor prospects have become more even and
the differences between them less accentuated.

More and more people characterised by long
spells of unemployment have joined the register;
and those with short spells have become less success-
ful in finding work. This has meant that aggregate
duration has risen markedly, from 8 to 21 weeks on
average for males and from 7 to 16 weeks for females.
These are the cohort measures of duration, which are
very much less than the stock measure. The stock
measure has risen from 51 weeks to 75 weeks for
males; from 32 weeks to 49 weeks for females.

These results are necessarily somewhat tentative. For instance, there is no straightforward
measure of goodness of fit. Experiments with a
Pearson chi-squared test reported in Baker and
Trivedi (1982) indicate an excellent fit which improves as the cycle becomes more recent. This is
confirmed by the visual fit obtained from a graph of
R(t) and predicted R(t). Only the residual sum of
squares is reported in the Tables.

There is also the question of whether the bi-
modal form is the only form that fits. Experiments
with the uni-modal form show that this cannot describe
the cumulative frequency distribution of uncompleted
spell. It would, however, be instructive to test
other modal forms, although Cripps and Tarling's
results which estimated an unconstrained inflow density function (see earlier) did pick out the two-
mode form.

Accepting these caveats, however, what conclusions may be drawn from the results ? The secular
increase in the register over the past twenty years
would appear to be duration dominated. The stock
of unemployed increased by a factor of 4 composed of
duration rising by a factor of 2.5 and flows by a
factor of 1.5. However, it is interesting to note
that this is a composition effect. The segment of
the cohort with poor prospects is flows dominated and
not duration dominated, and the weight of this segment among the cohort has been growing. Should

Cohort Characteristics: Males, Great Britain

Exit profile of the cohort derived from bimodal model.

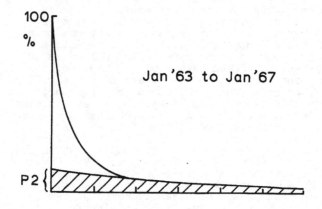

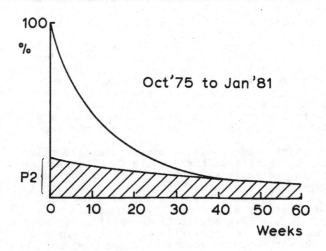

Figure 1

Hughes: Flows to and from Unemployment

Cohort Characteristics: Females, Great Britain

Exit profile of the cohort derived from bimodal model.

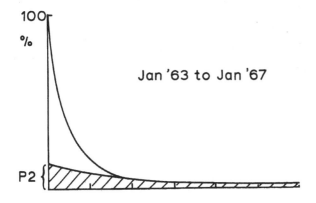

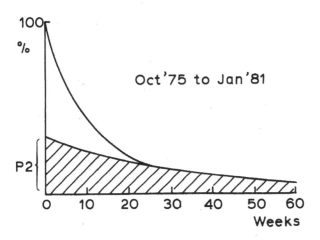

Figure 2

these trends continue, the register would cease to
be duration dominated (7).

APPLICATIONS OF THE BI-MODAL MODEL, SOME
IMPLICATIONS AND FURTHER RESEARCH

If the hypothesis of a bi-modal flow and a bi-modal
register is supported, then it would appear that the
register is composed of an increasing proportion of
people with relatively fixed (and low) probabilities
of escape.   Once on the register, these people are
likely to stay there.   Even a substantial expansion
in demand for labour could only operate slowly, presumably by cutting back the rate of inflow but not
having much effect on the prospects of outflow of a
large proportion of the register.
     The unemployed with the better prospects of
leaving the register would benefit quickly from an
expansion in demand.   Quite probably their duration
would drop sharply.   This might even promote an increase in the flow for purposes of job search;   and
the proportion among the cohort with the good prospects would rise.   The effect on the proportion
among the stock is uncertain: the register would
be expected to become less uniform again, and those
with the good characteristics would be expected to
leave the register more quickly than before.   Quite
possibly the proportion among the stock with the
poor characteristics would rise (8).
     For further research, it is proposed to test the
model at regional level to see if the good fit at
national level survives disaggregation.   If the
model fits at regional level (and results are encouraging in this respect) this will be further evidence
that the register is bi-modal.
     Finally, some examples are given of applications
of the bi-modal model.   First, it can be helpful in
assessing the costs of unemployment.   The category
with the better prospects of escape from the register
may be likened to the voluntary/frictional component
of the register that bears few costs;   the second
category (involuntary/structural/demand-deficient) is
likely to incur costs - these costs offset to a
diminishing extent by the value of leisure (see
Layard, 1981) (9).
     Second, the model may be used to complement the
work of researchers who have estimated the conditional probability that a person on the register will find
work or otherwise leave unemployment from cross-

section analysis.

Third and last, there are a variety of applications which are noted here for the sake of completeness, but for which no order of priority or of emphasis is proposed: these are Phillips curve applications (presumably the segment with the more favourable characteristics has greater labour market leverage than the less favoured segment); applications with regard to the problem of long term unemployment (if an expansion in labour demand can be expected to do little for the job prospects of those with the less favourable characteristics, could this suggest a screening for characteristics on entry to the register ?); and, finally, applications relating to the description and interpretation of secular trends in the composition of the unemployed.

ACKNOWLEDGEMENTS

In preparing this paper, I am grateful to Dr. Gillian Hutchinson, Q.M.C., for her help and advice and to Andrew Fontenelle for programming assistance. K. Hughes has helped me in checking the data set.

The paper has been revised in the light of the helpful suggestions made by the discussant, R. Disney, and by other conference participants, in particular J. Stern and J. Treble. Comments from A. R. Thatcher have also been incorporated.

NOTES

1. For a discussion of these issues, see Armstrong and Taylor (1982).

2. This dichotomisation is offered as a simplification of the true inflow structure. The true structure is believed to be heterogeneous in the sense that every inflow cohort member will experience a unique probability of exit. There has been some debate as to whether this unique probability will vary with the individual's duration of unemployment. For some evidence on this point see Nickell (1979b), Lancaster (1979), Lancaster and Nickell (1980), Narendranathan, Nickell and Stern (1982). What is suggested in this paper is that outflow probabilities will cluster around the two modal values. The parameter values are thus estimates of the central values of each cluster along with the associated weights.

3. A register is stationary if inflows equal outflows and the proportions among the inflow cohort

who remain on the register after a given number of
weeks remain constant.
    4. Obtained as (stock * X * P_1)/(stock * X * P_1
+ stock * (1 - X) * P_2).
    5. The distinction between expected duration of
the cohort and that of the stock is discussed in
Akerlof (1979) and Main (1981). The expectation of
the cohort summarizes the experience in duration of
the cohort, some of whose members will be experiencing very short spells of unemployment and whose likelihood of being on the register on a particular day
is quite slight. The second measure focusses on
the experience of those who are present on the register on a particular day; and therefore gives more
weight to those with longer unemployment spells.
    6. See Annex for Data on Duration of Unemploy-
ment and Flows.
    7. This result throws an interesting light on
a popular view - see, for instance, Nickell (1979a) -
that there is little relation between the inflow
and the stock of unemployed; hence it is sufficient
to model the duration of unemployment in order to
model the stock. The above results suggest that
the observed variance of the male inflow about a more
or less fixed point which characterized the late
1960s and early 1970s and which prompted the view
about duration dominance was a composition effect.
    8. If Z = proportion among the cohort with
characteristic P_1, then X (the proportion among the
stock) equals:

$$\frac{Z\int_0^\infty P_1(t)\ dt}{Z\int_0^\infty P_1(t)\ dt + (1 - Z)\int_0^\infty P_2(t)\ dt}$$

which is

$$\frac{Z * P_1\ duration}{Cohort\ duration}$$

If Z rises and the P_1 duration falls sufficiently,
then it is possible for X to fall. Compare, for
example, Jan. 72-Jan. 75 for males with Oct. 75-
Jan. 81.
    9. The above is one interpretation - another
(see Carlson and Horrigan, 1983) turns this argument
on its head: those for whom unemployment is most
costly will leave unemployment quickly while those
with a smaller cost and less incentive to leave un-

employment will tend to be the long term unemployed.
The very long spells of unemployment for the less
favoured segment reported in this paper would tend
to argue against the second of these interpretations.

APPENDIX: DATA ON DURATION OF UNEMPLOYMENT AND FLOWS

Duration of unemployment: Tables 1, 2, 3 and 4
The duration data is published data for Great Britain
over the period January 1963 to April 1981.   The
figures for numbers unemployed more than 0, 1, 2, 4,
6, 8, 13, 26, 39, and 52 weeks are as recorded by
the Department of Employment at each quarterly count
and are not adjusted for changes in administrative
practice such as, for instance, the exclusion of
adult students from October 1975 and inclusion of
casuals after May 1972.   There is no seasonal
adjustment.

D.H.S.S. Flows Series: Table 5

The D.H.S.S. flows are a monthly count of inflows
at Unemployment Benefit Offices.   They record the
number of claims to benefits (or credits for National
Insurance) made during the four or five weeks ending
on the Saturday which precedes the first Mondy in
each calendar month;   that is, it is a caldendar month
record and not a record of flows between the dats of
successive unemployment counts.   Adult students are
included in the series.

197

Table 1: Cumulative Duration of Unemployment and Representative Registers: Great Britain, January 1963 to January 1967   (Thousands)

	Jan 1963	Apr	Jul	Oct	Jan 1964	Apr	Jul	Oct	Jan 1965	Apr	Jul	Oct	Jan 1966	Apr	Jul	Oct	Jan 1967
Males																	
Total	481.6	421.4	332.3	333.9	356.5	299.5	232.8	247.7	274.1	238.8	208.0	230.4	261.6	230.8	201.9	288.8	420.8
Over 1	429.0	383.4	291.3	299.0	319.6	269.1	205.1	216.5	239.6	205.2	179.0	198.0	226.8	196.9	172.2	244.6	370.5
" 2	380.8	357.5	268.5	270.7	291.6	243.9	185.5	194.0	215.9	187.6	160.4	175.7	202.2	183.3	152.9	211.8	334.6
" 4	319.9	322.4	236.3	233.3	253.6	219.0	163.9	166.2	187.7	166.3	139.5	148.9	178.2	156.3	131.9	172.9	292.7
" 6	280.0	293.6	214.2	207.3	226.8	199.4	148.9	147.2	165.7	151.9	125.9	129.7	155.3	140.2	116.9	144.5	250.5
" 8	244.3	270.5	199.4	188.2	203.7	183.5	137.3	134.0	148.6	140.0	115.3	118.2	137.4	127.4	108.1	129.2	217.4
" 13	179.0	217.1	166.4	155.3	161.0	154.0	118.2	112.0	117.5	116.8	97.3	96.5	106.6	104.9	88.7	101.1	153.1
" 26	106.6	127.8	119.5	111.4	107.9	105.3	89.2	82.7	80.0	79.9	71.5	69.1	69.9	71.2	64.3	68.4	83.8
" 39	75.1	85.6	84.8	86.4	82.9	78.6	69.5	66.8	63.0	59.8	55.2	54.5	53.5	51.9	49.2	52.7	59.9
" 52	55.8	63.6	62.6	66.0	66.4	63.4	56.3	54.6	52.1	48.9	44.8	44.1	43.6	41.2	39.1	42.0	46.9
Females																	
Total	141.7	139.5	107.9	119.8	114.1	99.7	75.6	87.5	87.8	82.3	63.5	75.3	73.2	64.7	54.0	82.2	101.9
Over 1	122.2	120.8	94.6	103.7	98.7	87.2	64.7	73.9	73.4	67.9	52.2	62.0	59.8	53.3	44.2	65.7	85.7
" 2	107.4	109.7	85.2	111.2	87.4	76.7	57.1	63.7	64.4	60.6	45.5	53.0	51.8	48.1	38.3	54.7	75.4
" 4	89.5	93.8	72.7	74.0	75.4	66.7	48.4	50.7	56.0	51.4	38.2	45.6	45.6	40.1	31.7	41.0	65.8
" 6	77.6	81.1	63.8	61.4	66.1	58.4	42.1	41.9	48.3	44.7	33.4	41.3	39.1	34.3	27.0	31.8	55.5
" 8	66.4	71.6	58.0	52.9	57.6	51.6	37.4	35.6	41.5	39.5	29.4	28.7	34.1	29.6	24.1	27.1	47.1
" 13	45.6	52.6	44.1	39.3	41.5	38.8	29.4	26.4	29.1	29.2	22.7	20.8	23.8	22.1	18.1	18.4	30.5
" 26	21.4	27.9	25.7	24.1	22.4	22.6	18.2	16.6	15.4	16.6	13.8	13.2	12.4	13.2	11.2	11.4	14.0
" 39	13.5	15.7	16.3	15.8	15.1	14.2	12.5	11.6	10.8	10.4	9.6	9.2	8.8	8.3	7.9	8.0	9.3
" 52	9.0	10.7	10.4	11.1	10.5	10.3	8.9	8.6	8.0	7.8	7.0	7.0	6.5	6.2	5.7	6.0	6.8

Source: Dept. of Employment

Table 2: Cumulative Duration of Unemployment: Great Britain, Males

(Thousand)

1966 – 1970

Weeks	Jan 1966	Apr	Jul	Oct	Jan 1967	Apr	Jul	Oct	Jan 1968	Apr	Jul	Oct	Jan 1969	Apr	Jul	Oct	Jan 1970	Apr	Jul	Oct
Total	261.6	230.8	201.9	288.8	420.8	370.5	379.7	417.7	493.8	445.2	409.0	379.2	428.5	469.8	426.3	447.2	494.2	447.7	467.7	453.6
Over 1	226.8	196.9	172.2	244.4	370.5	340.6	339.8	377.5	445.2	409.0	378.1	341.6	390.5	428.5	390.1	402.2	447.5	408.8	419.9	409.9
" 2	202.2	183.3	152.9	211.8	340.6	308.3	305.6	340.6	390.0	365.9	345.6	296.3	345.9	390.4	345.6	365.5	409.0	370.4	379.9	368.7
" 4	178.2	156.3	131.9	181.9	305.6	270.1	270.5	305.6	344.6	306.9	290.8	232.2	296.5	345.1	303.3	326.8	367.2	330.3	336.3	322.5
" 6	155.3	134.9	116.9	142.9	270.1	236.5	239.0	260.0	281.6	246.5	232.5	207.6	254.3	290.6	265.0	294.8	317.2	279.1	295.7	255.7
" 8	137.1	127.4	108.2	129.2	246.5	189.2	257.7	237.7	230.6	221.7	207.8	200.8	232.2	232.5	237.6	276.5	294.0	254.3	268.7	225.1
" 13	106.6	104.9	101.1	101.2	194.8	124.2	148.5	189.2	178.2	148.5	141.9	141.8	148.1	154.2	141.1	181.1	141.8	115.0	220.1	154.8
" 26	69.7	71.2	64.3	68.4	111.3	89.5	117.7	124.2	137.6	102.6	103.4	107.5	110.1	107.3	135.7	151.5	112.1	89.1	152.2	114.5
" 39	55.6	51.9	49.2	52.7	83.8	63.5	97.2	89.5	97.2	75.8	108.0	81.3	83.7	110.1	135.7	112.7	89.1	92.9	114.5	116.9
" 52	43.6	41.2	39.1	42.0	53.3	63.5	54.3	51.3	72.0	75.8	76.6	79.6	82.5	83.7	61.8	81.3	89.1	92.9	88.6	116.9

1971 – 1975

Weeks	Jan 1971	Apr	Jul	Oct	Jan 1972	Apr	Jul	Oct	Jan 1973	Apr	Jul	Oct	Jan 1974	Apr	Jul	Oct	Jan 1975	Apr	Jul	Oct
Total	572.1	614.6	608.3	681.3	779.8	775.5	676.0	661.2	660.6	595.7	469.8	432.9	494.2	537.8	480.3	432.9	537.8	733.5	814.9	855.1
Over 1	518.0	557.3	571.9	628.5	727.3	718.0	620.5	615.1	613.7	530.7	425.9	396.5	447.5	485.9	427.6	402.3	—	693.2	755.5	782.5
" 2	472.7	515.2	522.5	579.6	679.3	687.0	572.0	573.7	578.2	490.1	391.8	365.6	409.9	436.6	386.5	366.6	—	628.6	680.8	736.5
" 4	428.3	454.3	459.2	509.9	617.1	617.1	517.7	517.7	524.5	406.4	352.1	326.8	364.6	378.2	339.3	326.8	—	531.1	574.3	661.1
" 6	374.4	404.8	406.5	451.2	567.6	567.6	467.9	468.1	478.5	362.2	322.6	294.8	324.4	345.1	303.3	294.8	—	473.2	512.3	589.4
" 8	334.1	367.8	375.3	397.4	513.3	524.9	436.6	441.9	441.9	304.0	304.0	276.5	290.6	317.7	281.8	276.5	—	427.1	465.4	545.5
" 13	259.6	292.0	291.0	333.2	404.3	436.6	381.8	384.8	366.2	265.0	265.0	237.6	229.0	261.7	238.4	237.6	—	342.3	374.5	427.6
" 26	165.6	176.2	162.0	156.0	251.3	201.2	261.7	205.3	281.0	186.1	186.6	151.5	148.1	161.1	181.1	151.5	—	241.7	241.7	273.0
" 39	123.2	132.7	142.0	142.6	172.5	150.1	150.1	162.0	161.5	152.7	166.5	151.5	110.1	141.1	135.7	135.7	—	171.0	171.5	192.5
" 52	96.0	102.0	108.0	118.5	130.0	143.8	150.0	150.0	130.0	137.3	137.3	129.2	82.5	83.7	112.7	129.2	—	122.9	129.2	164.5

1976 – 1980

Weeks	Jan 1976	Apr	Jul	Oct	Jan 1977	Apr	Jul	Oct	Jan 1978	Apr	Jul	Oct	Jan 1979	Apr	Jul	Oct	Jan 1980	Apr	Jul	Oct
Total	981.3	959.1	1030.7	—	1034.0	992.5	1081.3	1028.7	1070.2	999.7	1038.8	946.0	989.9	916.2	933.7	882.7	908.7	891.4	933.7	848.6
Over 1	934.0	915.9	966.4	—	991.9	962.0	1037.9	988.5	1032.7	966.5	978.8	908.2	950.6	891.4	865.2	848.5	908.1	891.4	929.9	848.6
" 2	903.2	870.1	895.7	—	940.3	903.9	967.0	993.8	1052.8	908.2	908.1	861.3	906.1	859.3	865.6	803.5	848.1	859.3	892.9	803.5
" 4	830.5	803.3	800.9	—	889.0	833.6	845.9	858.2	931.8	814.2	790.6	851.4	906.1	802.3	802.1	733.5	814.1	802.3	845.5	733.5
" 6	752.0	742.2	711.6	—	820.8	776.8	780.3	792.9	867.5	796.1	726.3	730.1	785.4	752.9	664.4	673.0	752.9	760.2	792.2	673.0
" 8	686.2	691.1	658.8	—	757.6	725.6	697.8	741.3	807.9	748.4	677.4	685.6	729.3	709.2	607.6	629.3	707.9	707.9	760.5	629.3
" 13	547.5	580.1	556.1	—	626.9	618.7	592.3	624.7	674.6	646.7	586.6	585.4	613.8	612.0	534.0	536.1	589.2	589.2	646.6	536.1
" 26	333.8	389.8	390.9	—	429.3	439.4	430.6	463.7	614.6	430.6	469.3	471.5	439.7	449.3	412.3	425.0	455.1	455.8	511.6	425.0
" 39	226.5	259.6	284.6	—	314.9	323.1	327.7	331.3	343.5	345.5	358.6	361.0	343.9	343.9	331.9	318.4	318.4	344.8	377.8	318.4
" 52	163.5	186.2	201.8	—	242.4	249.5	254.5	264.9	272.5	270.4	266.2	266.7	262.9	276.5	268.8	265.0	264.2	337.0	295.3	265.0

1980 – 1982

Weeks	Jan 1980	Apr	Jul	Oct	Jan 1981	Apr	Jul	Oct	Jan 1982	Apr	Jul	Oct	Jan 1983	Apr
Total	983.4	929.9	1011.0	1209.3	1353.1	1647.1	1749.3	1935.6	2028.6	2123.7	2083.1			
Over 1	981.4	929.9	1158.2	1302.0	1600.8	1702.8	1885.4	1982.3	2094.4	2096.8				
" 2	895.2	890.2	923.4	1231.0	1530.8	1641.3	1818.4	1925.2	2032.1	1999.4				
" 4	896.4	895.4	927.4	1131.8	1457.9	1549.7	1704.6	1820.4	1953.2	1910.3				
" 6	792.2	760.2	845.5	1031.4	1316.2	1461.2	1589.3	1701.9	1855.9	1832.5				
" 8	737.6	707.9	760.5	957.1	1258.4	1382.0	1481.9	1620.2	1762.2	1754.0				
" 13	622.6	589.2	646.6	789.2	1034.4	1192.4	1305.7	1439.3	1596.3	1558.0				
" 26	455.1	439.7	511.6	650.4	804.8	945.8	1065.4	1161.9	1239.2					
" 39	325.6	318.4	344.8	377.8	446.9	539.1	669.0	798.9	893.4	950.8				
" 52	262.9	264.2	268.7	295.3	337.0	384.1	464.2	584.6	682.6	754.3				

Source: Dept. of Employment

Table 3: Cumulative Duration of Employment: Great Britain, Females

(Thousands)

1966–1970

Weeks	Jan 1966	Apr	Jul	Oct	Jan 1967	Apr	Jul	Oct	Jan 1968	Apr	Jul	Oct	Jan 1969	Apr	Jul	Oct	Jan 1970	Apr	Jul	Oct
Total	73.2	64.7	54.0	82.2	101.9	104.1	88.7	102.2	101.2	93.0	75.9	88.5	86.8	80.4	75.1	86.4	85.1	85.0	81.2	93.0
Over 1	59.8	53.3	44.2	65.7	85.7	90.4	75.9	86.3	86.4	79.8	64.4	74.8	73.6	67.7	62.4	72.8	72.8	74.1	60.5	79.2
" 2	51.8	48.7	38.3	54.7	75.4	79.3	61.7	77.3	75.5	71.5	57.0	64.3	73.5	62.1	53.7	62.4	64.4	64.4	58.7	68.3
" 4	45.6	40.1	31.7	41.0	65.8	68.7	56.8	60.6	60.3	60.6	48.3	50.8	55.5	51.5	43.5	48.9	55.6	54.8	48.2	54.2
" 6	39.1	34.3	27.0	34.3	55.5	59.0	48.9	60.9	70.8	52.0	48.3	51.2	50.8	44.8	37.3	39.6	47.5	46.8	46.0	43.8
" 8	34.1	29.6	24.1	27.1	47.1	51.5	44.0	44.1	74.4	45.8	37.5	44.1	36.3	38.8	32.9	34.4	41.0	40.4	36.2	38.0
" 13	23.8	22.1	18.1	18.9	30.5	37.1	32.9	32.5	31.4	34.2	28.8	29.1	29.6	29.1	24.8	29.1	28.8	29.5	27.2	27.7
" 26	8.8	13.2	11.2	14.0	14.0	19.3	19.0	19.7	19.4	19.9	27.2	27.0	17.0	17.3	15.7	15.4	15.4	17.3	16.1	17.1
" 39	8.3	8.3	7.9	2.3	9.3	10.7	10.9	12.9	19.4	12.6	11.8	10.9	11.8	12.2	10.9	15.0	10.8	11.3	11.2	11.2
" 52	6.5	6.2	5.7	6.0	6.8	7.5	7.6	8.8	8.9	9.0	8.3	8.8	8.8	8.4	7.8	8.3	8.2	8.4	8.2	8.7

1971–1975

Weeks	Jan 1971	Apr	Jul	Oct	Jan 1972	Apr	Jul	Oct	Jan 1973	Apr	Jul	Oct	Jan 1974	Apr	Jul	Oct	Jan 1975	Apr	Jul	Oct
Total	99.6	112.4	112.6	134.8	144.7	149.0	134.7	138.6	135.4	124.0	91.5	83.4	—	115.9	93.3	—	—	186.9	227.2	243.5
Over 1	85.1	97.7	96.1	118.2	127.5	131.9	115.7	123.5	119.8	108.4	77.5	72.9	—	97.1	75.9	—	—	173.0	198.6	235.7
" 2	74.8	87.5	82.6	104.2	110.9	122.5	101.5	110.6	109.6	94.7	68.0	64.7	—	79.2	64.7	—	—	151.0	163.8	198.3
" 4	65.7	67.3	68.4	85.0	104.9	103.5	89.7	104.9	92.5	79.7	51.2	58.5	—	60.2	62.3	—	—	106.5	121.7	169.9
" 6	62.8	54.9	58.2	70.1	89.0	103.3	88.5	103.9	94.1	74.8	51.1	53.5	—	46.7	44.8	—	—	89.3	103.3	143.9
" 8	47.8	54.9	51.7	78.0	80.6	80.6	68.5	74.4	79.0	64.0	45.7	42.4	—	46.7	30.4	—	—	77.5	90.4	127.8
" 13	33.6	39.0	37.7	55.6	55.6	60.5	53.0	70.5	74.8	50.2	37.9	32.4	—	35.1	30.5	—	—	94.5	66.4	83.3
" 26	17.7	21.6	21.8	24.5	27.9	34.2	32.1	52.1	31.4	31.7	25.0	22.2	—	21.5	19.9	—	—	28.5	33.8	42.7
" 39	12.2	13.6	14.3	16.2	17.4	20.0	20.9	21.9	31.7	21.1	20.8	18.4	—	15.4	14.5	—	—	17.6	20.6	24.9
" 52	8.8	9.8	10.0	11.5	12.0	13.4	13.9	15.6	15.6	15.6	13.6	13.3	—	12.5	11.2	—	—	12.8	13.9	16.7

1976–1980

Weeks	Jan 1976	Apr	Jul	Oct	Jan 1977	Apr	Jul	Oct	Jan 1978	Apr	Jul	Oct	Jan 1979	Apr	Jul	Oct	Jan 1980	Apr	Jul	Oct
Total	270.5	272.1	371.8	—	356.2	343.1	466.2	427.0	444.5	391.6	473.7	438.5	401.3	363.6	458.3	420.0	434.0	443.7	602.7	639.9
Over 1	251.3	256.4	334.3	—	337.8	331.2	438.5	409.0	396.4	372.7	435.1	400.6	382.0	352.6	433.4	401.8	410.0	430.1	571.2	596.0
" 2	239.0	241.0	293.4	—	318.0	305.1	396.0	384.7	376.5	351.6	389.4	376.5	363.5	337.0	393.5	377.5	390.1	401.1	519.6	565.3
" 4	214.7	217.3	245.4	—	294.6	278.6	318.3	351.1	351.1	316.4	339.0	339.1	311.5	311.5	323.5	337.9	364.8	432.5	512.2	565.8
" 6	190.1	195.3	200.8	—	269.9	255.7	283.4	345.9	332.0	291.9	276.1	305.6	305.6	289.2	280.2	302.0	333.0	336.0	370.8	461.0
" 8	168.8	176.8	180.7	—	246.3	236.1	285.6	311.3	324.8	270.2	245.8	282.0	282.0	266.8	245.8	277.4	304.4	309.2	319.2	515.1
" 13	137.2	137.0	140.7	—	194.0	191.0	131.0	285.0	300.5	223.8	211.7	229.5	229.0	219.1	206.4	245.1	277.4	309.5	261.1	544.3
" 26	55.9	70.9	42.4	—	111.7	120.2	180.2	229.5	243.3	147.8	136.9	133.3	135.9	146.3	139.8	125.5	245.5	249.7	163.9	139.7
" 39	31.3	40.8	50.5	—	65.7	84.5	75.0	126.5	147.1	101.4	97.8	143.9	97.8	96.6	101.8	139.8	199.8	160.7	160.3	185.5
" 52	18.8	24.8	28.0	—	41.9	46.7	52.6	59.1	61.4	61.9	66.2	65.0	66.0	69.9	71.1	72.0	70.9	70.9	103.1	83.3

1981–1982

Weeks	Jan 1981	Apr	Jul	Oct	Jan 1982	Apr
Total	673.4	676.6	808.4	847.9	833.6	812.8
Over 1	649.8	656.9	776.9	825.1	814.9	800.2
" 2	612.7	631.2	734.5	795.8	783.2	770.0
" 4	580.2	541.4	665.8	735.4	747.4	785.8
" 6	541.4	550.2	601.3	660.3	708.2	687.5
" 8	500.4	515.7	544.3	617.4	665.3	681.1
" 13	409.7	419.9	309.5	544.3	562.6	562.6
" 26	239.8	277.5	309.5	347.3	347.1	406.0
" 39	142.7	168.0	207.8	236.3	261.1	276.9
" 52	93.3	104.5	129.7	162.0	179.9	195.4

Source: Dept. of Employment

Table·4: Representative Registers: Great Britain, Males and Females

(Thousands)

	Jan 63/ Jan 67 thous.	R(t) %	Apr 67/ Oct 71 thous.	R(t) %	Jan 72/ Jul 75 thous.	R(t) %	Oct 75/ Jan 81 thous.	R(t) %
Males								
Total	297.1	100.0	493.4	100.0	633.2	100.0	1044.6	100.0
Over 1	261.5	88.0	445.9	90.4	584.2	92.3	1001.2	95.8
" 2	236.3	79.5	407.8	82.6	539.3	85.2	948.4	90.8
" 4	205.2	69.1	359.3	72.8	478.2	75.5	869.8	83.3
" 6	182.2	61.3	319.3	64.7	433.8	68.5	798.1	76.4
" 8	164.8	55.5	290.0	58.8	400.8	63.3	739.1	70.7
" 13	132.1	44.5	232.2	47.1	332.6	52.5	621.2	59.5
" 26	88.7	29.9	152.2	30.8	231.4	36.5	431.3	41.3
" 39	66.4	22.4	110.1	22.3	173.9	27.5	321.7	30.8
" 52	52.4	17.6	83.9	17.0	137.6	21.7	251.8	24.1
Females								
Total	92.4	100.0	94.0	100.0	135.4	100.0	422.0	100.0
Over 1	78.2	84.7	80.3	85.5	118.5	87.5	400.3	94.8
" 2	70.1	75.8	70.4	75.0	103.7	76.6	372.8	88.3
" 4	57.8	62.5	58.9	62.6	84.3	62.3	332.9	78.9
" 6	49.4	53.5	49.9	53.1	73.0	53.9	298.9	70.8
" 8	43.1	46.6	43.7	46.4	64.9	47.9	271.4	64.3
" 13	31.3	33.9	31.8	33.8	48.7	36.0	218.3	51.7
" 26	17.6	19.1	18.3	19.5	28.4	20.9	132.2	31.3
" 39	11.6	12.5	12.1	12.9	18.9	13.9	85.4	20.2
" 52	8.3	9.0	8.7	9.2	13.6	10.0	57.9	13.7

Table 5: Claims to Unemployment Benefit: January 1963 to October 1981 (Claims per Quarter)

(Thousands)

Males

Males	1963	1964	1965	1966	1967	1968	1969	1970	1971	1972	1973
Jan	876.8	580.2	490.6	499.3	705.8	668.4	649.5	658.3	662.3	729.6	612.8
Apr	991.7	538.7	520.8	(507.8)	698.0	662.1	688.2	686.8	726.1	(739.2)	571.9
Jul	564.2	455.0	426.7	416.3	627.1	600.4	598.9	608.5	690.4	619.8	516.7
Oct	598.7	462.4	474.6	521.8	647.1	695.7	658.3	664.5	756.7	(716.6)	559.6

	1974	1975	1976	1977	1978	1979	1980	1981
Jan	584.6	531.3	796.6	—	707.2	664.8	686.3	830.7
Apr	567.8	785.0	780.7	698.9	687.6	665.4	686.8	815.7
Jul	571.3	774.0	870.3	851.0	790.8	714.4	888.8	781.2
Oct	768.3	956.9	903.2	915.0	856.3	800.6	967.4	930.7

Females

Females	1963	1964	1965	1966	1967	1968	1969	1970	1971	1972	1973
Jan	209.9	149.4	126.2	110.9	178.9	152.0	124.9	130.1	141.1	177.3	158.9
Apr	193.5	138.9	129.1	(104.9)	180.1	136.2	123.6	133.5	160.7	(174.1)	146.7
Jul	156.5	108.1	97.0	84.0	150.2	110.6	106.7	118.1	142.6	146.7	124.2
Oct	162.1	116.4	105.2	112.1	152.3	137.6	133.6	144.1	186.0	(192.0)	148.6

	1974	1975	1976	1977	1978	1979	1980	1981
Jan	140.1	138.0	283.2	—	286.6	286.1	310.7	352.6
Apr	136.9	230.4	275.9	246.6	273.8	273.5	310.0	361.0
Jul	136.2	224.2	360.8	376.6	371.9	367.9	476.8	358.0
Oct	224.8	375.9	412.0	439.5	453.5	452.1	500.8	509.9

Note: Figures in brackets are partly estimated: Apr. 1966 end month in quarter unavailable; Apr. and Oct. 1972 male/female split unavailable.

Source: D.H.S.S.

THE IMPACT OF DEMOGRAPHIC CHANGE ON UNEMPLOYMENT

RATES IN CANADA: 1953-1978

David Forrest

UPWARD TRENDS IN THE RATE OF UNEMPLOYMENT

In Canada, as in most Western economies, the rate of
unemployment was higher during the 1970s than during
the 1950s and 1960s.   Indeed, except for the unusually high figures of the period 1958-61, the unemployment rate showed a trend increase over the
whole of the 1953-78 period.
    The most prominent explanation for the increase
in unemployment in the 1970s centred on the role of
the unemployment insurance system.   The Unemployment Insurance Act (1971) extended eligibility for
benefit and considerably increased the size of payments to unemployed persons.   The consequent fall
in the opportunity cost of non-work activities was
predicted to raise the unemployment rate.   Previous
empirical studies (Grubel, Maki and Sax (1975),
Green and Coisineau (1976)) have estimated the size
of the impact of the Act and suggest that it raised
the unemployment rate to between 0.4 and 0.8 percentage points higher than it would otherwise have
been.
    The empirical studies cited do not then attrib-
ute all of the unemployment increases to changes in
unemployment insurance arrangements.   If we take
comparable trade cycles (defined from one peak in
the annual unemployment rate to the next) then the
mean rate over 1972-78, at 6.8%, was 1.4 percentage
points higher than that measured over 1968-72.   If
we accept the estimates of the impact of the Unemployment Insurance Act, there is therefore still a
marked residual rise in unemployment to be explained.
Moreover, even prior to the 1971 Act, a trend rise in
unemployment was perceivable (between 1961-68 and
1968-72 the mean unemployment rate increased from
4.5 to 5.3 percent).   So what factors other than

unemployment insurance were working to increase unemployment ?

In searching for additional explanations,
account must be taken of the fact that Canada was
not alone in facing increasing unemployment rates.
Within the Western economic bloc, rising unemployment
was very much an international phenomenon. Any
major plausible explanations for the increase in
Canadian unemployment should be capable of being used
also to explain rising unemployment across a wide
range of countries; distinct explanations for the
rise in unemployment in each country would be less
satisfactory since they would appear as ad hoc in
nature. Of course, part of the appeal of the
unemployment insurance hypothesis was that it was
indeed capable of being used to explain a rise in unemployment in several different countries, since several countries expanded benefit provision at about
the same time.

The criterion that any explanation of rising
Canadian unemployment should be potentially valid for
other countries also is met by the hypothesis advanced and tested in this paper. The hypothesis is
that demographic change was responsible for pushing
up unemployment rates. Specifically, it is argued
that Canada, like most Western countries, experienced an unusually high level of birth activity in the
10-20 years following World War II: when the
products of this post-war baby boom reached the age
for entering the labour force, the resulting change
in labour force age composition may have led to a
change in the equilibrium rate of unemployment.

WHY MIGHT CHANGES IN POPULATION AGE STRUCTURE

INFLUENCE THE RATE OF UNEMPLOYMENT ?

The overall unemployment rate is the weighted sum of
the unemployment rates of the several groups that
make up the labour force. In our context, it will
be useful to define the overall unemployment rate,
U, as follows:

$$U \equiv \sum_i w_i u_i \qquad i = 1, \ldots, n.$$

Here, u_i is the age specific unemployment rate of
group i; w_i, the labour force weight of group i, is
the proportion of the labour force accounted for by
members of the group; there are n age groups.

From this way of defining the overall unemployment rate, we can perceive various channels by which
an increase in the proportion of teenagers in the
working age population might influence overall unemployment.

First, if labour force participation rates are
taken as given for each demographic group, the population composition changes would generate proportionate changes in labour force composition. Even if
there were no consequential changes in age specific
unemployment rates, the overall unemployment rate
would nevertheless be affected so long as different
demographic groups have different unemployment rates.
In fact the younger age groups are systematically
more unemployment-prone than average - this arises
from an abnormally high frequency (rather than from
a long mean duration) of unemployment on the part of
the youth population; presumably this reflects a
pattern of search costs and benefits that favours
extensive job search (see Gower (1975)). Whatever
the detailed causes, the fact that the youth population in fact constitutes an exceptionally unemployment-prone group will mean that if a greater weight
is attached to that group within the labour force, as
a result of a bulge in their population, then overall
unemployment will increase as a result. This channel,
via which demographic change affects the overall
unemployment rate, we term here the 'weights effect'.

A second channel of influence of demographic
change we shall call the 'rates effect'. This
effect would operate if there were any way in which
a change in the age structure of the population
acted so as to change particular age-specific unemployment rates (the u_i in our identity). Wachter and
Kim (1979) predicted that the entry into the labour
force of large cohorts of young people would raise
youth unemployment rates; this was their 'cohort
overcrowding hypothesis'. The prediction can be
generated by assuming that young workers and old
workers are imperfect substitutes for one another.
As an approximation, in the short run, experienced
workers can be considered as a factor of production
in fixed supply; if young workers are viewed as a
variable factor, then any increase in their numbers
will result (according to the 'law' of diminishing
returns) in a fall in their marginal productivity;
their increased numbers can then be accommodated
fully only if their relative wages drop by enough to
compensate for the fall in marginal productivity.
In practice, there is evidence from the United States
that youth relative earnings indeed fell under

pressure of greater numbers in the 1970s (Welch, 1979).
However, there is no guarantee that youth wages are
sufficiently flexible to avoid some unemployment
increase in these circumstances: there are institutional impediments (such as minimum wage laws) that
make wages less than fully flexible in the downward
direction. Hence, it is appropriate to investigate
whether age-specific unemployment rates were sensitive
to changes in the demographic composition of the population.

If demographic changes were indeed found to have
influenced age-specific unemployment rates, then this
would open up the possibility of indirect weights
effects in addition to the direct weights effects
cited above. The well known added and discouraged
worker effects propose that participation rates
depend on unemployment rates. If demographic
change induces changes in unemployment rates, then
there will be changes in labour force weights in
addition to those proportionate changes associated
with population composition movements.

A simple model that highlights these channels by
which demographic change affects unemployment consists
of four equations:

$$U = \sum u_i w_i \tag{1}$$

$$w_i = p_i (PR_i / PR) \tag{2}$$

$$(PR_i / PR) = g (u_i, u) \tag{3}$$

$$u_i = h (X, w_i) \tag{4}$$

Here, X stands for 'other exogenous variables'
(including, e.g., the stage of aggregate demand in
the economy); p_i is the proportion of the working
age population accounted for by the group i; PR_i is
that group's labour force participation rate; PR is
the economy-wide participation rate; and w_i and u_i
have the same meaning as before.

In the model, (1) is simply the identity established above. Equation (2) is an identity stating
that the labour force weights depend on both population weights and participation rates. Equation (3)
states that the participation rate for a group is
influenced by its rates of unemployment (this link
would be via the discouraged worker effect). In
equation (4), the proposition is that a group's rate
of unemployment is dependent on its weight in the

labour force and on certain exogenous variables.

DECOMPOSITION OF CHANGES IN THE OVERALL RATE OF UNEMPLOYMENT

This section sets a framework within which it will be possible to evaluate the hypothesis that changes in age composition affected the overall unemployment rate in Canada. The framework utilises the identity $U = \sum w_i u_i$. From this identity, it can easily be established that the change in the aggregate unemployment rate (U) between any two periods, 0 and 1, may be divided arithmetically into three parts. The first part of the change is that unambiguously attributable to changes in the labour force weights, w_i. This may be written as:

$$\sum_i u_i^0 (w_i^1 - w_i^0) \tag{5}$$

where u and w have the same meaning as before and where superscripts refer to the periods 0 and 1.
The second element in the change in U between the two periods is that unambiguously attributable to changes in the group-specific unemployment rates, u_i. This element may be written as

$$\sum_i w_i^0 (u_i^1 - u_i^0) \tag{6}$$

There now remains a third element in the change in U between periods 0 an 1. This is given by the expression:

$$\sum_i (w_i^1 - w_i^0)(u_i^1 - u_i^0) \tag{7}$$

which is known as the 'interaction' term. This reflects the joint effects of the w_i and u_i varying together and is therefore known sometimes as the 'covariance term'.
We have now divided the change in U between two periods into three components:

$$U^1 - U^0 = \sum_i u_i^0(w_i^1 - w_i^0) + \sum_i w_i^0 (u_i^1 - u_i^0)$$
$$+ \sum_i (w_i^1 - w_i^0)(u_i^1 - u_i^0)$$

The first component of change we shall take as our estimate of the 'weights effect'.

The second component includes the effects on U of change in age-specific unemployment rates, whatever the source of those changes. We shall use multiple regression analysis to estimate how much of this component originated in changes in population age composition.

The third component is more difficult to interpret. Should any or all of this component of the change in unemployment be attributed to demographic change ? The answer depends on the view one takes of the dominant direction of causation between Δw and Δu. If changes in population proportions are the primary determinant of changes in w, then if there is also strong causation running from w to u, this would imply that a substantial part of the covariance term could indeed be attributed to demographic change. However, our model shows a chain of causation running not only from w to u (equation (4)), but also (via equations (2) and (3)) from u to w. Therefore not all of the covariance term can be attributed to demographic change. How much of it should be so attributed is a tricky problem but fortunately it is not one that we need confront directly. It will be demonstrated below that our multiple regression analysis will allow us to estimate together those parts of the second and third components ($w\Delta u$ and $\Delta w\Delta u$) that arise as a result of changes in population age composition.

Table 1 presents the decomposition (into three components) of changes in the mean unemployment rate across four Canadian trade cycles. The decomposition was based on a division of the Canadian Labour Force into four age groups (15-19 years, 20-24 years, 25-44 years, 45 and above). The principal feature of this table is that the bulk of variations in the unemployment rate occur because of variations in age-specific unemployment rates rather than because of changes in labour force weights; weights effects (and the covariance term) are small relative to total changes in unemployment. The limited effect of demographic change working via weights effects may be gauged by centering on the increase of unemployment that occurred during the late 1970s. Comparing the 1968-72 and 1972-78 trade cycles, the mean unemployment rate between the two periods increased by 1.4 percentage points. Weights effects are estimated to have contributed only one-tenth of a percentage point to this rise, only 6-7% of the total change.

Table 1: Decomposition of changes in the Unemployment Rate across four Canadian Trade Cycles

Trade Cycles	(1) Total Changes in U	(2) $\sum_i u_i^0(w_i^1-w_i^0)$	(3) $\sum_i w_i^0(u_i^1-u_i^0)$	(4) $\sum_i (u_i^1-u_i^0)(w_i^1-w_i^0)$	(5) Sum of columns (2), (3) and (4)
1954-8 to					
1961-68	+0.32	+0.02	+0.22	+0.01	+0.25
1968-72	+1.12	+0.07	+0.95	+0.05	+1.07
1972-78	+2.55	+0.16	+2.19	+0.17	+2.52
1961-8 to					
1968-72	+0.80	+0.06	+0.73	+0.03	+0.82
1972-78	+2.23	+0.11	+1.97	+0.15	+2.23
1968-72 to					
1972-78	+1.43	+0.09	+1.28	+0.04	+1.41

Notes:

1. For definitions, see text.

2. 'Trade cycles' are defined from one peak in the annual unemployment rate to the next.

3. Column (5) differs from column (1) because of rounding errors in the calculation of the three components of change.

It follows from these findings that if the
demographic changes being discussed are to be accor-
ded any great significance in explaining the increases in unemployment, then it can only be via our
rates effects(1).   The bulk of the paper must
therefore be devoted to assessing the extent to
which demographic change may have influenced age-
specific unemployment rates.

MODELLING THE EFFECTS OF CHANGE IN AGE STRUCTURE ON AGE SPECIFIC UNEMPLOYMENT RATES

Let p_i be the proportion of the working age
population in demographic group i (2); let w_i be
the proportion of the labour force in demographic
group i; and let PR_i and u_i be respectively the
participation rate and unemployment rate of group i.
In estimating the model, eight demographic groups
will be delineated: we have the same four age
groups groups as were specified in estimating the
weights effect and these are now further divided by
sex.   Male groups are denoted by i = 1 to i = 4
(corresponding to the groups 15-19, 20-24, 25-44,
45 years and above); female groups are denoted
by i = 5 to i = 8 (corresponding to the same age-
groups as in the male case).   We shall discuss first
a model of male unemployment.

We hypothesise that the unemployment rate for a
demographic group will depend upon the relative
numbers of that group in the labour force (3).   It
will of course depend also on a set of other variables.   Amongst these we include the rate of unemployment of prime males (4), u_3.   This is a common
indicator of overall tightness in the labour market
(5): its advantage is that it will reflect both
variations in aggregate demand conditions and variations in policies (e.g. employment taxes) that have
their specific effects on the labour market.

Also included in the equation explaining variations in u_i are variables designed to represent
the effects of minimum wage laws and unemployment
insurance conditions.   We shall use a male minimum
wage index (wm) to pick up the impact of changes in
minimum wage laws and a dummy variable (d) to examine the effects of changes in unemployment insurance
conditions.   The precise specification of these
variables will be discussed below.

We propose, then, that age-specific unemployment rates (for male groups other than the prime age

group) may be explained by relationships of the form

$$u_i = f_1 \ (w_i, \ u_3, \ wm, \ d) \quad i = 1, \ 2, \ 4 \qquad (8)$$

In turn, the relative size of group i in the labour force will depend on both the group's relative size in the population and on its rate of labour force participation. The relationship derives from the identity

$$w_i = p_i \ (PR_i/PR) \qquad (9)$$

According to the evidence from empirical studies of the discouraged worker effect (6), there may be a relationship through which participation rates are influenced by unemployment rates. Thus PR_i depends on u_i; and PR, the economy-wide participation rate depends on U, the economy-wide unemployment rate. We therefore include in our model the relationship

$$PR_i/PR = f_3 \ (u_i, \ U) \qquad (10)$$

Substitution of equations (9) and (10) into equation (8) now yields the reduced form equation

$$u_i = F_1 \ (p_i, \ u_3, \ wm, \ d, \ U) \quad i = 1, \ 2, \ 4 \quad (11)$$

This equation bears the problem, from an estimation viewpoint, that u_3 and u are very highly correlated (since prime-males are the largest demographic groups in the labour force, u_3 is a major component in U). Thus, for convenience, we shall omit U and have as our reduced form for estimation

$$u_i = F_2 \ (p_i, \ u_3, \ wm, \ d) \quad i = 1, \ 2, \ 4 \qquad (12)$$

It remains to discuss the determination of prime male unemployment. This is specified as for the other male age groups except that a new controlling cyclical variable will be required. For the moment, we shall write this as g (7), so that this equation reads

$$u_3 = F_3 \ (p_3, \ g, \ wm, \ d) \qquad (13)$$

The four equations described by (12) and (13) then constitute our model for male unemployment. They will be estimated below by simultaneous methods of regression analysis.

From our viewpoint of estimating the impact of demographic change, the key variable is p_i. The coefficient on p_i in the reduced form equation (12) is in fact a composite, reflecting the coefficients on w_i in equation (8), on p_i in equation (9) and on u_i in equation (10). The composite coefficient measures the total impact of a change in p_i on the group-specific unemployment rate, u_i: it incorporates both the direct effect of changes in p_i (8) and the effects insofar as they occur by modifying the group-specific participation rates (PR_i). It is therefore appropriate to use estimates of this coefficient to estimate the sum of the rates effect and that part of the covariance term associated with demographic change. Referring back to the decomposition of unemployment changes, those parts of components (6) and (7) that we need to separate out can thus be estimated by reference to our regression equations. The combined estimate we shall term the 'augmented rates effect' of demographic change. To assess the total effect of demographic change, we shall add together this estimate and our earlier estimate of the weights effect. The latter we shall henceforth term the 'pure weights effect' because (to avoid double counting) we have not included any part of the interaction term in our measure of it.

Female Unemployment

Thus far, variations in participation rates in our model have been regarded as being generated by variations in unemployment rates. This seems to be an inadequate view so far as females are concerned: while unemployment rates may be viewed as playing a role in the short and medium term, such short and medium term fluctuations have been over-shadowed in the case of Canada and other countries by long term trends in the participation rates of women. Such long term trends cannot be ignored in our empirical analysis. Whatever the source of the trend increase in participation, it has served to raise the proportion of the labour force accounted for by female groups in almost every successive year. In examining the impact of changes in the population proportion (p_i), for a female demographic group, the omission of a variable representing these long term forces may yield misleading results: we refer here to the possibility that the role of long run (for our purposes) exogenous changes in the PR_i have overshadowed the role of changes in the p_i in

explaining changes in the female w_i.   We therefore
adapt our model of unemployment to take account of
changes in female participation rates.
   For the female groups (i = 5 to i = 8) we hypothesise (as for the male model) that the group unemployment rate depends on the proportion of the
group in the labour force (w_i), the rate of prime
male unemployment (u_3), unemployment insurance conditions (represented by d) and minimum wage conditions (represented now by a female   minimum wage
series, wf):

$$u_i = h_1 \ (w_i, \ u_3, \ wf, \ d) \quad i = 5, \ 6, \ 7, \ 8 \quad (14)$$

   As before, participation rates and population
proportions determine labour force weights:

$$w_i = p_i \ (PR_i/PR) \hspace{5cm} (15)$$

   The distinctive feature for females, we have
suggested, is that some exogenous, long term factors
are important in the determination of participation
rates.   We represent these factors by a time trend,
t (9) so that

$$PR_i/PR = h_3 \ (u_i, \ U, \ t) \quad i = 5, \ 6, \ 7, \ 8 \quad (16)$$

   Estimates of this system of equation will be
used, along with the estimates of the male system,
for assessing the size of the augmented rates effect
of demographic change.

Specification of Variables

The period covered by the regression analysis is
1953-78 and observations are annual.   The group
employment rates for this period were those generated
by Professor Frank Denton and his colleagues at
McMaster University.   For the 1953-74 period, these
figures differed slightly from the official data because they were adjusted to make them comparable with
post -1975 data (a new Labour Force Survey, introduced in 1975, changed the form of questions asked
about unemployment status).
   Population proportion figures were based on
estimates published by Statistics Canada.   The
estimates pertain to the 1st July in each year.
   The cyclical variable used in the prime male unemployment equation may be termed the 'G.N.P. gap'

(g). It was generated by taking a series 'G.N.P. measured in 1972 dollars' and fitting a log linear trend to the 26 years of data. Residuals were then retrieved and used as the G.N.P. gap variable (with positive values representing shortfalls of real G.N.P. from trend and negative values representing real G.N.P. figures above the fitted trend).

Our minimum wage indices (calculated separately for males and females) are those described in Swidinsky (1980). Professor Swidinsky kindly supplied the indices for the period 1953-75 and these were then updated to 1978 using his methods and sources. The index, whether for males or females, takes account of both the level of the minimum wage (relative to the average wage) in each province and of the rate of coverage of the law in each province. It is given by:

$$W = \sum_{i=1}^{10} \frac{L_i}{L_c} \cdot \frac{MW_i}{AHE_i} \cdot C_i$$

where the subscripts i refer to the ten provinces and the subscript c refers to Canada. MW is the minimum hourly wage, C is the proportion of the provincial non-agricultural labour force to which the law applies, L is the non-agricultural labour force, and AHE is average hourly earnings in manufacturing (10). Note that the MW figure is that applicable to adults. From time to time, provinces have had special regulations on the employment of juveniles but a separate index for juveniles proved impossible to construct given the complexity of the rules and the inadequacy of the data. It has to be assumed therefore that movements in youth wage minima were reflected adequately by variations in the minimum wage index for Canada.

The final variable used in the regression equations is intended to represent variations in unemployment insurance conditions. The Unemployment Insurance Act (1971) radically altered the rules governing unemployment benefits in Canada in the direction of making more generous payments to those without a job. If the replacement ratio for Canada is calculated, by far the greater part of the variation in its value is accounted for by the introduction of the rules set out in this 1971 Act (11). It was therefore decided to use a dummy variable to take account of the influence of this legislation. The dummy is set equal to zero for each year up to 1970, to 0.5 for 1971 (the year during which, on

1st July, the Act came into force) and to one for
each year from 1972 on. It was felt preferable to
include a dummy variable rather than the calculated
replacement ratio because the latter was available
only for unemployed people generally. It may have
had very different values across age groups because
of the nature of the eligibility rules and because
of variations in the average wage across age groups.
By including a dummy, it should be possible to control
for the differential impact of the Act on the several
demographic groups.

REGRESSION RESULTS: MALE UNEMPLOYMENT (1953-78)

The model discussed above consists of the four
equations

$$u_i = F_i \ (p_i, \ u_3, \ wm, \ d) \quad i = 1, \ 2, \ 4$$

$$u_3 = F_3 \ (p_3, \ g, \ wm, \ d)$$

One problem with estimating these equations as they
stand is that the dependent variable in each case is
not free to vary between minus and plus infinity as
the classical regression model requires. A logis-
tic transformation was therefore undertaken so that,
instead of the unemployment rate, we had the log.
of the odds of being unemployed as the dependent
variable in each equation. This new dependent variable is given the symbol y where

$$y = \ln(\frac{u}{1-u})$$

Marginally better results in terms of explanatory power were obtained by transforming the relevant
right hand side variables to the log. of odds form
also; this procedure had the additional advantage of
making simultaneous estimation of the four equations
a simpler matter. Thus, the regression equations
embodied here take the final form

$$\hat{y}_i = \alpha + \beta_1 x_i + \beta_2 y_3 + \beta_3 wm + \beta_4 d \quad i = 1, \ 2, \ 4$$

$$\hat{y}_i = \alpha + \beta_1 x_i + \beta_2 g + \beta_3 wm + \beta_4 d \quad i = 3$$

where

215

$$x_i = \ell n \left(\frac{p_i}{1-p_i}\right).$$

Estimation by single equation O.L.S. would have been inappropriate: since this is a simultaneous equations model, estimation by such methods would have yielded inconsistent results. The system was instead estimated by the method of three stage least squares (3SLS) (12). Estimates are presented in Table 2. It should be noted that in the equation for y_3, each variable (V_i) included had first been transformed as follows:

$$V_{i_t}^* = V_{i_t} - 0.66\, V_{i_{t-1}} + 0.10\, V_{i_{t-2}}.$$

The reason for this transformation being made was that tests had indicated the presence of second order autocorrelation in the equation for y_3. Unfortunately, a statistical package allowing correction for autocorrelation within the context of 3SLS was not available. The ad hoc procedure adopted instead was to estimate the y_3 equation using a Cochrane-Orcutt transformation procedure for second order serial correlation (CORC2). From this CORC2 single equation estimation of the y_3 equation, the values of the first and second order coefficients of autocorrelation (RHO1 and RHO2) were retrieved: RHO1 = 0.66, RHO2 = -0.10. These values for RHO1 and RHO2 were then used to transform the variables in the y_3 equation prior to 3SLS estimation of the whole system.

The final results of the exercise (Table 2) indicate some support for the cohort crowding hypothesis: the coefficient on the population proportion variable, x_i, was positive and significant (at the 5% level) for three of our four male groups. For the prime age group (25-44 years), the coefficient was not significantly greater than zero but this is not surprising since the group is so large that, relative to its total size, fluctuations in its relative importance in the population have been small. Interpretation of these findings is postponed until after presentation of the regression results for females.

We consider now the findings with respect to the other variables included in the model. The cyclical variable was very strongly significant in each case. Variations in prime male unemployment 'explained' most of the variation in the unemployment rates of other male groups; the 'G.N.P. gap' variable performed strongly in the prime male equation.

216

Table 2: Male Unemployment - 3SLS Estimation with Correction for Autocorrelation in the Prime Male Equation

Dependent Variable	Constant	x_i	y_3	g	wm	d	y_3^A	$\bar{R}^2$	D.W.
y_1	2.50* (4.50)	0.63* (3.46)	0.90* (26.44)		0.41* (1.95)	-0.005 (-0.24)		.98	2.04
y_2	1.79* (3.29)	0.34* (1.95)	1.08* (25.92)		0.28 (1.82)	0.19* (5.54)		.99	1.89
y_3	-1.49 (-2.00)	0.71 (0.42)		9.04* (6.90)	-1.10 (-1.42)	0.40* (3.17)	0.70* (3.82)	.82	2.03
y_4	4.69* (3.17)	3.28* (3.64)	0.80* (16.35)		0.29* (1.98)	-0.08 (-1.69)		.93	1.94

Note: In the y_3 equation, each independent variable was transformed by the formula

$$v_1^* = v_{i_t} - 0.66\, v_{i_{t-1}} + 0.10\, v_{i_{t-2}}$$

$$y_{3_t}^A = -0.66\, y_{3_{t-1}} + 0.10\, y_{3_{t-2}}$$

(see text for explanation).

Symbols are explained in the text. t-statistics appear in brackets. Asterisks indicate statistical significance at the 5% level (one- or two-tailed test as appropriate).

217

Turning to the minimum wage index, increases were predicted to affect most adversely the unemployment rates of low paid age groups. For 'non prime' equations, the coefficient on wm was therefore expected to be positive. For prime males, there was no a priori expectation as to sign for, while some members of the group may lose jobs as a result of the minimum wage, others may benefit because of substitution between them and groups whose price has been artificially raised. In fact, for all groups but prime males, the coefficient turned out to be positive and significant at the 5% level (one-tailed test); for prime males it was negative but not significantly different from zero at the 5% level of significance.

So far as unemployment insurance is concerned, teenagers are limited in the extent to which they are able to participate in the Canadian scheme; this accounts for the zero coefficient on the unemployment insurance dummy in the equation for y_1. For the other groups, the coefficient on d was expected to be positive. In fact, it was strongly positive for the 20-24 and 25-44 age groups. However, for '45 and above' it was negative, though not significantly less than zero at the 5% significance level. No explanation is readily apparent for this result in the y_4 equation.

REGRESSION RESULTS: FEMALE UNEMPLOYMENT (1953-78)

The model estimated in this section consists of the four equations

$$\hat{y}_i = \alpha + \beta_1 x_i + \beta_2 y_3 + \beta_3 wf + \beta_4 d + \beta_5 t$$

$$i = 5, 6, 7, 8$$

It is similar to that used for the analysis of male unemployment except that the minimum wage index is not one calculated specifically for females (wf). For the reasons given above, an additional variable, a time trend (t), is also included in each equation. As in the case of the model for males, the unemployment and demographic variables are in the log. of odds form. As before also, estimation by single equation O.L.S. would have been inappropriate because of the likelihood that error terms across the four equations would be correlated. Estimation is therefore by the method of seemingly unrelated regression equations (SURE).

218

Table 3 presents the results of estimation by SURE.
The cohort crowding hypothesis suggests that
the coefficient on the population proportions variable should be positive. In fact, in this female
model, the estimate of this coefficient was positive,
and significantly greater than zero at the 5% level,
for the 15-19 and 20-24 year old groups. It proved
not to be significantly different from zero for
either the 25-44 or the 45 and above age groups.
For the model on male unemployment, the estimates of the coefficients on x_i were expected to be
greater than zero for three of the four age groups.
For females, support for the cohort crowding hypothesis is thus more limited, since the estimates are
significant for only two of the age groups. Perhaps
it would be expected that female age specific unemployment rates would be less sensitive to cohort size
than corresponding male rates: there may be greater
ease of substitution between workers of different
ages in typical female occupations (13).
Turning to other variables, the coefficient on
the cyclical variable, y_3, was strongly significant
in all four female equations and the time trend was
significantly positive (5% level) in three of them.
The coefficient on the unemployment insurance dummy
was significantly positive for the two middle groups.
However, the estimated coefficient on the minimum
wage series, wf, was not significantly different
from zero in any of the four equations. This failure of the variable wf is particularly puzzling in
the case of the youngest age group since minimum
wage laws have been predicted to impinge with
especial severity on teenagers. A possible explanation could of course be a failure of our index,
based on adult female minimum wage rates, to track
female youth minimum wage rates with sufficient
accuracy.

INTERPRETATION OF MALE AND FEMALE REGRESSION RESULTS

The results presented in the last two sections included equations in the form

$$\ln \left(\frac{u_i}{1-u_i}\right) = \alpha + \beta_1 \ln \left(\frac{p_i}{1-p_i}\right) + \beta_2 \ln \left(\frac{u_3}{1-u_3}\right) +$$

$$\{\beta_k Z_k\}$$

Table 3: Female Unemployment - Estimation by seemingly unrelated regression method.

Dependent Variable	Constant	x_i	y_3	wf	d	t	$\bar{R}^2$	D.W.
y_5	2.55 (1.28)	1.17* (2.05)	0.75* (10.49)	0.63 (0.55)	0.03 (0.37)	0.03* (2.65)	.97	1.61
y_6	1.47 (1.53)	0.88* (2.94)	0.78* (14.72)	-0.66 (-0.08)	0.26* (5.05)	0.03* (4.85)	.98	1.87
y_7	-2.00* (-3.20)	-0.03 (-0.44)	0.55* (8.48)	-0.38 (-0.38)	0.42* (6.78)	0.02 (2.35)	.97	1.56
y_8	-6.34 (-1.43)	-1.97 (-0.85)	0.50* (6.01)	2.53 (1.45)	1.16 (1.53)	0.02 (1.58)	.89	2.17

Symbols are explained in the text. t-statistics appear in brackets.

Asterisks indicate statistical significance at the 5% level (one- or two-tailed test as appropriate).

$$i = 1, 2, 4, 6, 7, 8$$

$$\{Z\} = \text{other variables}$$

$$k \text{ signifies the kth variable}$$

As they stand, the coefficients in such an equation are hard to interpret. Ideally, we would instead like to have values for expressions such as

$$\frac{\partial u_i}{\partial p_i} \quad \text{and} \quad \frac{\partial u_i}{\partial u_3}$$

Fortunately, these may be derived by totally differentiating the above equations to obtain the results that

$$\frac{\partial u_i}{\partial p_i} = \beta_1 \frac{u_i(1-u_i)}{p_i(1-p_i)} \quad ;$$

$$\frac{\partial u_i}{\partial u_3} = \beta_2 \frac{u_i(1-u_i)}{u_3(1-u_3)} \quad ; \quad \text{and}$$

$$\frac{\partial u_i}{\partial d} = \beta \; u_i(1-u_i).$$

All these expressions were evaluated at the means of variables for each cases where the estimate of the relevant regression coefficient was statistically significant (at the 5% level). The results of the exercise are tabulated in Table 4. The table also presents the corresponding elasticities.

The results indicate, for example, that a one percentage point rise in the proportion of the 15-69 year old population accounted for by 15-19 year old males was associated with a 1.1 percentage points rise in their group unemployment rate. Females of the same age were somewhat more prone to suffer from cohort crowding; and the elasticity was greatest of all for the oldest male group. This last group was benefiting from falling numbers; presumably, to the extent that new workers were being absorbed by the labour market, there was a corresponding rise in the demand for complementary inputs (including experienced labour).

Within the male group, the finding that the elasticity of the unemployment rate with respect to

221

Table 4: Interpretation of Regression Results

Group	Population Variable		Cyclical Variable		U.I. Variable
	$\frac{\partial u_i}{\partial P_i}$	Elasticity of Unemployment rate w.r.t. Pop. Prop.	$\frac{\partial u_i}{\partial u_3}$	Elasticity of Unemployment rate w.r.t. Prime Male Unemployment	Effect on u_i of setting U.I. Dummy to one
Male 15-19	1.10	0.59	2.71	0.82	n.s.
Male 20-24	0.44	0.34	2.09	1.04	+1.23
Male 25-44	n.s.	n.s.	-	-	+1.51
Male 45-	0.93	3.76	0.82	0.80	n.s.
Female 15-19	1.60	1.14	1.72	0.71	n.s.
Female 20-24	0.83	0.94	1.04	0.76	+1.31
Female 24-44	n.s.	n.s.	0.62	0.70	+1.78
Female 45-	n.s.	n.s.	0.43	0.50	n.s.

n.s.: Not significant.

the population proportion was greatest for the youngest and oldest group was expected. It is easiest to cope with changing relative numbers in middle-aged groups, because for these groups, it is relatively easy to interchange tasks with members of adjacent age groups in either slightly earlier or slightly later stages of a typical career progression. In the case of the youngest and oldest groups, there is less scope for flexibility because each group has only one adjacent age group with which there can be an easy reallocation of tasks.

As between male and female groups, it had been expected that female unemployment rates would be relatively less sensitive to cohort size because of greater ease of substitutability between workers of different ages in typical female jobs. In the event, any such difference between males and females was evident only in the results for the 45 and above age group.

It is also of interest to note our results on the responsiveness of age-specific unemployment rates to the rate of unemployment of prime males. Table 4 has the striking result that for all females and (to a lesser extent) for the youngest and oldest males, the elasticity of group unemployment with respect to prime male unemployment is significantly less than one. In other words, unemployment for groups comprised mainly of secondary workers is less sensitive to variations in the trade cycle than is the unemployment rate for prime workers; perhaps this result is associated with the abnormal concentration of secondary workers in the service sector (itself less cyclical in its levels of activity than manufacturing).

Finally, it may be noted from Table 4 that quite strong unemployment increases are attributed to the introduction of the new unemployment insurance system in 1971. With the dummy set equal to one, the unemployment rate for females aged 25-44 years was raised by nearly two full percentage points.

ASSESSMENT OF AUGMENTED RATES EFFECT AND THE OVERALL EFFECT OF DEMOGRAPHIC CHANGE

The previous sections have yielded some indication of the importance of demographic change in each age sex group. In this section we pull the evidence together to obtain an estimate of the total impact of age structure change on the rate of unemployment in

Canada. The derivation of the estimate begins in
Table 5. This table presents information for each
group for which the coefficient on the demographic
variable was significant in the regression equation.
Take, as an illustration of the method used, the
group consisting of males aged 15-19 years. The
first column tells us that a rise of one percentage
point in this group's population proportion was expected to raise its rate of unemployment by 1.10
percentage points. The next four columns given the
mean values of the group's population proportion
across each of our four Canadian trade cycles. It
will be noted, for example, that 15-19 year old
males increased in relative numbers by 1.298 percentage points between the first two cycles.
Multiplying this change in p_i by our estimate of the
value of

$$\frac{\partial u_i}{\partial p_i}$$

gives us an estimate of the change in group unemployment rate attributable to a change in group size. In
this case, the change in group size raised the male
teenage unemployment rate by 1.43 percentage points
between the 1954-58 and 1961-68 cycles. Next, the
implication of this for the overall unemployment
rate in Canada was obtained by multiplying the
figure of 1.43 by the mean proportion of the labour
force taken up by 15-19 year old males over the combined periods 1954-1958 and 1961-68. This exercise
yields the number 0.08 in the eleventh column of
the table - this then is our estimate of the impact
on overall unemployment arising from a 'cohort
crowding' effect amongst teenage males. An identical procedure was followed for the other demographic groups and for comparisons as between other pairs
of Canadian trade cycles. The total augmented
rates effects shown in the table were obtained by
aggregation across age groups.
    It will be noted from the results in Table 5
that the augmented rates effects had a rather negligible impact on the overall rate of unemployment.
Their influence was, however, non-trivial on the
unemployment rates for particular age groups;
teenage girls, for example, suffered significantly
higher unemployment in 1961-68 as a result of the
influx of new labour market entrants. Older males,
on the other hand, benefitted from their fall in
relative numbers and this partially offset the

Table 5: The augmented rates effect of age structure change over four Canadian trade cycles

Group	$\frac{\partial U_i}{\partial P_i}$	Mean values of P_i				Change in u_i attributed to Change in P_i					Effect on Overall U				
		1954-8	1961-8	1968-72	1972-8	1954-8 to 1961-8	1961-8 to 1968-72	1968-72 to 1972-8	1954-8 to 1972-8	1961-8 to 1972-8	1954-8 to 1961-8	1961-8 to 1968-72	1968-72 to 1972-8	1954-8 to 1972-8	1961-8 to 1972-8
15-19 Male	1.10	5.896	7.194	7.682	7.567	+1.43	+0.48	-0.07	+1.48	+0.41	+0.08	+0.03	-0.004	+0.11	+0.02
20-24 Male	0.44	5.648	5.701	6.562	6.720	+0.02	+0.38	+0.07	+0.47	+0.45	0.00	+0.03	+0.006	+0.04	+0.04
45- Male	0.93	16.457	16.502	16.252	15.874	+0.04	-0.23	-0.35	-0.57	-0.58	+0.01	-0.06	-0.07	-0.13	-0.13
15-19 Female	1.60	5.756	7.004	7.398	7.291	+2.00	+0.63	-0.17	+2.45	+0.45	+0.09	+0.03	-0.001	+0.14	+0.02
20-24 Female	0.830	5.600	5.737	6.552	6.690	+0.11	+0.68	+0.11	+0.90	+0.79	+0.01	+0.04	+0.007	+0.05	+0.05
Augmented Rates Effect											+0.19	+0.07	-0.06	+0.21	0.00

adverse impact on overall unemployment coming from
the rise in the teenage rate.   In other words,
rates effects were more important in redistributing
the burden of unemployment than in increasing the
overall rate.
     In this paper, the overall impact of demograph-
ic change on the unemployment rate in Canada has been
viewed as the sum of weights effects and rates
effects.   The former were estimated in the section
on decomposition of changes and in Table 6 these are
added to the augmented rates effects estimated in the
present chapter.   These additions yield the 'total
effects' shown in the table.   Between 1954-58 and
1961-68, demographic change raised the unemployment rate by 0.21 percentage points (65.6% of the
overall increase between the two periods).   Between
1961-68 and 1968-72, demographic change raised the
unemployment rate by 0.13 percentage points (16.2%
of the overall increase between the two periods).
Between 1968-72 and 1972-78, demographic change
raised the overall unemployment rate by only 0.03
points (this was only 2% of the overall increase
between the two periods).   Thus, demographic change
appears to explain most of the modest increase in
unemployment between the nineteen fifties and the
nineteen sixties;   in the late nineteen sixties, it
was still playing some part in raising unemployment;
but the evidence attributes no significant role to
it in the nineteen seventies when the sharpest rise
in unemployment occurred.   This negative conclusion
with regard to the nineteen seventies contrasts with
our finding that unemployment insurance changes
induced a sharp rise in unemployment.   The effect
of unemployment insurance changes was estimated
using a procedure exactly analogous to that used for
estimating rates effects.   The procedure of taking
estimated regression coefficients on the U.I. dummy
for each group for which they were significant, and
combining these with the appropriate labour force
weights, yielded an estimate that the 1971 Unemployment Insurance Act raised the Canadian unemployment
rate by 0.73 percentage points (14).

CONCLUSION

The results indicate that one must be very sceptical
about claims that the entry into the labour force
of unusually large cohorts of teenagers was responsible for large changes in Canadian unemployment in
the nineteen seventies.   Examining the possible

226

Table 6: The total effect of age-structure change over four Canadian trade cycles

	Effect on Overall Unemployment Rate				
	1954-8 to 1961-8	1961-8 to 1968-72	1968-72 to 1972-8	1954-8 to 1972-8	1961-8 to 1972-8
Augmented Rates Effect	+0.19	+0.07	-0.06	+0.21	0.00
Pure Weights Effect	+0.02	+0.06	+0.09	+0.16	+0.11
Total Effect	+0.21	+0.13	+0.03	+0.37	+0.11
(% of total increase in U)	(65.6%)	(16.2%)	(2.1%)	(14.1%)	(5.0%)

channels by which this could have occurred, we find no evidence for the hypothesis. The impact of this demographic change impinged more upon the structure of unemployment than upon the overall rate of unemployment (15).

ACKNOWLEDGEMENTS

The paper is based on a Ph.D. dissertation submitted to the University of Western Ontario. My thanks are due to my advisory committee (Chris Robinson, David Laidler, Edward Saraydar). I also acknowledge, with gratitude, helpful comments made by present and former colleagues at McMaster, Liverpool and Manchester Universities.

NOTES

1. Previous studies (eg. Council of Economic Advisors (1974), Denton et al (1975)) may have underestimated the impact of demographic change because they considered only what we call the weights effect.
2. The working age population will be defined to include all persons aged 15-69 years.
3. This is the 'cohort overcrowding hypothesis'.
4. Those aged 25-55 years.
5. Used, for example, by Ragan (1981).
6. E.g. Perry (1977), Corry and Roberts (1974),
7. Its specification will be discussed below.
8. I.e. the effect there would be if participation rates were unaffected.
9. This is a common device for picking up the effects of long term changes in female participation behaviour - cf. Ragan (1981). The present author has experimented with including other variables (e.g. real hourly earnings) instead of a time trend. Results are changed only in detail (and are available on request).
10. Canadian minimum wage rates do not apply to agriculture.
11. See, for example, Holden and Peel (1979, p. 614).
12. The method was presented by Zellner and Theil (1962).
13. This would be because a relatively small number of females work in occupations with a well defined career structure where different tasks are performed by workers at different stages of their career progression.

14.   This estimate is broadly similar to that of other studies of the effect of the 1971 Act - see first section.

15.   The author also carried out an empirical study of the impact of the youth bulge in the United States.   The aggregate effect was a little greater than in Canada, largely because of greater 'weights effects'.   The regression model, based on 1948-78 data, used fewer variables than the Canadian model (minimum wages and the unemployment insurance variables were finally excluded) but was otherwise similar and yielded a similar degree of support for the cohort overcrowding hypothesis - the only exception being that no cohort overcrowding effect was apparent in the U.S. model within the 20-24 year old female category.

EMPLOYMENT FUNCTIONS FOR GREAT BRITAIN: A NEW APROACH

M. Chatterji and S. Price

SECTION 1: INTRODUCTION

The dismal record of recent unemployment trends in the U.K. is well known to the general public, economists and policy makers. The subject receives constant attention in the media and economists have made significant (at least in quantity if not in quality) contributions to the debate. Numerous recent studies on unemployment are testimony to this (1). What is generally not so widely appreciated is the equally gloomy employment situation in recent years in the U.K. Perhaps paralleling this, the analysis and forecasting of employment in the U.K. has recently received relatively less attention by economists (2). Yet between March 1977 and March 1982, employment fell from 21,969,000 to 20,626,000, a drop of some 1,343,000. Obviously, the unemployment situation is of great concern in its own right. Nonetheless, the concern is magnified by the fact that the massive increase in unemployment has been accompanied by job loss on a fairly large scale rather than by constant or rising employment. Indeed, over the same period, measured unemployment (3) rose by some 1,448,000. Thus, almost all the rise in unemployment may be due to job loss and not simply to increased registration due to an alleged increase in the laxity of the unemployment benefit system. The aim of this paper is to attempt to fill this gap by analysing and estimating a simple model for explaining employment in the U.K.

Despite the current paucity, models which explain and forecast employment in Great Britain have a long pedigree. The pioneering work of Ball and St. Cyr (1966) and Brechling (1965) established the employment function as a permanent feature of British applied macroeconomics. In fact, very little theoretical development has taken place since their pioneering effort, although several wrinkles and much greater econometric sophistication has been added. These developments are well documented in an excellent review article by Hazeldine (1981). In our view, the conventional employment function approach has a number of unsatisfactory features, mostly connected with the use of output as a regressor. These are discussed in Section 2. Section 3 outlines our theoretical approach to the problem. The main novelty is in our eschewing the use of current output and our focus on the way in which international factors directly impinge on employment. In Section 4 we present and discuss the estimates of our model and Section 5 concludes the paper. Appendix 1 contains a discussion of model selection procedures which are germane to this paper. The data used is defined in Appendix 2.

SECTION 2: CONVENTIONAL EMPLOYMENT FUNCTIONS

As stated above, the essence of these is an equation which determines aggregate employment as a function of output, lagged employment and occasionally the real wage. In most of these studies (see Hazeldine, op.cit.) the real wage variable is usually found to play a very minor role. Purely from the viewpoint of estimation, having a current endogenous variable like output as a regressor presents no serious problems. The equation can be estimated by IV or, if embedded in a system, then a systems estimator can be used (4). The problem is one of interpretation of the equation and its usefulness as a forecasting device.
    There are at least two different ways in which the use of current output as a regressor can be rationalised. The first is to treat output as exogenously determined by demand and then treat the representative firm as a cost minimiser given this exogenous output level. This is essentially the approach of Ball and St. Cyr (op.cit.) and Brechling (op.cit.). The other common method is to regard output as endogenous and determined by a profit maximising firm together with employment. In this case, the first order conditions (real wage equals marginal product) involve the level of the capital stock which is typically not observable and even if observable, would involve non-linear estimation for a C.E.S. production function. Thus the level of the capital stock is substituted out of the first order conditions

by using the production function.   This yields a
desired employment level in terms of output and the
real wage.   Once again a partial adjustment mechanism completes the exercise and produces an employment equation with output, real wage and lagged employment as the regressors.   An example of this type
of approach is Lucas and Rapping (1969).   However,
given the fact that the real wage typically turns
out to be of minor importance, it is difficult to
distinguish these two formulations.   Furthermore,
both these approaches characterise employment as
being determined by the demand for labour alone (5).
Little attention is paid to the supply of labour be-
yong the implicit recognition in the partial adjustment mechanism that supply shortages could affect
the employment level.   This point is noted by
Hazeldine (op.cit.) who states that "the use of such
a simple representation on the supply side of the
labour market does, as one might expect, spur a
number of queries and objections".

The final point regarding conventional employment functions is their usefulness as a forecasting
device.   In order to generate employment forecasts
one first needs to generate an output forecast.
Within the context of a full system this is not a
conceptual problem though the complication of working with a full system rather than a single equation
reduced form is fairly obvious (6).   If one of the
objectives is to analyse the influence of exogenous
international forces, e.g. the level of world trade,
on employment, then the conventional employment
function is not the appropriate tool.   Indeed if one
uses a conventional employment function, then the
only way in which any exogenous component of demand
can affect employment is through output.   Not only
is one unable to analyse the direct impact of such
forces on employment (if any) but also the impact
via any route other than output (if any) cannot be
analysed.   As we shall show in the next section,
this is a fairly restrictive paradigm which fails
to take account of a number of interesting possibilities.

SECTION 3:   TOWARDS A NEW APPROACH

The essence of our approach lies in modelling both
the demand for labour and the supply of labour.
Various exogenous forces are seen as shifting either
or both of these fundamental functions.   In the long
run, employment and wages are simultaneously deter-

232

mined with the other endogenous variables like output, the price level, etc.   Our approach is to
analyse the reduced form of the equation determining
employment in the long run.   Short run employment
is then viewed as being determined by an admittedly
ad hoc procedure, viz. some suitably restricted distributed lag of the various exogenous variables.
    We start by assuming that the cost function of
the representative firm is given by:

$$C = f(w, m, A).X, \quad f_1 > 0, \; f_2 > 0, \; f_3 < 0,$$

$$f_{13}, f_{23} < 0.$$

where X is output, w is the nominal wage, m the
sterling price of oil and A is a neutral shift parameter of the production function.   The above cost
function is, of course, consistent with a constant
returns to scale production function.   Increases in
the shift parameter lower total and marginal costs.
The conditional input demand functions are given by:

$$N_D = \frac{\partial C}{\partial w} = X.f_1 \tag{1}$$

$$M_D = \frac{\partial C}{\partial m} = X.f_2 \tag{2}$$

where N_D and M_D are the demand for labour and oil
given all input prices and the level of output.
    The firm's product is sold at home and abroad
and it is assumed that, due to transport costs, legislation and other barriers to trade, these markets
are separated.   Furthermore, the firm faces competition from foreign producers who manufacture a close
but not perfect substitute.   Thus the firm is assumed to behave like a discriminating monopolist.
    The home private demand and foreign demand for
the domestically produced good are given by:

$$X_1 = \phi\left(\frac{e\pi_1^*}{p_1}, \frac{y-T}{p_1}\right), \quad \phi_1 > 0, \quad \phi_2 > 0 \tag{3}$$

and

$$X_2 = \psi\left(\frac{e\pi_2^*}{p_2}, \frac{y^*}{\pi_2^*}\right), \quad \psi_1 > 0, \quad \psi_2 > 0 \tag{4}$$

where X_1, X_2 are home and foreign demand respectively, π_1^*, π_2^* are home and foreign prices respectively (both in dollars - the !foreign' currency of the competing good), y, y* are nominal incomes at home and abroad measured in their own currencies and e is the exchange rate defined by £e = \$1 so that an increase in e is a devaluation of domestic currency.

Since the firm is a discriminating monopolist, profit maximising behaviour requires the firm to set marginal revenue in each market equal to marginal cost of production. This yields

$$\frac{\partial(p_1 X_1)}{\partial X_1} = \frac{\partial C}{\partial X} = f(w, m, A) \tag{5}$$

and

$$\frac{\partial(p_2 X_2)}{\partial X_2} = \frac{\partial C}{\partial X} = f(w, m, A) \tag{6}$$

(5) and (6) determine prices at home and abroad and the allocation of output to the two markets given the input prices.

Labour supply is given by a homogeneous function of real wages and benefits as:

$$N_S = \alpha\left[\frac{w}{p_1 + e\pi_1^*}, \frac{w}{B}\right] , \quad \alpha_1 > 0, \quad \alpha_2 > 0 \tag{7}$$

where B is nominal benefits.

Labour market clearing implies

$$N_S = N_D \tag{8}$$

The government is assumed to have two discretionary categories of expenditure. The first G_C is government consumption (net of benefit payments) and the second is G_K which is government capital spending (on roads, hospitals, etc.) which is assumed to increase A and for convenience may be taken as synonymous with A. No attempt is made to model the government's budget deficit which, in any case, is endogenous to the system. Any attempt to do so would necessarily involve greatly complicating the model by the addition of a monetary sector.

Finally, total output is given by

$$X = X_1 + X_2 + G_C/p_1 + G_K/p_1 \tag{9}$$

In order to close the model, some attention must be paid to what are endogenous and what are exogenous variables. This will depend in part on the structure of the economy and the exchange rate regime. Three cases will be distinguished. The first is the period until 1971 when the U.K. was an oil importer and the exchange rate was fixed. In this case the endogenous variables are

$$X_1, \ X_2, \ X, \ p_1, \ p_2, \ N_D, \ N_S, \ M_D, \ w \text{ and } y$$

and the model is closed by the national income identity

$$y = p_1 X_1 + p_2 X_2 + \frac{G_C + G_K}{p_1} - mM \qquad (10)$$

The factor payments on M are deducted since they are paid to foreigners (7).

In 1971 the pound was floated and in 1980, North Sea oil production was sufficient for net exports to occur. We shall deal with the endogeneity of the exchange rate by an ad hoc method for the same reason as we ignored the government budget constraint, viz. the extra complication of a full blown monetary sector. The export of oil now adds an extra dimension to national income. Implicitly treating oil production as costless, the national income identity 10 is now replaced by

$$y = p_1 X_1 + p_2 X_2 + \frac{G_C + G_K}{p_1} + m X_m \qquad (10a)$$

where X_m is net oil exports and is treated as exogenous. It may be argued that X_m depends on y^*/π_2^*, world real income, but X_m may be an important determinant of the exchange rate too and thus should be included as an explanatory variable anyway. After 1971 we shall proxy the exchange rate by a crude monetary measure, viz. relative money supplies as in monetary theories of exchange rate determination (e.g. Dornbusch (1976)). In addition, post 1980 the net oil export probably exerted pressure on the exchange rate but, since this is already included via (10a), little further comment is necessary.

Thus we have three distinct regimes: (I) up until 1971 for which the model consists of (1) to (10). (II) From 1971 until 1980 for which the

model consists of (1) to (10) with the exchange rate
endogenised in the rather crude way suggested earlier; and (III) post 1980 where the model consists
of (1) to (10a) with the exchange rate endogenised
as in regime (II).
    No attempt has been made to solve the model.
Rather, the model was used to suggest what the approx-
imate exogenous variables should be. Indeed without
a great deal more structure, little can be said a
priori about the effects of changes in the various
exogenous variables on the endogenous variables and,
in particular, on the variable of interest, viz. employment. A fortiori, there is no real hope of ob-
taining any cross equation or within equation restrictions either. Accordingly we follow a very flexible procedure of estimating the reduced equation
for employment, imposing no a priori restrictions.
Equations (1) to (10) (or (10a)) are seen as determining long run equilibrium employment. We have no
explicit theory of short run behaviour. Rather we
allow short-run dynamics to be artibrarily determined
by the data by estimating the reduced form equation
for employment using a long distributed lag model.

SECTION 4: EMPIRICAL RESULTS

In this section we present some results. Our data
set consisted of British quarterly unadjusted data,
and was available for the period 1957(I) to 1982(III).
The variables we used are discussed briefly in
Section 3 and are defined precisely with sources in
the Appendix. As all explanatory variables are
exogenous, we used ordinary least squares and the
Cochrane-Orcutt transformation throughout.
    Employment itself has not been a homogeneous
quantity over the sample period. Figure 1 shows how
the total (our dependent variable) has moved in relation to two of its components, male and female employment. There has also been a large rise in part-
time employment (see Robertson and Briggs (1979) for
some recent history). In 1961, 1.1% of males and
25.0% of females worked part-time in Britain (8) and
twenty years later the proportions were 4.1% and
44.0% respectively (9). We are therefore attempt-
ing a somewhat difficult task in trying to explain
the total, whose industrial composition has also
changed dramatically.
    As is argued above, there is little that one
can specify a priori about the short run dynamics of
any process under examination and these are freely

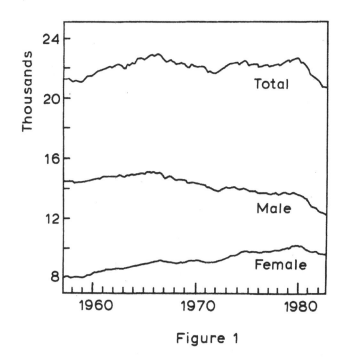

Figure 1

estimated from the data.   The problem with this
approach is that the sequential, iterative process
involved will invalidate formal tests.   However,
the number of iterations involved was low.

Another issue of some importance is whether the
various policy determined variables, in particular
government spending on consumption and capital goods,
are exogenous.   In our equations, they are treated
as such.   However, if they react in some counter-
cyclical way, then this assumption is not valid.
This is an important but largely unsettled issue.
Certainly it can be argued that total government
expenditure moves counter-cyclically.   However,
since a large part of this may be explained by transfer payments (e.g. unemployment benefits) and these
are explicitly excluded from both our government
spending variables, it is not clear whether our results are seriously biased.   In any event, whatever
the uncertainty regarding the appropriate reaction
function to explain total government expenditure,
the specification of reaction functions for two very
different components of government expenditure is
even more hazardous.

Our methodology was the error correction approach popularised by Davidson et al. (1978).
Section 3 informs us about the long run properties of
our model but not about the short run dynamics of
the process.   We therefore estimated a restricted
version of the following general specification:

$$\Delta_1 y_t = \alpha_0 + \sum_{i=1}^{n-1} \left\{ \sum_{j=0}^{4} \alpha_{ji} \Delta_1 x_{it} + \alpha_{5i} x_{it-1} \right\}$$

$$+ \alpha_6 x_{nt} + \alpha_7 x_{nt-1} + \alpha_8 y_{t-1} + \varepsilon_t \qquad (11)$$

where Δ_1 indicates a first-difference, ε_t is an error
term and there are n exogenous variables, the x_i.
All variables are in natural logs (except for the
standard rate of income tax).   The nth variable,
x_{nt}, was net oil exports, which was only employed
for the last nine quarters.   The dynamics on this
variable were restricted to a maximum of one lag.
In order to preserve degrees of freedom, a maximum
lag of 4 periods was employed elsewhere.   This
specification enables us to solve for a long run
solution for y^*.   Given equilibrium or long run
values of the exogenous variable x_i^* and with all dif-
ferenced terms equal to zero in the long run, we have
a long run solution for y^*.

$$y^* = -\alpha_8^{-1}(\alpha_o + \sum_{i=1}^{n} \alpha_{5i} x_i^*)$$

In addition to this specification, we experimented with lagged dependent variables, and specification in fourth differences. Although the restricted estimates that resulted from these alternative specifications were qualitatively similar, they suffered from a degree of autocorrelation which we took as evidence of dynamic misspecification.

Our final equations are presented in Table 1. We normalised by the population aged between 15 and 64 for men and 15 and 59 for women. In Section 3, three regimes are identified where parameters are likely to vary on critical variables, in particular on the exchange rate. As discussed above, we treated these regimes by constraining the exchange rate to have no effect after 1971 (III), the relative money supply to have no effect before 1971 (III) and the level of net oil exports to have no effect before 1980(II). We look first at the OLS results. The complete set of restrictions implicit in the equation is comfortably accepted (χ^2_{37} = 35.9) against the general specification (11). When tested, the normalising restriction cannot be rejected (10). The $\bar{R}^2$ is respectable for a specification in first differences. The results are of some interest. There is a positive short run impact of government expenditure on employment but a long run crowding out effect which is quite substantial, with an elasticity of -0.34. This is far larger than any other estimated effect. The short run effect is only just significant at 90%. However, government expenditure is significant at 95% (χ^2_2 = 7.45). Supply side variables are important. Our results indicate the short run effect of an increase in income tax is to <u>increase</u> employment, but the long run effect is significantly negative, though small. This variable is, of course, a very imperfect measure of the effective marginal tax rate. The level of unemployment benefits has an overall negative short run effect but no long run effect. The results confirm the importance of external factors to Britain. World trade has a positive short and long run effect (long run elasticity = 0.09). The long run effect is apparently insignificant. However, jointly it is highly significant with the short run effect (χ^2_2 = 30.5). The oil price has a negative short and long run effect. Relative money supplies have a long run positive effect, which we argue is due to the

Table 1: Dependent Variable: Δ_1 log (employment/population)$_t$

Independent Variable	OLS Coefficient	(t)	CORC Coefficient	(t)
Constant	0.056	(2.13)	0.065	(2.88)
Seasonal: 2nd quarter	0.0072	(6.68)	0.0075	(6.98)
Seasonal: 3rd quarter	0.0087	(7.00)	0.0085	(6.90)
Log (employment/population)$_{t-1}$	-0.070	(2.28)	-0.057	(2.14)
Δ_1 log (government current expenditure)$_{t-1}$	0.019	(1.67)	0.013	(1.11)
Log (government current expenditure)$_{t-1}$	-0.024	(2.43)	-0.025	(2.95)
Δ_1 log (oil price)$_t$	-0.016	(3.43)	-0.017	(3.90)
Log (oil price)$_{t-1}$	-0.0043	(1.86)	-0.0040	(1.98)
Log (UK £M1/US $M1)$_{t-1}$	0.0014	(2.64)	0.0014	(3.23)
Log (net oil exports)$_t$	-0.0021	(3.09)	-0.0020	(3.10)
Log (net oil exports)$_{t-1}$	0.00028	(0.38)	-0.00040	(0.56)
Δ_1 log (benefits)$_t$	-0.017	(2.62)	-0.017	(2.69)
Δ_1 log (benefits)$_{t-3}$	0.013	(1.94)	0.013	(1.92)
$\sum_0^2 \Delta_1$ log (world trade)$_{t-1}$	0.041	(5.34)	0.044	(6.04)
Log (world trade)$_{t-1}$	0.0065	(1.36)	0.0066	(1.61)
Δ_1 (income tax)$_t$	0.00073	(2.17)	0.00073	(2.27)
Δ_1 (income tax)$_{t-1}$ + Δ_1(income tax)$_{t-4}$	0.0010	(3.66)	0.0010	(3.70)
income tax$_{t-1}$	-0.00081	(3.05)	-0.00080	(3.50)

Test Statistics	OLSQ	CORC
$\bar{R}^2$	0.74	0.74
D.W.	2.35	2.03
Q_{12} (Box-Pierce), χ_{12}^2, χ_{11}^2	15.4	13.2
LM_{12}, χ_{12}^2	21.6	18.8
LM_8, χ_8^2	8.33	5.36
LM_4, χ_4^2	7.43	4.80
LM_1, χ_1^2	3.55	0.20

Long run Solution

log (employment/population) = 0.92 - 0.34 log (government expenditure)
                                      (0.22)

         + 0.019 log (UK £M1/US$M1) - 0.026 log (net oil exports)
           (0.012)   (0.015)

         + 0.093 log (world trade) - 0.012 (income tax)
           (0.077)   (0.005)

         - 0.062 (oil price)
           (0.037)

standard errors in parentheses.

exchange rate, while net oil exports have also reduced employment through the same route. However,
the exchange rate before 1971(III) has no effect. If
the lagged exchange rate is added to the equation,
it is insignificant, as are all the terms individually
and jointly (χ_6^2 = 3.33) when the lagged level and current and lagged differences are added up to four lags.
Another variable excluded by the data is government
capital expenditure. Adding the lagged level and
current and lagged differences up to four lags, no
coefficients are individually or jointly significant
at 90% (χ_6^2 = 6.50). Despite some experimentation,
this variable was never found to be significant.
Throughout, the short run impact of all the variables
comes through very rapidly. It should be noted,
however, that the implied long run impact is far
slower. If the equation is rewritten in levels

$$y_t = (1 + \hat{\alpha}_8)y_{t-1} + \hat{\alpha}_o + \hat{AX}$$

$$= 0.93y_{t-1} + \hat{\alpha}_o + \hat{AX} \tag{12}$$

where AX summarises the effect of the explanatory
variables, it is clear that the adjustment process is
slow. The median lag for a disturbance on an exogenous variable lagged one period (the oil price, for
example) is 10.55 quarters for an equation like (12).
    As a test on the final specification, for each
variable all the excluded terms were in turn added
to the equation, variable by variable. In no case
were the coefficients individually or jointly significant. Examination of the residuals may suggest
a problem. · The equation fails the LM test for up to
12th order autocorrelation at the 95% level, although
it passes the Box Pierce test at 90%. This appears
to be due to an outlier at 9 lags. Such a high
order lag is difficult to ascribe to misspecification
and may be due to chance. More seriously, there is
some evidence for first order autocorrelation. We
therefore corrected for this by the Cochrane-Orcutt
technique. The results were scarcely different
from the OLS results and are not discussed further.
    With all variables defined in differences set to
zero, the long run proportion of the potential population in employment with variables defined in levels set equal to their means is 70.3%, as compared
with the sample mean of 67.7%. The system is
clearly stable as the coefficient on the lagged level
of the dependent variable is negative and greater than
-2.

SECTION 5: CONCLUSIONS

The thrust of this paper has been to estimate an
aggregate employment function which is suitable for
forecasting.   The main innovation was to eschew the
use of output as an endogenous variable - an approach
common to earlier employment functions.   We were
particularly concerned to model the effects of the
international environment and the results justify
this.   The price of oil, net oil exports post 1980,
the exchange rate since floating began in 1971 and,
to a lesser extent, world trade, were all found to
have a long run influence on employment.   These
results merely serve to emphasise that Britain is a
small open economy and that any discussion of employment policy must take this central fact into account.
The major policy implications of our results are
that (1) the authorities should try and manipulate
the exchange rate to a more appropriate level, and
(2) a subsidy on the price of oil should be offered
to domestic industrial users.   These tentative policy proposals must be viewed with some caution in
the light of certain peculiarities in our results,
particularly those relating to the effects of government expenditure variables.
      The most puzzling of these is that the long run
elasticity of current government expenditure (net of
unemployment benefits) is -0.34.   Even though in a
model of monopolistic competition, it is possible
for current government expenditure to have a long run
influence of either sign, the size of this impact does
seem very large, especially in relation to the other
long run coefficients.   Furthermore, neither unemployment benefits nor government capital expenditure
appear to have any long run influence suggesting that
our long run equation may be under parameterised.
There are two reasons why this might be the case.
First, it could be the case that the lags involved
in the transmission mechanism for government capital
expenditure may be longer than the 5 quarters we
allowed for.   Also, our methodology of using an
error correction mechanism to tie down the long run
with a one quarter lag in levels may also result in
some under paramterisation (11).
      A number of other caveats and qualifications
should also be mentioned.   No structural break tests
or post sample fitting tests were conducted.   Given
that we had explicitly tried to model the well known
structural breaks that had actually occurred, we did
not feel that further ad hoc testing would be useful.
Data considerations ruled out post sample fitting

tests which are, of course, the acid test of a forecasting model.   Since positive net oil exports
started only in 1980(II) and the model was estimated
till 1982(IV), there was not much scope for post
sample predictions.
   A number of potentially important features were
omitted from the model.   These include payroll taxes
and the potential effects of capital formation.   But
perhaps most importantly, our specification was derived from a model which allowed explicitly only for
traded goods.   No attempt was made to model other
employment categories, e.g. government employment or
employment in the non-traded goods sector although,
to some extent, the exogenous variables affecting
non-traded good employment will be included in our
specification.   Nonetheless, given the importance of
non-traded goods, specific modelling of the non-traded
goods sector is called for.   This is the direction
our future research will take.
   Despite these qualifications, our results raise
some important issues.   First, as already emphasised,
they show our dependence on international factors.
Policy designed at permanently improving our employment performance must take into account such constraints and, possibly, try and shift them.   Secondly,
they suggest the relative unimportance of supply side
factors like benefits and tax rates.   Finally, and
perhaps most importantly, they suggest that it is
possible to provide an adequate explanation of employment without the customary reliance on output as
a regressor.   Given the conceptual advantage of
this methodology, we are hopeful that these results
will stimulate further research along similar lines.

ACKNOWLEDGEMENT

We are grateful to the SSRC for financial support
under Grant HR7274/1.   We would like to thank our
colleagues Tim Hatton and Raja Junankar for helpful
advice and comments.   We would also like to thank
Sheila Ogden for her efficient typing.   We, of
course, remain responsible for any deficiencies.

NOTES

   1. For a recent partial survey of research in
this area, see Nickell (1982).
   2. Exceptions are Nickell (1981), Symons (1981),
Henry and Wren Lewis (1983) and Muellbauer and Mendis

(1983).   However, these have, in the main, concentrated on manufacturing rather than aggregate employment.
    3.   New basis: data <u>Employment Gazette</u>, various.
    4.   This is precisely the approach adopted by
the major forecasters.   See Henry (1981).
    5.   Lucas and Rapping add a supply of labour
equation to this model.
    6.   Nickell (1981) and Henry and Wren Lewis
(1983) generate "rational forecasts" of output using
a fairly arbitrary equation for output which does not
explicitly incorporate the simultaneous determination
of output and employment.
    7. M_D and M are assumed equal.
    8.   <u>Historical Abstract of Labour Statistics.</u>
    9.   <u>Employment Gazette</u>, November 1982.
    10.   A regression using Δ_1 log (employment)$_t$ as
the dependent variable and with Δ_1 log (population)$_{t-1}$
on the right hand side yields a coefficient on population that is not significantly different from
unity, although it is very badly determined.
    11.   See Appendix 1 for a fuller discussion of
this point.

APPENDIX 1:   ALTERNATIVE PARAMETERISATIONS

Consider the following alternative but equivalent
parameterisations of the same model:

$$y_t = \alpha + \alpha_o x_t + \alpha_1 x_{t-1} + \alpha_2 x_{t-2} + \delta y_{t-1} \qquad (A1)$$

$$\Delta y_t = \alpha + \alpha_o \Delta x_t - \alpha_2 \Delta x_{t-1} + \beta z_{t-1} + \pi y_{t-1} \qquad (A2)$$

$$\Delta y_t = \alpha + \alpha_o \Delta x_t + b_1 \Delta x_{t-1} + \beta x_{t-2} + \pi y_{t-1} \qquad (A3)$$

where

$$\beta = \alpha_o + \alpha_1 + \alpha_2, \; b_1 = \alpha_o + \alpha_1; \; \pi = \delta - 1.$$

The long run solution is given by:

$$y = \frac{\alpha}{1-\delta} + \frac{\alpha_o + \alpha_1 + \alpha_2}{1 - \delta} x.$$

In other words, (assuming $\delta \neq 1$), whether x has a
long run influence on y depends only on $\beta = (\alpha_o + \alpha_1 + \alpha_2)$.   Testing the hypothesis $\beta = 0$ could be done

using estimates of (A1) which is an ECM with the 1st lag tying down the long run or using estimates of (A3) which is an ECM with the 2nd lag tying down the long run. The t statistic of $\hat{\beta}$ obtained from the above two procedures will clearly be different as they will be based on different $(X'X)$ matrices. Thus the choice of parameterisation can affect the model selection process and lead to under parameterisation in some cases.

APPENDIX 2: DATA SOURCES AND DEFINITIONS

All data are seasonally unadjusted except where stated.

1. Employment
Total G.B. Employment, end quarter. Sources British Labour Statistics Historical Abstract and Year Books and Employment Gazette.

2. World Trade
Quantum index of market economies exports 1970 = 100. Source: U.N. Monthly Bulletin.

3. Government Consumption
Real government consumption on total current expend- iture less government expenditure on national insur- ance benefits and government grants to personal sec- tor. Sources: C.S.O. Macroeconomic data bank table 2008. G.D.P. Deflator: Economic Trends and Monthly Digest.

4. Government Capital Spending
Real government capital expenditure in 1975 prices. Sources: Economic Trends and Monthly Digest.

5. Tax Rate
Standard (or basic) rate of income tax expressed as a percentage. Source: Annual Abstract of Statistics.

6. Flat Rate and E.R.S. Unemployment Benefit
Flat rate plus E.R.S. benefits for a notional mar- ried male with dependent wife and two children def- lated by previous periods' retail prices. Source: D.H.S.S. Abstract of Statistics for Index of Retail Prices, Average Earnings, Social Security Benefits and Contributions.

7. Oil Price
Crude petroleum export price index 1975 = 100

deflated by unit value index of exports of market
economies, 1970 = 100, dollar prices.   Sources: U.N.
Statistical paper series M. no. 29, rev. 2 and U.N.
Monthly Bulletin.

8. Exchange Rate
Inverse of the mid quarter dollar exchange rate.
Source: Financial Statistics and Monthly Digest of
Statistics.

9. Population
Total G.B. population aged between 15 and 64 for men
and 15 to 59 for women.   Quarterly figures linearly
interpolated between mid year bench marks.   Source:
O.P.C.S.

10. Relative Money Supply
U.K. Sterling M1 divided by U.S. dollar M1, seasonally
adjusted.   Sources: Federal Reserve Bulletin and
Economic Trends.

11. Net Oil Exports
Value of all U.K. net exports of oil and oil products.   Source: Energy Trends.

LIST OF COMMON REFERENCES

Akerlof, G. A., (1970), 'The Market for Lemons', Quarterly Journal of Economics, 84, pp. 488-500.
—————————, (1979), 'The case against Conservative Macroeconomics: An Inaugural Lecture', Economica, 46, pp. 219-237.
—————————,and H. Miyazaki, (1980), 'The Implicit Contract Theory of Unemployment meets the Wage Bill Argument', The Review of Economic Studies, XLVII, pp. 321-338.
Allen, F., (1982), 'Optimal Linear Income Taxation with General Equilibrium Effects on Wages', Journal of Public Economics, 17, 135-143.
Altonji, J. G., (1982), 'Intertemporal Substitution in Labour Supply: Evidence from Micro Data', Columbia University Working Paper.
—————————— and O. Ashenfelter, (1980), 'Wage Movements and the Labour Market Equilibrium Hypothesis', Economica, 47, pp. 217-245.
Anderson, R. W., (1979), 'Perfect Price Aggregation and Empirical Demand Analysis', Econometrica, 47, pp. 1209-1230.
Armstrong, H. and J. Taylor, (1982), 'Unemployment Stocks and Flows in the Travel-to-Work Areas of the N.W. Region, 1970-80', Lancaster University Mimeo.
Ashenfelter, O., (1980), 'Unemployment as Disequilibrium in a Model of Aggregate Labour Supply', Econometrica, 48, pp. 547-564.
—————————— and J. J. Heckman, (1974), 'The Estimation of Income and Substitution Effects in a Model of Family Labour Supply', Econometrica, 42, pp. 73-85.
Atkinson, A. B. and N. H. Stern, (1980), 'On the Switch from Direct to Indirect Taxation', Journal of Public Economics, 14, pp. 195-224.

247

List of Common References

Baker, G. M. and P. K. Trivedi, (1982), 'Methods for
    Estimating the Duration of Periods of Unemploy-
    ment: A Comparative Study', Department of
    Economics, Australian National University,
    Working Paper No. 076, October 1982.
Ball, R. J. and E. B. A. St. Cyr, (1966), 'Short Term
    Employment Functions in British Manufacturing
    Industry', Review of Economic Studies, 33,
    pp. 179-197.
Barmby, T., R. W. Blundell and I. Walker, (1983),
    'Estimating a Life Cycle Consistent Model of
    Family Labour Supply with Cross Section Data',
    University of Manchester, mimeo.
Barro, R. J. and H. I. Grossman, (1974), 'Suppressed
    Inflation and the Supply Multiplier', Review of
    Economic Studies, 41, pp. 87-104.
    ——————————————————, (1976), Money,
    Employment and Inflation, Cambridge University
    Press.
Bartholomew, D. J., (1978), Stochastic Models for
    Social Processes, Chapter 6, John Wiley and
    Sons, 2nd edition.
Barton, M., R. G. Layard and A. Zabalza, (1980).
    'Married Women's Participation and Hours',
    Economica, 47, pp. 51-72.
Beenstock, M. and P. Warburton, (1982), 'An Aggregate
    Model of the U.K. Labour Market', Oxford Economic
    Papers, 34, pp. 253-275.
Begg, D. K. H., (1982), 'Rational Expectations, Wage
    Rigidity and Involuntary Unemployment', Oxford
    Economic Papers, 34, pp. 23-47.
Benjamin, D. K. and L. A. Kochin, (1979), 'Searching
    for an Explanation of Unemployment in Interwar
    Britain', Journal of Political Economy, 87,
    pp. 441-478.
Blackorby, C., R. Boyce and R. R. Russell, (1978),
    Duality, Separability and Functional Structure,
    North-Holland, New York.
Blanchard, O. J., (1982), 'Price Desynchronisation
    and Price Level Inertia', Hoover Institute
    Working Paper No. E-82-11.
Blinder, A. S., (1974), Toward an Economic Theory of
    Income Distribution, MIT Press, Cambridge, Mass.
Blundell, R. W., (1980), 'Estimating Continuous
    Consumer Equivalence Scales in an Expenditure
    Model with Labour Supply', European Economic
    Review, 14, pp. 145-157.
    ——————————— and I. Walker, (1982), 'Modelling the
    Joint Determination of Household Labour Supplies
    and Commodity Demands', Economic Journal, 92,
    pp. 351-364.

248

List of Common References

Bodkin, A. C., (1969), 'Real Wages and Cyclical Variations in Employment: A Re-examination of the Evidence', Canadian Journal of Economics, 2, pp. 353-374.

Bornhoff, Edward J., (1982), 'Predicting the Price Level in a World that Changes all the Time', Carnegie-Rochester Conference series on Public Policy, Vol. 7, pp. 7-38.

Bowden, R., (1978), The Econometrics of Disequilibrium, North-Holland, Amsterdam.

Bowers, J. K., (1982), 'The Duration of Unemployment by Age and Sex 1976-1981', University of Leeds mimeo.

Brechling, F., (1965), 'The Relationship between Output and Employment in British Manufacturing Industries', Review of Economic Studies, 32, pp. 187-216.

Browning, M. J., A. S. Deaton and M. Irish, (1982), 'A Profitable Approach to Labour Supply and Commodity Demands Over the Life Cycle', University of Bristol, mimeo.

Birtless, G. and J. Hausman, (1978), 'The Effects of Taxes on Labour Supply: Evaluating the Gary NIT Experiment', Journal of Political Economy, 86, pp. 1103-1131.

Calmfors, Lars, (1982), 'Employment Policies, Wage Formation, and Trade Unions in a Small Open Economy', The Scandanavian Journal of Economics, 84, pp. 345-373.

——————————, (1983), 'Stabilisation Policy and Wage Formation in the Smaller European Economies with Strong Trade Unions', mimeo.

Carlson, J. A. and M. W. Horrigan, (1983), 'Measures of Unemployment Duration as Guides to Research and Policy', Department of Economics, Williams College, Massachusetts, mimeo.

Chirinko, R. S., (1980), 'The Real Wage Rate Over the Business Cycle', Review of Economics and Statistics, LXII, pp. 459-465.

Cogan, J., (1980), 'Labour Supply with Time and Money Costs of Participation', in J. P. Smith (ed.), Female Labour Supply: Theory and Estimation, Princeton University Press.

Corry, B. A. and J. A. Roberts, (1974), 'Activity Rates and Unemployment, The U.K. Experience: Some Further Results', Applied Economics, 6, pp. 1-21.

Council of Economic Advisors, (1974), Economic Report of the President, 1974, U.S. Government Printing Office, Washington, D.C.

List of Common References

Creedy, J. and R. Disney, (1981), 'Eligibility for
    Unemployment Benefit in Great Britain', Oxford
    Economic Papers, 33, pp. 256-273.
Cripps, T. F. and R. J. Tarling, (1974), 'An Analysis
    of the Duration of Male Unemployment in G.B.,
    1932-1973', Economic Journal, 84, pp. 289-316.
Currie, D., (1981), 'Some Long Run Features of
    Dynamic Time Series Models', Economic Journal,
    91, pp. 704-715.
Davidson, J. E. H., D. F. Hendry, F. Srba and S. Yeo,
    (1978), 'Econometric Moddelling of the Aggregate
    Times Series Relationship between Consumer's
    Expenditure and Income in the U.K.', Economic
    Journal, 88, pp. 661-692.
Dawson, A., (1983), 'The Performance of Three Wage
    Equations in Postwar Britain', Applied Economics,
    pp. 91-105.
Deaton, A. S., (1980), 'Demand Analysis', forthcoming
    in Z. Griliches and M. Intriligator (eds.),
    Handbook of Econometrics, JAI Press.
Denton, Frank, Christine Feaver and Leslie A. Robb,
    (1975), Patterns of Unemployment Behaviour in
    Canada, Discussion Paper No. 36, Economic
    Council of Canada, Ottawa.
Dertouzos, J. N. and J. H. Pencavel, (1981), 'Wage
    and Employment Determination under Trade Union-
    ism: The International Typographical Union',
    Journal of Political Economy, 89, pp. 1162-81.
Diewert, W. E.,(1974a), 'The Effects of Unionization
    in a General Equilibrium Model', Economic
    Inquiry, 12, pp. 319-339.
    —————————,(1974b), 'Unions in a General Equili-
    brium Model', Canadian Journal of Economics, 7,
    pp. 475-495.
Dunlop, J. T., (1938), 'The Movement of Real and
    Money Wage Rates', Economic Journal, 48,
    pp. 413-434.
Engle, R. F., D. F. Hendry and J.-F. Richard, (1983),
    'Exogeneity', Econometrica, 51, pp. 277-304.
Feldstein, M., (1976), 'Temporary Layoffs in the
    Theory of Unemployment', Journal of Political
    Economy, 84, pp. 937-57.
Forbes, A. and C. Leicester, (1976), 'An Analysis of
    Duration of Unemployment in Great Britain 1966-
    1973', Institute of Manpower Studies, University
    of Sussex Working Paper No. GN93.
Fowler, R. F., (1968), 'The Duration of Unemployment
    on the Register of Wholly Unemployed', Studies
    in Official Statistics, Research Series No. 1,
    Dept. of Employment and Productivity, H.M.S.O.

List of Common References

Frisch, A., (1932), New Methods of Measuring Marginal Utility, J.C.B. Mohr, Tubigen.

Geary, P. T. and J. Kennan, (1982), 'The Employment-Real Wage Relationship: An International Study', Journal of Political Economy, 90, pp. 854-871.

Ghez, G. R. and G. S. Becker, (1975), The Allocation of Time and Goods Over the Life Cycle, N.B.E.R., New York.

Gorman, W. M., (1968), 'Conditions for Additive Separability', Econometrica, 36, pp. 605-609.

Gower, David E., (1975), 'Job Search Patterns in Canada', Special Labour Force Studies, Series A, No. 10, Statistics Canada Labour Division, Ottawa.

Green, C., (1967), Negative Taxes and the Poverty Problem, Brookings Institution.

Green, C. and J.-M. Cousineau, (1976), Unemployment in Canada: The Impact of Unemployment Insurance, Economic Council of Canada, Ottawa.

Grossman, S. and O. Hart, (1981), 'Implicit Contracts, Moral Hazard, and Unemployment', Papers and Proceedings of the American Economic Association, pp. 301-307.

Grossman, S. J. and L. Weiss, (1982), 'Heterogeneous Information and the Theory of the Business Cycle', Journal of Political Economy, 90, pp. 699-727.

Grubb, D., R. Jackman and R. Layard, (1983), 'Wage Rigidity and Unemployment in O.E.C.D. Countries', European Economic Review, 21, pp. 11-39.

Grubel, H. G., D. R. Maki and S. Sax, (1975), 'Real and Insurance-Induced Unemployment in Canada', Canadian Journal of Economics, 8, pp. 174-197.

Hall, R. E., (1978), 'Stochastic Implications of the Life Cycle Permanent Income Hypothesis', Journal of Political Economy, 86, pp. 971-988.

—————————, (1980), 'Employment Fluctuations and Wage Rigidity', Brookings Papers on Economic Activity, 11, pp. 91-123.

————————— and D. M. Lilien, (1979), 'Efficient Wage Bargains under Uncertain Supply and Demand', American Economic Review, 69, pp. 868-79.

Ham. J., (1982), 'Estimation of a Labour Supply Model with Censoring Due to Unemployment and Underemployment', Review of Economic Studies, 49, pp. 335-354.

—————————, (1983), 'Testing for the Absence of Constraints in a Life Cycle of Labour Supply', University of Manchester Econometrics Discussion Paper ES 143.

251

List of Common References

Harsanyi, J. C., (1956), 'Approaches to the Bargaining Problem Before and After the Theory of Games: A Critical Discussion of Zeuthen's, Hicks', and Nash's Theories', _Econometrica_, 24, pp. 144-157.
——————, (1977), _Rational Behaviour and Bargaining Equilibrium in Games and Social Situations_, Cambridge University Press.
Hart, O., (1983), 'Optimal Labour Contracts under Asymmetric Information: an Introduction', _Review of Economic Studies_, 50, pp. 3-36.
Hausman, J. A., (1980), 'The Effects of Wages, Taxes and Fixed Costs on Women's Labour Force Participation', _Journal of Public Economics_, 14, pp. 161-194.
Hazeldine, T., (1981), '"Employment Functions" and the Demand for Labour in the Short Run', in Z. Hornstein et al., _The Economics of the Labour Market_, H.M.S.O., London.
Heady, C., D. T. Ulph and A. A. Carruth, (1982), 'Optimal Income Taxation and Comparative Advantage', University College London, mimeo.
Heckman, J. J., (1974a), 'Life Cycle Consumption and Labour Supply: An Explanation of the Relationship between Income and Consumption over the Life Cycle', _American Economic Review_, 64, pp. 188-194.
——————, (1974b), 'The Effect of Child Care Programs on Women's Work Effort', _Journal of Political Economy_, 82, pp. 5136-5163.
——————, (1974c), 'Shadow Prices, Market Wages and Labour Supply', _Econometrica_, 42, pp. 679-694.
——————, M. Killingsworth and T. E. MaCurdy, (1981), 'Empirical Evidence on Static Labour Supply Models: A Survey of Recent Developments', in Z. Hornstein, J. Grice and A. Webb (eds.), _The Economics of the Labour Market_, H.M.S.O., London.
—————— and T. E. MaCurdy, (1980), 'A Life Cycle Model of Female Labour Supply', _Review of Economic Studies_, 47, pp. 47-74.
Hendry, D. F. and A. Spanos, (1980), 'Disequilibrium and Latent Variables', Paper presented to the Fourth World Congress of the Econometric Society.
Henry, S. G. B., (1982), 'Empirical Models of Real Wages with Applications to the U.K.", National Institute for Economic and Social Research, mimeo.
—————— and S. Wren-Lewis, (1983), 'Manufacturing Employment and Expected Output', N.I.E.S.R. Discussion Paper, No. 55.

List of Common References

Holden, K. and D. A. Peel, (1979), 'The Benefit-Income Ratio for Unemployed Workers in the United Kingdom', International Labour Review, 118, pp. 607-615.

Holmes, J. M. and D. J. Smyth, (1979), 'Excess Demand for Labour, Unemployment, and the Theories of the Phillips' Curve', Journal of Macroeconomics, 1, pp. 347-37

Hughes, P. , (1982) 'Flows on and off the Unemployment Register', Employment Gazette, 90, pp. 527-530.

Jackman, R. and R. Layard, (1982), 'Trade Unions, The N.A.I.R.U., and a Wage-Inflation Tax', London School of Economics, Discussion Paper 100.

Jackson, D., H. A. Turner and F. Wilkinson, (1975), Do Trade Unions Cause Inflation ?, Cambridge University Press.

Johnson, H. G. and P. Mieskowski, (1970), 'The Effects of Unionization on the Distribution of Income: A General Equilibrium Approach', Quarterly Journal of Economics, 84, pp. 539-561.

Jones, R. W., (1971), 'Distortions in Factor Markets and the General Equilibrium Model of Production', Journal of Political Economy, 79, pp. 437-459.

Kalai, E. and M. Smorodinsky, (1975), 'Other Solutions to Nash's Bargaining Problem', Econometrica, 43, pp. 513-518.

Killingsworth, M., (1981), 'A Survey of Labour Supply Models: Theoretical Analysis and First-Generation Empirical Results', in R. G. Ehrenberg (ed.), Research in Labour Economics, 4, JAI Press.

Keynes, J. M., (1936), The General Theory of Employment,Interest and Money, Macmillan Press, London.

Kuh, E., (1966), 'Unemployment, Production Functions, and Effective Demand', Journal of Political Economy, 74, pp. 238-249.

Lancaster, T., (1979), 'Econometric Methods for the Duration of Unemployment', Econometrica, 47, pp. 939-956.

—————, and S. Nickell, (1980), 'The Analysis of Re-employment Probabilities for the Unemployed', Journal of the Royal Statistical Society, A143, pp. 141-165.

Layard, R., (1981), 'Measuring the Duration of Unemployment: A Note', Scottish Journal of Political Economy, 28, pp. 273-277.

—————, (1982), 'Is Incomes Policy the Answer to Employment ?', Economica, 49, pp. 219-241.

—————, and S. J. Nickell, (1980), 'The Case for Subsidizing Extra Jobs', Economic Journal, 90, pp. 51-73.

List of Common References

Leontieff, W., (1946), 'The Pure Theory of the
    Guaranteed Annual Wage Contract', *Journal of*
    Political Economy, 56, pp. 76-79.
Lerner, A., (1978), 'A Wage-increase Permit Plan to
    Stop Inflation', *Brookings Papers on Economic*
    Activity, 1, pp. 491-505.
Lewis, P. E. T. and G. H. Makepeace, (1981a), 'The
    Estimation of Aggregate Demand and Supply Curves
    for Labour in the U.K.', *Applied Economics*, 13,
    pp. 289-298.
——————————————————————————, (1981b),
    'Cyclical Unemployment in the U.K. During the
    Post-War Period', Hull University Discussion
    Paper No. 81.
Lucas, R. E., (1981), 'Tobin and Monetarism: A
    Review Article', *Journal of Economic Literature*,
    19, pp. 558-67.
—————————— and L. A. Rapping, (1970), 'Real Wages,
    Employment and Inflation', in E. S. Phelps et
    al., *Microeconomic Foundations of Employment*
    and Inflation Theory, Norton, New York.
Lundberg, S., (1982), 'Involuntary Unemployment as a
    Constraint on Household Labour Supply', Univer-
    sity of Pennsylvania, mimeo.
MaCurdy, T. E., (1981), 'An Empirical Model of Labour
    Supply in a Life Cycle Setting', *Journal of*
    Political Economy, 89, pp. 1059-1085.
——————————————, (1982), 'Interpreting Empirical
    Models of Labour Supply in an Intertemporal
    Framework with Uncertainty', Stanford Research
    Papers in Economics of Factor Markets, 23.
——————————————, (1983), 'A Simple Scheme for Estima-
    ting an Intertemporal Model of Labour Supply and
    Consumption in the Presence of Taxes and Uncer-
    tainty', *International Economic Review*, 24,
    pp. 265-289.
Main, B. G. M., (1981), 'The Length of Employment
    and Unemployment in Great Britain', *Scottish*
    Journal of Political Economy, 28, pp. 146-164.
Malinvaud, E., (1977), *The Theory of Unemployment*
    Reconsidered, Basil Blackwell, Oxford.
Marshall, G. P., (1978), 'The U.K. Retirement Pension
    and Negative Taxation', *Bulletin of Economic*
    Research, 30, pp. 31-38.
Mayer, L. H. and C. Webster, Jr., (1982),
    'Monetary Policy and Rational Expectations: A
    Comparison of Least Squares and Bayesian
    Learning', *Carnegie-Rochester Conference Series*
    on Public Policy, 17, pp. 67-97.
McCallum, B. T., (1974), 'Wage Rate Changes and the
    Excess Demand for Labour: An Alternative

254

Formulation', *Economica*, 41, pp. 269-277.

McDonald, I. M. and R. Solow, (1981), 'Wage Bargaining and Employment', *American Economic Review*, 71, pp. 896-908.

―――――――――――――――――, (1983), 'Wages and Employment in a Segmented Labour Market', University of Melbourne Department of Economics Research Paper No. 91.

Meade, J., (1961), 'Mauritius: a Case Study in Malthusian Economics', *Economic Journal*, 71, pp. 521-534.

―――――――. (1964), *Efficiency, Equality and the Ownership of Property*, George Allen and Unwin, London.

Minford, A. P. L., (1982), 'Labour Market Equilibrium in an Open Economy', University of Liverpool, mimeo.

Mirrlees, J. A., (1971), 'An Exploration in the Theory of Optimum Income Taxation', *Review of Economic Studies*, 38, pp. 175-208.

Modigliani, F., (1975), 'The Life Cycle Hypothesis of Saving Twenty Years Later', in M. Parkin and A. R. Nobay (eds.), *Contemporary Issues in Economics*, Manchester University Press.

―――――――――― and R. Brumberg, (1955), 'Utility Analysis and the Consumption Function: An Interpretation of Cross Section Data', in K. K. Kurihara (ed.), *Post Keynesian Economics*, George Allen and Unwin, London.

Muellbauer, J. and L. Mendis, (1983), 'Employment Functions and Productivity Change: Has there been a British Productivity Breakthrough ?", *C.L.E. Unemployment Seminar*.

Mussa, M., (1981), 'Sticky Prices and Disequilibrium Adjustment in a Rational Model of the Inflationary Process', *American Economic Review*, 71, pp. 1020-1027.

Narendranathan, W., S. Nickell and J. Stern, (1982), 'Unemployment Benefits Revisited', C.L.E. Working Paper No. 462.

Nash, J. F., Jr., (1950), 'The Bargaining Problem', *Econometrica*, 18, pp. 155-162.

Nickell, S. J., (1979a), 'The Effect of Unemployment and Related Benefits on the Duration of Unemployment', *Economic Journal*, 89, pp. 34-49.

―――――――――, (1979b), 'Estimating the Probability of Leaving Unemployment', *Econometrica*, 47, pp. 1249-1266.

―――――――――. (1981), 'An Investigation of the Determinants of Manufacturing Employment in the United Kingdom', C.L.E. Discussion paper No. 105.

List of Common References

Nickell, S. J., (1982a), 'A Bargaining Model of the
    Phillips Curve', C.L.E. Discussion Paper No. 130.
────────────, (1982b), 'Research into Unemployment:
    A Partial View of the Economics Literature',
    C.L.E. Discussion Paper No. 131.
──────────── and R. Andrews, (1983), 'Unions, Real
    Wages, and Employment in Britain 1951-1979',
    C.L.E. Discussion Paper.
Oswald, A., (1979), 'Wage Determination in an Economy
    with Many Trade Unions', Oxford Economic Papers,
    31, pp. 369-385.
────────────, (1982a), 'The Micro-economic Theory of the
    Trade Union', Economic Journal, 92, pp. 576-595.
────────────, (1982b), 'Optimal Intervention in an
    Economy with Trade Unions', Balliol College,
    Oxford, mimeo.
────────────, (1983), 'The Economic Theory of Trade
    Unions: An Introductory Survey', Paper given at th
    the SSRC Labour Economics Study Group Conference,
    Hull, University, 20-22 July.
──────────── and D. T. Ulph, (1982), 'Unemployment and
    the Pure Theory of the Trade Union', Discussion
    Papers in Economics, 30, University College London.
Patterson, K. D. and J. Ryding, (1982), 'Deriving and
    Testing Rate of Growth and Higher Order Growth
    Effects in Dynamic Economic Models', Bank of
    England Discussion Paper (revised version).
Perry, G. L. , (1977), 'Potential Output and Product-
    ivity', Brookings Papers on Economic Activity,
    1, pp. 11-47.
Pettengill, J., (1979), 'Labour Unins and the Wage
    Structure: a General Equilibrium Approach',
    Review of Economic Studies, 46, pp. 675-693.
────────────, (1980), Labor Unions and the
    Inequality of Earned Income, North-Holland,
    Amsterdam.
Phelps, E. S., (1978), 'Disinflation without Recession:
    Adaptive Guideposts and Monetary Policy',
    Weltwirtschaftliches Archiv, 114, pp. 783-809.
Quandt, R. E., (1982), 'Econometric Disequilibrium
    Models', Econometric Abstracts, pp. 7-64.
Ragan, J. F., Jr., (1981), 'The Effect of a Legal Min-
    imum Wage on the Pay and Employment of Teenage
    Students and Non-Students', in S. Rottenberg (ed.),
    The Economics of Legal Minimum Wages, American
    Enterprise Institute, Washington, D.C., pp. 11-41.
Robertson, J. A. S. and J. M. Briggs, (1979), 'Part
    time Working in Great Britain', Employment
    Gazette, 87, pp. 671-677.
Rosen, S., (1970), 'Unionization and the Occupational
    Wage Structure in the United States', Inter-

List of Common References

national Economic Review, 11, pp. 269-286.
Rosen, H. S. and R. E. Quandt, (1978), 'The Estima-
tion of a Disequilibrium Aggregate Labour Market'
Review of Economics and Statistics, 60, pp. 371-
379.
Rotemberg, J. J., (1982), 'Sticky Prices in the United
States', Journal of Political Economy, 90,
pp. 1187-1211.
Ruggles, R., (1940), 'The Relative Movements of Real
and Money Wage Rates', Quarterly Journal of
Economics, 55, pp. 130-149.
Sachs, J., (1979), 'Wages, Profits and Macroeconomic
Adjustment: A Comparative Approach', Brookings
Papers on Economic Activity, 10, pp. 269-319.
Sampson, A. A., (1983), 'Employment Policy in a
Model with a Rational Trade Union', Economic
Journal, 93, pp. 297-311.
Sargan, J. D., (1964), 'Wages and Prices in the
United Kingdom: A Study in Econometric Method-
ology', in P. E. Hart, G. Mills and J. K. Whit-
aker (eds.), Econometric Analysis for National
Economic Planning, Colston Papers No. 16,
Butterworths, London.
Sargent, T. J. and Neil Wallace, (1976), 'Rational
Expectations and the Theory of Economic Policy',
Journal of Monetary Economics, 2, pp. 169-183.
Smith, J. P., (1977), 'Family Labour Supply over the
Life Cycle', Explorations in Economic Research,
4, pp. 205-276.
Smyth, D. J., (1983), 'The British Labour Market in
Disequilibrium: Did the Dole Reduce Employment
in Interwar Britain ?', Working Paper, Dept. of
Economics, Wayne State University, Detroit.
Spence, A. M., (1973), 'Job Market Signalling',
Quarterly Journal of Economics, 87, pp. 355-374.
Spindler, Z. A. and D. Maki, (1979), 'More on the
Effects of Unemployment Compensation on the
Rate of Unemployment in Great Britain', Oxford
Economic Papers, 31, pp. 147-164.
Swidinsky, R. , (1980), 'Minimum Wages and Teen-
age Unemployment', Canadian Journal of Economics,
13, pp. 158-170.
Symons, J. S. V., (1981), 'The Demand for Labour in
British Manufacturing', C.L.E. Discussion Paper
No. 91.
Tarshis, L., (1939), 'Changes in Real and Money Wage
Rates', Economic Journal, 49, pp. 150-154.
Taylor, J. B., (1979), 'Staggered Wage Setting in a
Micro Model', American Economic Review, Papers
and Proceedings 68, pp. 108-113.
————————————, (1980), 'Aggregate Dynamics and

List of Common References

Staggered Contracts', _Journal of Political Economy_, 88, pp. 1-23.

Ulph, A.M. and D. T. Ulph, (1982), 'Unions and the Distribution of Earned Income - a Critique of Pettengill', Discussion Paper in Economics 31, University College, London.

——————————————————————, (1983), 'Trade Unions and the Distribution of Income and Employment', University College, London, mimeo. (Paper presented at the European Econometric Society Conference, Pisa, 1983).

Wachter, M. L. and C. Kim, (1979), 'Time-Series Changes in Youth Joblessnes', National Bureau of Economic Research Working Papers, No. 384.

Weiss, Y., (1972), 'On the Optimal Lifetime Pattern of Labour Supply', _Economic Journal_, 82, pp. 1293-1315.

Welch, F. (1979), 'Effects of Cohort-Size on Earnings: The Baby Boom Babies' Financial Bust', _Journal of Political Economy_, 87, pp. 65-98.

Zabalza, A., (1983), 'The C.E.S. Utility Function, Non-Linear Budget Constraints and Labour Supply. Results in Female Participation and Hours', _Economic Journal_, 93, pp. 312-330.

Zellner, A. and H. Theil, (1962), 'Three-Stage Least Squares: Simultaneous Estimation of Simultaneous Relations', _Econometrica_, 30, pp. 54-78.

Zeuthen, F., (1930), _Problems of Monopoly and Economic Welfare_, George Routledge and Sons, London.

Printed in the United States
by Baker & Taylor Publisher Services